2nd Workshop on Argumentation Mining 2015

Held at NAACL HLT 2015

Denver, Colorado, USA
4 June 2015

ISBN: 978-1-5108-0442-5

Printed from e-media with permission by:

Curran Associates, Inc.
57 Morehouse Lane
Red Hook, NY 12571

CURRAN ASSOCIATES INC.
proceedings.com

Some format issues inherent in the e-media version may also appear in this print version.

Printed by Curran Associates, Inc. (2015)

Association for Computational Linguistics
209 N. Eighth Street
Stroudsburg, Pennsylvania 18360

Phone: 1-570-476-8006
Fax: 1-570-476-0860

acl@aclweb.org

Additional copies of this publication are available from:

Curran Associates, Inc.
57 Morehouse Lane
Red Hook, NY 12571 USA
Phone: 845-758-0400
Fax: 845-758-2634
Email: curran@proceedings.com
Web: www.proceedings.com

NAACL HLT 2015

2nd Workshop on Argumentation Mining

Proceedings of the Workshop

June 4, 2015
Denver, Colorado, USA

Order print-on-demand copies from:

Curran Associates
57 Morehouse Lane
Red Hook, New York 12571
USA
Tel: +1-845-758-0400
Fax: +1-845-758-2633
curran@proceedings.com

Background

The goal of this workshop is to provide a follow-on forum to last year's very successful Argumentation Mining workshop at ACL, the first research forum devoted to argumentation mining in all domains of discourse.

Argumentation mining is a relatively new challenge in corpus-based discourse analysis that involves automatically identifying argumentative structures within a document, e.g., the premises, conclusion, and argumentation scheme of each argument, as well as argument-subargument and argument-counterargument relationships between pairs of arguments in the document. To date, researchers have investigated methods for argumentation mining of legal documents (Mochales and Moens 2011; Bach et al. 2013; Ashley and Walker 2013; Wyner et al. 2010), on-line debates (Cabrio and Villata 2012), product reviews (Villalba and Saint-Dizier 2012; Wyner et al. 2012), user comments on proposed regulations (Park and Cardie 2014), newspaper articles and court cases (Feng and Hirst 2011). A related older strand of research (that uses the term 'argumentative structure' in a related but different sense than ours) has investigated automatically classifying the sentences of a scientific article's abstract or full text in terms of their contribution of new knowledge to a field (e.g., Liakata et al. 2012, Teufel 2010, Mizuta et al. 2005). In addition, argumentation mining has ties to sentiment analysis (e.g., Somasundaran and Wiebe 2010). To date there are few corpora with annotations for argumentation mining research (Reed et al. 2008) although corpora with annotations for argument sub-components have recently become available (e.g., Park and Cardie 2014).

Proposed applications of argumentation mining include improving information retrieval and information extraction as well as end-user visualization and summarization of arguments. Textual sources of interest include not only the formal writing of legal text, but also a variety of informal genres such as microtext, spoken meeting transcripts, product reviews and user comments. In instructional contexts where argumentation is a pedagogically important tool for conveying and assessing students' command of course material, the written and diagrammed arguments of students (and the mappings between them) are educational data that can be mined for purposes of assessment and instruction (see e.g., Ong, Litman and Brusilovsky 2014). This is especially important given the wide-spread adoption of computer-supported peer review, computerized essay grading, and large-scale online courses and MOOCs.

As one might expect, success in argumentation mining will require interdisciplinary approaches informed by natural language processing technology, theories of semantics, pragmatics and discourse, knowledge of discourse of domains such as law and science, artificial intelligence, argumentation theory, and computational models of argumentation. In addition, it will require the creation and annotation of high-quality corpora of argumentation from different types of sources in different domains.

We are looking forward to a full day workshop to exchange ideas and present onging research on all of the above!!!

Organizers:

Claire Cardie (Chair), Cornell University, USA
Nancy Green, University of North Carolina Greensboro, USA
Iryna Gurevych, Technische Universität Darmstadt, Germany
Graeme Hirst, University of Toronto, Canada
Diane Litman, University of Pittsburgh, USA
Smaranda Muresan, Columbia University, USA
Georgios Petasis, N.C.S.R. "Demokritos", Greece
Manfred Stede, Universität Potsdam, Germany
Marilyn Walker, University of California Santa Cruz, USA
Janyce Wiebe, University of Pittsburgh, USA

Program Committee:

Stergos Afantenos, IRIT Toulouse, France
Kevin Ashley, University of Pittsburgh, USA
Floris Bex, University of Utrecht, The Netherlands
Elena Cabrio, INRIA Sophia-Antipolis Méditerranée, France
Claire Cardie, Cornell University, USA
Chrysanne Dimarco, University of Waterloo, Canada
Debanjan Ghosh, Rutgers University, USA
Massimiliano Giacomin, University of Brescia, Italy
Matthias Grabmair, University of Pittsburgh, USA
Floriana Grasso, University of Liverpool, UK
Nancy Green, University of N.C. Greensboro, USA
Iryna Gurevych, Universität Darmstadt, Germany
Ivan Habernal, DIPF institute Frankfurt, Germany
Graeme Hirst, University of Toronto, Canada
Vangelis Karkaletsis, N.C.S.R., Greece
Valia Kordoni, Humboldt Universität zu Berlin, Germany
Joao Leite, FCT-UNL - Universidade Nova de Lisboa, Portugal
Beishui Liao, Zhejiang University, China
Maria Liakata, University of Warwick, UK
Diane Litman, University of Pittsburgh, USA
Bernardo Magnini, FBK Trento, Italy
Robert Mercer, University of Western Ontario, Canada
Marie-Francine Moens, Katholieke Universiteit Leuven, Belgium
Smaranda Muresan, Columbia University, USA
Fabio Paglieri, CNR, Italy
Alexis Palmer, Saarland University, Germany
Joonsuk Park, Cornell University, USA
Simon Parsons, University of Liverpool, UK

Table of Contents

This page intentionally left blank.

Conference Program

Thursday, June 4, 2015

07:30–08:45 **Breakfast**

08:45–09:00 ***Introductions***

09:00–09:40 ***Setting the Stage: Overview on Argumentation Mining by Manfred Stede, Nancy Green and Ivan Habernal***

09:40–10:05 *Linking the Thoughts: Analysis of Argumentation Structures in Scientific Publications*
Christian Kirschner, Judith Eckle-Kohler and Iryna Gurevych

10:05–10:30 *Identifying Argumentation Schemes in Genetics Research Articles*
Nancy Green

10:30–11:00 **Break**

11:00–11:20 *Extracting Argument and Domain Words for Identifying Argument Components in Texts*
Huy Nguyen and Diane Litman

11:20–11:30 ***Poster Madness: 1-minute presentation for each poster***

11:30–12:30 ***Poster Session***

Towards relation based Argumentation Mining
Lucas Carstens and Francesca Toni

A Shared Task on Argumentation Mining in Newspaper Editorials
Johannes Kiesel, Khalid Al Khatib, Matthias Hagen and Benno Stein

Conditional Random Fields for Identifying Appropriate Types of Support for Propositions in Online User Comments
Joonsuk Park, Arzoo Katiyar and Bishan Yang

A Computational Approach for Generating Toulmin Model Argumentation
Paul Reisert, Naoya Inoue, Naoaki Okazaki and Kentaro Inui

Thursday, June 4, 2015 (continued)

	Argument Extraction from News Christos Sardianos, Ioannis Manousos Katakis, Georgios Petasis and Vangelis Karkaletsis
	From Argumentation Mining to Stance Classification Parinaz Sobhani, Diana Inkpen and Stan Matwin
	Argument Discovery and Extraction with the Argument Workbench Adam Wyner, Wim Peters and David Price
12:30–2:00	**Lunch**
02:00–02:25	*Automatic Claim Negation: Why, How and When* Yonatan Bilu, Daniel Hershcovich and Noam Slonim
02:25–02:50	*Learning Sentence Ordering for Opinion Generation of Debate* Toshihiko Yanase, Toshinori Miyoshi, Kohsuke Yanai, Misa Sato, Makoto Iwayama, Yoshiki Niwa, Paul Reisert and Kentaro Inui
02:50–03:10	*Towards Detecting Counter-considerations in Text* Andreas Peldszus and Manfred Stede
03:10–03:30	*Identifying Prominent Arguments in Online Debates Using Semantic Textual Similarity* Filip Boltužić and Jan Šnajder
03:30–04:00	**Break**
04:00–04:25	*And That's A Fact: Distinguishing Factual and Emotional Argumentation in Online Dialogue* Shereen Oraby, Lena Reed, Ryan Compton, Ellen Riloff, Marilyn Walker and Steve Whittaker
04:25–04:50	*Combining Argument Mining Techniques* John Lawrence and Chris Reed
04:50–05:30	***Wrap-up Discussion***

Linking the Thoughts: Analysis of Argumentation Structures in Scientific Publications

Christian Kirschner[◇†], **Judith Eckle-Kohler**[◇], **Iryna Gurevych**[◇†]

◇ UKP Lab, Technische Universität Darmstadt
† German Institute for Educational Research
http://www.ukp.tu-darmstadt.de

Abstract

This paper presents the results of an annotation study focused on the fine-grained analysis of argumentation structures in scientific publications. Our new annotation scheme specifies four types of binary argumentative relations between sentences, resulting in the representation of arguments as small graph structures. We developed an annotation tool that supports the annotation of such graphs and carried out an annotation study with four annotators on 24 scientific articles from the domain of educational research. For calculating the inter-annotator agreement, we adapted existing measures and developed a novel graph-based agreement measure which reflects the semantic similarity of different annotation graphs.

1 Introduction

Argumentation mining aims at automatically identifying arguments and argumentative relations in argumentative discourse, e.g., in newspaper articles (Feng and Hirst, 2011; Florou et al., 2013), legal documents (Mochales-Palau and Moens, 2011), or scientific publications. Many applications, such as text summarization, information retrieval, or faceted search could benefit from a fine-grained analysis of the argumentation structure, making the reasoning process directly visible. Such an enhanced information access would be particularly important for scientific publications, where the rapidly increasing amount of documents available in digital form makes it more and more difficult for users to find specific information nuggets without investing a lot of time in reading (parts of) documents which are not relevant.

According to well-established argumentation theories in Philosophy and Logic (e.g. Toulmin (1958), Freeman (2011), Walton et al. (2008)), an *argument* consists of several *argument components* which often are of a specific type, such as premise or claim. *Argumentative relations* are usually directed relations between two argument components. Different relation types are distinguished, like *support* or *attack* (Peldszus and Stede, 2013) which indicate that the source argument component is a reason or a refutation for the target component. Argument components and argumentative relations together form the *argumentation structure*. Figure 1 shows the argumentation structure of one argument consisting of 6 argument components and 6 relations between them. Previous work has developed approaches to classify

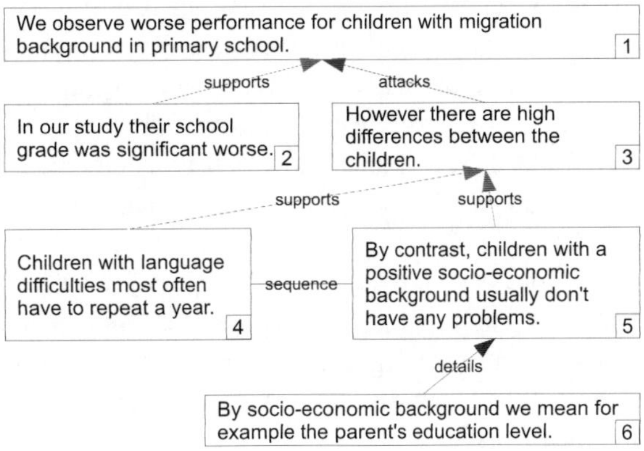

Figure 1: Illustration of one argument consisting of 6 argument components.

Proceedings of the 2nd Workshop on Argumentation Mining, pages 1–11,
Denver, Colorado, June 4, 2015. ©2015 Association for Computational Linguistics

sentences in scientific papers according to their argumentative role (Teufel, 1999; Liakata et al., 2012), distinguishing up to seven types of argumentative roles (e.g., Background, Other, Own). However, this results in a coarse-grained analysis of the argumentation structure present in a scientific paper, which merely reflects the more or less standardized way scientific papers are written in many domains (e.g., Natural Sciences or Computer Science). Such a coarse-grained analysis does not reveal how an author connects his thoughts in order to create a convincing line of argumentation. To the best of our knowledge, there exists no prior work which tries to identify argumentative relations between argument components on such a fine-grained level in scientific full-texts yet. This is a challenging task since scientific publications are long and complex documents, and even for researchers in a specific field it can be hard to fully understand the underlying argumentation structures.

We address this gap and aim at developing methods for the automatic identification of argumentation structures in scientific publications. We chose scientific journal articles from the educational research as a prototypical domain, because it is of particular interest not only for educational researchers, but also for other groups in the society, such as policy makers, teachers or parents.

This paper presents the results of our annotation of 24 articles from educational research (written in German) – a crucial step towards developing and testing automatic methods. Our contributions can be summarized as follows: (i) We introduce an annotation scheme and an annotation tool for the fine-grained analysis of argumentation structures in scientific publications, which represents arguments as small graph structures. (ii) We developed a novel graph-based inter-annotator agreement measure, which is able to reflect the semantic similarity of different annotation graphs. (iii) Finally, we present the results of a detailed quantitative and qualitative analysis of the annotated dataset where we characterize the argumentation structures in scientific publications and identify major challenges for future work.

The rest of the paper is organized as follows: First we discuss related work (section 2). In section 3, we describe our annotation scheme and the annotation study, and in section 4 the inter-annotator agreement measures are introduced. The results of the quantitative and qualitative analysis are discussed in section 5. Section 6 concludes.

2 Related Work

This section discusses related work regarding the annotation of argumentation structure on the one hand, and annotating scientific articles on the other hand. We give an overview of (i) annotation schemes for annotating argumentation and discourse structure, (ii) inter-annotator agreement (IAA) metrics suitable for this annotation task, (iii) previous annotation studies.

Annotation Schemes Previously, annotation schemes and approaches for identifying arguments in different domains have been developed. For instance, Mochales-Palau and Moens (2011) identify arguments in legal documents, Feng and Hirst (2011) focus on the identification of argumentation schemes (Walton, 1996) in newspapers and court cases, Florou et al. (2013) apply argumentation mining in policy modeling, and Stab and Gurevych (2014) present an approach to model arguments in persuasive essays. Most of the approaches focus on the identification and classification of argument components. There are only few works which aim at identifying argumentative relations and consequently argumentation structures. Furthermore it is important to note that the texts from those domains differ considerably from scientific publications regarding their length, complexity, purpose and language use.

Regarding argumentation mining in scientific publications, one of the first approaches is the work called *Argumentative Zoning* by Teufel (1999) which was extended by Teufel et al. (2009). According to the extended annotation scheme, each sentence in a scientific publication is annotated with exactly one of 15 categories (e.g. Background or Aim), reflecting the argumentative role the sentence has in the text. Mapping this scheme to our terminology (see section 1), a sentence corresponds to an argument component. The aim of this annotation scheme is to improve information access and to support applications like automatic text summarization (Teufel and Moens, 2002; Ruch et al., 2007;

Contractor et al., 2012). While the authors themselves do not consider argumentative relations, Angrosh et al. (2012) transfer the argumentation inherent in the categories of the *Argumentative Zoning* to the Toulmin model (Toulmin, 1958) and therefore describe how argument components of several types relate to each other. For example, research findings are used to support "statements referring to the problems solved by an article" and "statements referring to current work shortcomings" support "statements referring to future work". However, the paper focuses on citation contexts and considers relations only on a coarse-grained level.

Several similar annotation schemes for scientific publications exist. For instance, Liakata et al. (2012) proposed *CoreSC* ("Core Scientific Concepts"), an annotation scheme consisting of 11 categories[1]. Mizuta and Collier (2004) provide a scheme consisting of 7 categories (plus 5 subcategories) for the biology domain. In addition Yepes et al. (2013) provide a scheme to categorize sentences in abstracts of articles from biomedicine with 5 categories.

Furthermore, Blake (2010) describes approaches to identify scientific claims or comparative claim sentences in scientific articles (Park and Blake, 2012). Again these works do not consider argumentative relations on a fine-grained level, but focus on the classification of argument components. While all of these works use data from the natural sciences, there are only few works in the domain of social sciences (e.g. Ahmed et al. (2013)), and to the best of our knowledge no previous work has addressed scientific publications in the educational domain.

A field that is closely related to the annotation of argumentation structures is the annotation of discourse structure which aims at identifying discourse relations that hold between adjacent text units, e.g. sentences, clauses or nominalizations (Webber et al., 2012). Often, the text units considered in discourse analysis correspond to argument components, and discourse relations are closely related to argumentative relations. Most previous work in automated discourse analysis is based on corpora annotated with discourse relations, most notably the Penn Discourse Treebank (PDTB) (Prasad et al., 2008) and the Rhetorical Structure Theory (RST) Discourse Treebank (Carlson et al., 2001). However, the data consists of newspaper articles (no scientific articles), and only relations between adjacent text units are identified. In addition, it is still an open question how the proposed discourse relations relate to argumentative relations (the difference of the relations is best illustrated by the work of Biran and Rambow (2011)). Nevertheless, annotated corpora like this can be valuable resources for training automatic classifiers later.

IAA Metrics Current state-of-the-art annotation studies use chance corrected measures to compute IAA, i.e., random agreement is included in the calculation. The values can be in the range of -1 to 1, a value of 0 indicates random agreement and a value of 1 perfect agreement (negative values indicate a negative correlation). One of the most popular chance corrected measures for two raters is Cohen's κ (Cohen, 1960). While Cohen's κ assumes different probability distributions for each rater, there exist other approaches which assume a single distribution for all raters (Scott, 1955). In addition, extensions to multiple raters exist. Multi-π is the extension of Scott's π by Fleiss (1971). Multi-κ is the extension of Cohen's κ by Hubert (1977).

All of these measures are well suited for tasks where we have a fixed set of independent and uniformly distributed entities to annotate. However, as soon as the annotation of one entity depends on the annotation of another entity, or some entities have a higher overall probability for a specific annotation than others, the measures may yield misleadingly high or low values (see section 4). Apart from that, chance-corrected measures are criticized because they "are often misleading when applied to unbalanced data sets" (Rehbein et al., 2012) and can be "problematic in categorization tasks that do not have a fixed number of items and categories" (van der Plas et al., 2010). Therefore, many researchers still report raw percentage agreement without chance correction.

Annotation Studies Table 1 gives an overview of previous annotation studies performed for scientific publications. In all of these studies, the annotators have to label argument components (typically, each sentence represents exactly one argument component) with one out of 3 - 15 categories. In most of

[1]For a comparison between Argumentative Zoning and CoreSC, see Liakata et al. (2010).

Author	Data	Annotators	#Cat	Guidelines	IAA
Teufel (1999)	22 papers (CL)	3 (semi-experts)	3	6 pages	0.78
	26 papers (CL)	3 (semi-experts)	7	17 pages	0.71
	3x1 paper (CL)	3x6 (untrained)	7	1 page	0.35-0.72
Teufel et al. (2009)	30 papers (Chemistry)	3 (different)	15	111 pages	0.71
	9 papers (CL)	3 (experts)	15	111 pages	0.65
Liakata et al. (2012)	41 papers (Biochemistry)	3 (experts)	11	45 pages	0.55
Blake (2010)	29 papers (Biomedicine)	2 (students)	5	discussion	0.57-0.88

Table 1: Comparison of annotation studies on scientific full-texts (CL = computational linguistics, #Cat = number of categories which can be annotated, IAA = chance-corrected inter-annotator agreement).

the studies, the annotators are at least semi-experts in the particular domain and get detailed annotation guidelines. Regarding the IAA, Teufel et al. (2009) report that untrained annotators performed worse than trained expert annotators. All of the agreement measures in table 1 are chance corrected and therefore comparable.

There are also annotation studies outside the domain of scientific articles which deal with argumentative relations. Mochales-Palau and Moens (2011) report an IAA of Cohen's $\kappa = 0.75$ (legal documents) but only for the identification of argument components (here claims and premises) and not for argumentative relations. Stab and Gurevych (2014) report an IAA of Fleiss' $\pi = 0.8$ for argumentative support and attack relations in persuasive essays. However, these relations are annotated between pre-annotated premises and claims, which simplifies the task considerably: annotators already know that premises have outgoing support and attack relations and claims incoming ones, i.e., they only have to annotate the target or source components of the relations as well as their type. Furthermore, compared to scientific articles, persuasive essays are much shorter and less complex regarding language use.

3 Annotation Study

This section describes our annotation study: we introduce the dataset, the annotation scheme and describe the annotation tool we developed.

Dataset For the annotation study, we selected 24 publications from 5 controversial educational topics (teaching profession, learning motivation, attention deficit hyperactivity disorder (ADHD), bullying, performance rating) from different journals in the domain of educational psychology and developmental psychology.[2] All of the articles are in German, about 10 pages of A4, describe empirical studies, and are composed of similar sections (introduction, methods, results, discussion). In our annotation study, we annotated the introduction and discussion sections and left out the methods and results sections, because these sections usually just describe the experimental setup without any assessment or reasoning.

The dataset contains the following annotatable[3] text units: 529 paragraphs (22 per document), 2743 sentences (114 per document), 79680 tokens (3320 per document). On average, we have a comparably high number of 29 tokens per sentence, which indicates the high complexity of the texts (Best, 2002).

At least three annotators with different backgrounds annotated the journal articles, some documents were annotated by a forth annotator. Two of the annotators were students (psychology and sociology), one was a PhD student (computer science) and the forth annotator had a PhD degree (computational linguistics). We developed annotation guidelines of about 10 pages of A4[4] and trained the annotators on these guidelines. In a pre-study, the annotators annotated five documents about language learning (not included in the dataset described above). During this pre-study, the annotations were discussed several times and the annotation guidelines were adapted. All in all, the annotation study extended over several months part time work. The annotation of one single document took about two hours.

Annotation Scheme Our annotation scheme specifies argument components and binary relations

[2]published by Hogrefe & Huber Verlagsgruppe, http://psycontent.metapress.com

[3]without headings, abstract, method/results section.

[4]We plan to make the guidelines publicly available.

between argument components. Every sentence correponds to an argument component. Our observations show that most of the arguments can be found on the sentence level. This simplification helps to keep the identification of argumentative relations manageable: Scientific publications are highly complex texts containing argumentation structures that are often hard to understand even for researchers in the respective field.

There are four types of relations: the directed relations *support*, *attack*, *detail*, and the undirected *sequence* relation. The *support* and *attack* relations are argumentative relations, which are known from related work (Peldszus and Stede, 2013), whereas the latter two correspond to discourse relations used in Rhetorical Structure Theory (RST) (William and Thompson, 1988). The *sequence* relation corresponds to "Sequence" in RST, the *detail* relation roughly corresponds to "Background" and "Elaboration". We added the *detail* relation, because we observed many cases in scientific publications, where some background information (for example the definition of a term) is given, which is important for understanding the overall argumentation.

A *support* relation between an argument component A and another argument component B indicates that A supports (reasons, proves) B. Similarly, an *attack* relation between A and B is annotated if A attacks (restricts, contradicts) B. The *detail* relation is used, if A is a detail of B and gives more information or defines something stated in B without argumentative reasoning. Finally, we link two argument components with the *sequence* relation, if two (or more) argument components belong together and only make sense in combination, i.e., they form a multi-sentence argument component.[5]

Annotation Tool We developed our own web-based annotation tool DiGAT which we think is better suited for annotating relations in long texts than existing tools like WebAnno (Yimam et al., 2013), brat (Stenetorp et al., 2012) or GraPAT (Sonntag and Stede, 2014). Although all of them allow to annotate relations between sentences, the view quickly becomes confusing when annotating relations. In WebAnno and brat, the relations are drawn with arrows directly in the text. Only GraPAT visualizes the annotations in a graph. However, the text is included in the nodes directly in the graph, which again becomes confusing for texts with multiple long sentences.

DiGAT has several advantages over existing tools. First, the full-text with its layout structure (e.g., headings, paragraphs) is displayed without any relation annotations on the left-hand side of the screen. The argumentation structure which emerges by adding relations is visualized as a graph on the right-hand side of the screen. Second, the tool automatically marks each sentence in an argumentative paragraph by a different color for better readability. In addition, discourse markers in the text are highlighted to support the annotation of relations.[6]

4 IAA Measures for Relations

This section introduces the measures we used for calculating IAA. We will describe the adaption of measures discussed in section 2 to relation annotations. We also motivate and introduce a novel graph-based measure.

Adaptation of the Dataset to use Chance-corrected IAA Measures In this work, we focus on binary argumentative relations between two argument components. In order to use the chance-corrected measures introduced in section 2, we have to consider each possible pair of argument components in a document as either being connected via a relation (of different types) or not. Then we calculate the IAA with the multi-κ measure (Hubert, 1977) because it is suitable for multiple raters and assumes different probability distributions for each rater.

One drawback of this approach is that the probability of a relation between two argument components decreases with the distance between the components in the text. It is much more likely that two consecutive argument components are related than two components which are in different paragraphs (we observe about 70% of all relations to be between adjacent argument components). Consequently, we get a very high number of non-relations and a very unbalanced dataset because for a document with n=100 argument components, we get

[5]This is necessary because we fixed the size of one argument component to exactly one sentence.

[6]A previous annotation study showed that often discourse markers are signals of argumentative relations (Kluge, 2014).

$\frac{(n-1)*n}{2} = 4950$ pairs, only 1-2% of which are usually related.

Therefore, we limited our evaluation to pairs with a distance of d<6 argument components, since we observed only very few relations with a higher distance. We define the *distance* between two argument components as the number of argument components between them in the text flow. Thus, two adjacent argument components have the distance 0. For a document with n=100 argument components, this reduces the number of pairs to $(n - d) * (d) = 564$. Since we still have a higher probability for a relation with a small distance compared to a relation with a larger distance, we additionally calculated the agreement individually considering only relations with a particular distance (d=0, d=1, d=2, d>2) and averaged over the results weighting them according to the average probability for the distances (69.5% d=0, 18.5% d=1, 7% d=2, 5% d>2). We call this value *Weighted Average* (WA) in the next sections.

Adapted Percentage Agreement / F_1-Score As pointed out in section 2, many researches still report raw percentage agreement. Usually percentage agreement is calculated by dividing the number of annotation items where all annotators agreed by the total number of all annotation items. The high number of non-relations would result in a high agreement that would be meaningless. Therefore, we divide the number of annotation items where the annotators agreed by the number of annotation items where at least one annotator found a relation. We call this approach *adapted percentage agreement* (APA), also called "positive agreement" (Cicchetti and Feinstein, 1990).

We have to keep two things in mind: First, this APA approach leads to worse agreement results than usual percentage agreement because the agreement for non-relations is not considered at all. Second, the APA decreases with an increasing number of annotators because the number of pairs where all annotators agree decreases, and simultaneously the number of pairs where at least one anotator found a relation increases. Therefore, we average over the pairwise APA. This approach is quite similar to the F_1-Score $= \frac{2TP}{2TP+FP+FN}$ (TP = true positives = both annotators found a relation, FP/FN = false positives/false negatives = the annotators disagree). The only difference is the factor 2 for the true positives both in numerator and denominator which gives more weight to the agreements. For the two annotation graphs in figure 2, we get an APA of $\frac{1}{3} = 0.33$ or a F_1-Score of $\frac{2*1}{2*1+2} = 0.5$ (ignoring the direction of the relations).

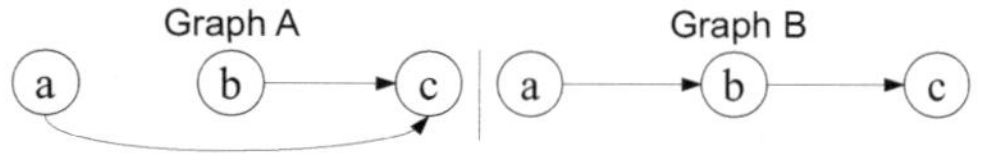

Figure 2: Two simple annotation graphs (each node represents an argument component).

New Graph-based IAA Measure The measures described above consider each pair of argument components independently in isolation. However, we do not annotate pairs of argument components in isolation, but we consider the complete text-flow and represent the argumentation structure in an annotation graph consisting of the argument components as nodes and the relation annotations as edges between them. This means that the annotation of one entity can influence the annotation of a second entity. So the measures do not consider the overall annotation graph structure. For example, in figure 2 both annotators think that the nodes a and b directly or indirectly support/attack node c which we cannot capture if we only consider pairs of argument components in isolation.

Consequently, we also need a method to calculate the IAA for annotation graphs, considering the graph structure. To the best of our knowledge, such a graph-based IAA metric has not been developed so far. There are approaches in graph theory which aim at calculating the similarity of graphs. However, most of these approaches are very complex because they target larger graphs and a matching of the nodes is required (which is not necessary in our case). Hence, we propose a novel graph-based agreement measure, which can identify different annotations with similar meaning. For example, it considers that in figure 2 both annotators directly or indirectly found a relation from node a to node c. Hence, the new measure results in a higher agreement than the standard measures.

The measure determines to what extent graph A is included in graph B and vice versa (note that relation types are ignored in this approach). To calculate to what extent graph A is included in graph B, we average over the sum of the inverse of the shortest path distance between two nodes which are connected by a relation of graph A in graph B:

$$\frac{1}{|E_A|} \sum_{(x,y) \in E_A} \frac{1}{SP_B(x,y)}$$

E_A is the set of edges in graph A with the elements (x,y) whereas x is the source and y the target node. $SP_B(x,y)$ is the shortest path between the nodes x and y in graph B.

We illustrate the process with an example (see figure 2). Starting from graph A (1), we find the two edges $a - c$ (distance 2 in graph B) and $b - c$ (distance 1 in graph B). Starting from graph B (2), we find the two edges $a - b$ (distance ∞ in graph A) and $a - c$ (distance 1 in graph A). So the graph-based agreement is:

(1) $\frac{1}{2} * (\frac{1}{2} + \frac{1}{1}) = 0.75$

(2) $\frac{1}{2} * (\frac{1}{1} + \frac{1}{\infty}) = 0.5$

On average, the graph-based agreement for the graphs A and B is $\frac{(0.75+0.5)}{2} = 0.625$. Considering (1) and (2) as precision and recall, we can also calculate F_1-Score = $\frac{2*precision*recall}{precision+recall}$. This measure has the advantage that it becomes higher for similar precision and recall values (also called "harmonic mean"). So in the example from figure 2 the F_1-Score is $\frac{2*0.5*0.75}{0.5+0.75} = 0.6$.

5 Results and Discussion

In this section, we will perform both a quantitative and a qualitative analysis of the annotated argumentative relations and the argumentation structure.

5.1 Quantitative Analysis

We analyze the IAA for the relations identified by the annotators. Table 2 gives an overview of the class distributions for each annotator (A1 - A4). While the distribution of relation distances is quite homogeneous (about 70% of identified relations are between adjacent argument components), there are large differences regarding the number of identified relations and the distribution of relation types. Especially A4 found more relations than the other annotators. In part, this is due to the fact that A4 annotated only 5 of the 24 documents which had above-average length. Nevertheless, we observe that A3 found only few relations compared to the other annotators, especially of the types sequence and detail (also in absolute numbers) and annotated most of the relations as support which is still less than the other annotators in absolute numbers.

Table 3 presents the IAA for the relations. We get multi-κ values up to 0.63 considering all distances d<6, which is a fair agreement considering the difficulty of the task. We already observed in the individual statistics that A3 identified much fewer relations than the other annotators. This is reflected in the agreement values which are lower for all pairs of annotators where A3 is involved. However, an analysis of the relations annotated by A3 using the graph-based measure reveals that most of these relations where also identified by the other annotators: the graphs by A3 are to a large extent contained in the graphs of the other annotators (0.63 - 0.68). The other way round, the graphs by A3 only marginally contain the graphs of the other annotators (0.29 - 0.41). This indicates that A3 only annotated very explicit argumentative relations (see section 5.2).

There are only small differences between the graph-based measure which considers the argumentation structure, and multi-κ which considers each pair of argument components in isolation. This can be attributed to the fact that about 50% of all argument components are in connected graph components[7] with only two nodes, i.e., there is no argumentation structure to consider for the graph-based measure.

In contrast, if we only consider graph components with at least 3 nodes for any pair of annotators, the graph-based IAA improves by about 0.15 (while the other measures do not change). This clearly demonstrates the advantages of our new graph-based approach for detecting different annotations with similar meaning.

Table 5 shows IAA when considering the relation types. This annotation task requires to decide between 5 different classes (support, attack, detail, sequence, none). The chance-corrected multi-κ values downgrade by about 0.1. If we consider the individual distances (WA measure), we get significantly lower results compared to considering all distances together (d<6).

Table 4 shows the multi-κ values for the different

[7] In a connected graph component, there exists a path between all nodes (assuming undirected edges).

Annotator	Relations									Distance between relations							
	#Sup	%	#Att	%	#Seq	%	#Det	%	#ALL	#d=0	%	#d=1	%	#d=2	%	#d>2	%
A1	45.0	58.8	8.9	11.6	12.0	15.7	10.7	13.9	76.7	51.5	67.2	14.1	18.4	5.9	7.7	5.1	6.7
A2	40.0	43.7	11.5	12.5	26.9	29.3	13.3	14.5	91.7	61.1	66.6	19.3	21.1	6.9	7.5	4.4	4.8
A3	36.5	73.6	3.6	7.2	5.5	11.0	4.1	8.2	49.7	37.7	75.8	8.0	16.1	2.3	4.6	1.7	3.4
A4	54.8	45.7	15.2	12.7	28.6	23.9	21.2	17.7	119.8	82.0	68.4	21.8	18.2	10.0	8.3	6.0	5.0
ALL	44.1	55.4	9.8	11.0	18.2	20.0	12.3	13.6	84.5	58.1	69.5	15.8	18.5	6.3	7.0	4.3	5.0

Table 2: Individual statistics for identified relations (#Sup/Att/Seq/Det = average number of support/attack/sequence/detail relations per document; #ALL = average number of relations per document; #d = average number of relations with distance d per document).

Annotators	Weighted Average (WA)			d<6			Graph-based			
	APA	F_1	multi-κ	APA	F_1	multi-κ	1-2	2-1	Avg.	F_1
A1-A2	0.5030	0.6380	0.4668	0.4681	0.6327	0.5822	0.5102	0.6460	0.5781	0.5607
A1-A4	0.5040	0.6467	0.4421	0.4859	0.6492	0.5988	0.5083	0.7343	**0.6213**	**0.5959**
A4-A2	**0.5553**	**0.6855**	**0.4744**	**0.5265**	**0.6873**	**0.6335**	0.5730	0.6069	0.5900	0.5881
A3-A1	0.3776	0.5261	0.3613	0.3693	0.5345	0.4903	0.6285	0.4059	0.5172	0.4795
A3-A2	0.3813	0.5189	0.3388	0.3629	0.5257	0.4767	**0.6815**	0.3380	0.5097	0.4424
A3-A4	0.3251	0.4690	0.2459	0.3152	0.4782	0.4229	0.6770	0.2868	0.4819	0.3992
ALL	0.4270	0.5559	0.3912	0.4044	0.5683	0.5257	-	-	0.5387	0.4984

Table 3: IAA for relation annotation, relation type is ignored (APA = adapted percentage agreement, weighted average = averaged results for relations with distance 0, 1, 2 and >2, weighted according to their probability; d<6 = agreement for all relations with a distance d<6; 1-2 or 2-1 (graph-based) = measures how much the annotation of annotator 1 is included in the annotation of annotator 2 or vice versa).

Annotators	multi-κ					
	d=0	d=1	d=2	d>2	WA	d<6
A1-A2	0.5426	0.3346	0.2625	0.1865	0.4668	0.5822
A1-A4	0.4756	0.3868	0.3729	0.2768	0.4421	0.5988
A4-A2	0.5388	0.3349	0.3878	0.2151	0.4744	0.6335
A3-A1	0.4079	0.2859	0.2562	0.1949	0.3613	0.4903
A3-A2	0.4002	0.2234	0.1779	0.1369	0.3388	0.4767
A3-A4	0.2889	0.1397	0.1353	0.1950	0.2459	0.4229
ALL	0.4488	0.2856	0.2488	0.1801	0.3912	0.5257

Table 4: IAA for relation annotation with multi-κ measure for different distances (relation type is ignored).

Annotators	Weighted Average (WA)			d<6		
	APA	F_1	multi-κ	APA	F_1	multi-κ
A1-A2	0.3144	0.4588	0.3784	0.2980	0.4516	0.4742
A1-A4	**0.3624**	**0.5124**	**0.4105**	**0.3479**	**0.5111**	**0.5153**
A4-A2	0.3126	0.4611	0.3546	0.3024	0.4594	0.4911
A3-A1	0.2838	0.4275	0.3341	0.2756	0.4278	0.4299
A3-A2	0.1986	0.3167	0.2535	0.1933	0.3187	0.3615
A3-A4	0.1884	0.3048	0.2065	0.1835	0.3078	0.3335
ALL	0.2699	0.4002	0.3246	0.2582	0.4023	0.4285

Table 5: IAA for relation annotation (relation type is considered).

distances in detail. As we can see, the agreement degrades significantly with increasing distance and even for distance d=0 the values are lower than for d<6. The reason for this is the high number of non-relations compared to relations, especially for distances with d>2.

5.2 Qualitative Analysis

In order to get a better understanding of the reasons for the partially low IAA, we performed a qualitative analysis. We focused on support and attack relations and compared instances annotated with high agreement[8] with instances where annotators disagreed.

Relations annotated with high agreement: Support or attack relations annotated with high agreement can be considered as explicit argumentative relations. We identified different types of argument components with explicit incoming support relations, which are typically marked by surface indicators (e.g. sentence mood, discourse markers, stylistic devices): a claim (expressed e.g. as a rhetorical question), an opinion statement marked by words expressing sentiment (e.g. *überraschend (surprisingly)*), a hypothesis marked by a conjunctive sentence mood and modal verbs (e.g. *könnte (could)*), a conclusion or summarizing statement marked by discourse markers (e.g. *daher (therefore)*), or a generalizing statement marked by adverbial expressions (e.g. *gemeinsam sein (have in common)*).

Another explicit support relation was annotated for argument components supporting an observation that is based on a single piece of evidence; here the supporting argument component contained lexical indicators such as *konform gehen (be in line with)*. Explicit attack relations, on the other hand, appeared

[8] High agreement means that 3 or 4 annotators agreed.

to be marked by a combination of discourse markers expressing concession (e.g., *jedoch, allerdings (however), aber (but)*) and negation or downtoning markers (e.g. *kaum (hardly)*). We found negation to be expressed in many variants, including not only explicit negation, such as *nicht (not), kein (no)*, but also (implicit) lexicalized negation, e.g. verbs such as *ausstehen (is pending)*.

Relations where annotators disagreed: Our analysis of support relations that were annotated only by one of 3 (4) annotators revealed that there are many cases, where the disagreement was due to an alternation of support and detail or support and sequence relation. These cases can be regarded as weakly argumentative, i.e. the argument component with the incoming relation is not considered by all annotators as a statement that requires argumentative support.

We performed the same qualitative analysis for attack relations and found that in most cases either a concession marker in the attacking argument component is present, or some form of negation, but not both as in the explicit case of the attack relation.

Ambiguity as the main reason for disagreement: One of the main challenges in identifying argumentative relations on a fine grained level in scientific publications is ambiguity (Stab et al., 2014). All the measures used to calculate IAA assume that there is one single correct solution to the annotation problem. Actually, we believe that in many cases several correct solutions exist depending on how the annotators interpret the text. In our qualitative analysis, we found that this is especially true for argument components that are lacking discourse markers or other surface indicators. For example, the following text snippet can be interpreted in two ways:

*"School grades have severe consequences for the academic career of students.**(a)** Students with good grades can choose among numerous career options.**(b)** According to Helmke (2009), judgments of teachers must therefore be accurate, when qualification certificates are granted.**(c)**"*[9]

According to one interpretation, there is a relation chain between a, b, and c (a supports b and b supports c), while the other interpretation considers a and b as a sequence which together supports c (a supports c and b supports c).

Another source of ambiguity is the ambiguity of discourse markers, which sometimes seems to trigger annotation decisions that are based on the presence of a discourse marker, rather than on the semantics of the relation between the two argument components. A prototypical example are discourse markers expressing concession, e.g. *jedoch, allerdings (however)*. They are often used to indicate attacking argument components, but they can also be used in a different function, namely to introduce counter-arguments. In this function, which has also been described by (Grote et al., 1997), they appear in an argument component with incoming support relations.

Apart from ambiguity, we found that another difficulty are different granularities of some argument components. Sentences might relate to coarse-grained multi-sentence units and this is not representable with our fine-grained annotation scheme. This is illustrated by the following example where *against this background* relates to a long paragraph describing the current situation: *Against this background, the accuracy of performative assessment received growing attention recently.*

6 Conclusion

We presented the results of an annotation study to identify argumentation structures on a fine-grained level in scientific journal articles from the educational domain. The annotation scheme we developed results in a representation of arguments as small graph structures. We evaluated the annotated dataset quantitatively using multiple IAA measures. For this, we proposed adaptions to existing IAA measures and introduced a new graph-based measure which reflects the semantic similarity of different annotation graphs. Based on a qualitative analysis where we discussed characteristics of argument components with high and low agreement, we identified the often inherent ambiguity of argumentation structures as a major challenge for future work on the development of automatic methods.

[9] Südkamp and Möller (2009), shortened and translated.

Acknowledgements

This work has been supported by the German Institute for Educational Research (DIPF) as part of the graduate program "Knowledge Discovery in Scientific Literature" (KDSL). We thank Stephanie Bäcker and Greta Koerner for their valuable contributions.

References

Shameem Ahmed, Catherine Blake, Kate Williams, Noah Lenstra, and Qiyuan Liu. 2013. Identifying claims in social science literature. In *Proceedings of the iConference*, pages 942–946, Fort Worth, USA. iSchools.

M.A. Angrosh, Stephen Cranefield, and Nigel Stanger. 2012. A Citation Centric Annotation Scheme for Scientific Articles. In *Australasian Language Technology Association Workshop*, pages 5–14, Dunedin, New Zealand.

Karl-Heinz Best. 2002. Satzlängen im Deutschen: Verteilungen, Mittelwerte, Sprachwandel. In *Göttinger Beiträge zur Sprachwissenschaft 7*, pages 7–31.

Or Biran and Owen Rambow. 2011. Identifying justifications in written dialogs by classifying text as argumentative. *International Journal of Semantic Computing*, 05(04):363–381.

Catherine Blake. 2010. Beyond genes, proteins, and abstracts: Identifying scientific claims from full-text biomedical articles. *Journal of biomedical informatics*, 43(2):173–189.

Lynn Carlson, Daniel Marcu, and Mary Ellen Okurowski. 2001. Building a Discourse-tagged Corpus in the Framework of Rhetorical Structure Theory. In *Proceedings of the Second SIGdial Workshop on Discourse and Dialogue*, pages 1–10, Aalborg, Denmark.

Domenic V. Cicchetti and Alvan R. Feinstein. 1990. High agreement but low kappa: II. Resolving the paradoxes. *Journal of Clinical Epidemiology*, 43(6):551 – 558.

J. Cohen. 1960. A Coefficient of Agreement for Nominal Scales. *Educational and Psychological Measurement*, 20(1):37.

Danish Contractor, Yufan Guo, and Anna Korhonen. 2012. Using Argumentative Zones for Extractive Summarization of Scientific Articles. In *Proceedings of the 23th International Conference on Computational Linguistics (COLING 2012)*, pages 663–678, Mumbai, India.

Vanessa Wei Feng and Graeme Hirst. 2011. Classifying Arguments by Scheme. In *Proceedings of the 49th Annual Meeting of the Association for Computational Linguistics: Human Language Technologies*, pages 987–996, Portland, USA.

Joseph L. Fleiss. 1971. Measuring nominal scale agreement among many raters. *Psychological bulletin*, 76(5):378.

Eirini Florou, Stasinos Konstantopoulos, Antonis Koukourikos, and Pythagoras Karampiperis. 2013. Argument extraction for supporting public policy formulation. In *Proceedings of the 7th Workshop on Language Technology for Cultural Heritage, Social Sciences, and Humanities*, pages 49–54, Sofia, Bulgaria.

James B. Freeman. 2011. *Argument Structure: Representation and Theory*, volume 18 of *Argumentation Library*. Springer.

Brigitte Grote, Nils Lenke, and Manfred Stede. 1997. Ma(r)king concessions in English and German. *Discourse Processes*, 24(1):87–118.

Lawrence Hubert. 1977. Kappa revisited. *Psychological Bulletin*, 84(2):289.

Roland Kluge. 2014. Automatic Analysis of Arguments about Controversial Educational Topics in Web Documents, Master Thesis, Ubiquitious Knowledge Processing Lab, TU Darmstadt.

Maria Liakata, Simone Teufel, Advaith Siddharthan, and Colin R Batchelor. 2010. Corpora for the Conceptualisation and Zoning of Scientific Papers. In *Proceedings of the 7th Conference on Language Resources and Evaluation (LREC)*, pages 2054–2061, Valletta, Malta.

Maria Liakata, Shyamasree Saha, Simon Dobnik, Colin Batchelor, and Dietrich Rebholz-Schuhmann. 2012. Automatic recognition of conceptualization zones in scientific articles and two life science applications. *Bioinformatics*, 28(7):991–1000.

Yoko Mizuta and Nigel Collier. 2004. Zone identification in biology articles as a basis for information extraction. In *Proceedings of the International Joint Workshop on Natural Language Processing in Biomedicine and its Applications*, pages 29–35, Geneva, Switzerland.

Raquel Mochales-Palau and Marie-Francine Moens. 2011. Argumentation mining. *Artificial Intelligence and Law*, 19(1):1–22.

Dae Hoon Park and Catherine Blake. 2012. Identifying comparative claim sentences in full-text scientific articles. In *Proceedings of the Workshop on Detecting Structure in Scholarly Discourse*, pages 1–9, Jeju, Republic of Korea.

Andreas Peldszus and Manfred Stede. 2013. From Argument Diagrams to Argumentation Mining in Texts: A Survey. *International Journal of Cognitive Informatics and Natural Intelligence (IJCINI)*, 7(1):1–31.

Rashmi Prasad, Nikhil Dinesh, Alan Lee, Eleni Miltsakaki, Livio Robaldo, Aravind Joshi, and Bonnie Webber. 2008. The Penn Discourse TreeBank 2.0. In *Proceedings of the Sixth International Conference on Language Resources and Evaluation (LREC'08)*, pages 28–30, Marrakech, Morocco.

Ines Rehbein, Joseph Ruppenhofer, Caroline Sporleder, and Manfred Pinkal. 2012. Adding nominal spice to SALSA-frame-semantic annotation of German nouns and verbs. In *Proceedings of the 11th Conference on Natural Language Processing (KONVENS12)*, pages 89–97, Vienna, Austria.

Patrick Ruch, Celia Boyer, Christine Chichester, Imad Tbahriti, Antoine Geissbühler, Paul Fabry, Julien Gobeill, Violaine Pillet, Dietrich Rebholz-Schuhmann, Christian Lovis, et al. 2007. Using argumentation to extract key sentences from biomedical abstracts. *International journal of medical informatics*, 76(2):195–200.

William A Scott. 1955. Reliability of Content Analysis: The Case of Nominal Scale Coding. *Public Opinion Quarterly*, 19(3):321–325.

Jonathan Sonntag and Manfred Stede. 2014. GraPAT: a Tool for Graph Annotations. In *Proceedings of the Ninth International Conference on Language Resources and Evaluation (LREC'14)*, Reykjavik, Iceland.

Christian Stab and Iryna Gurevych. 2014. Annotating Argument Components and Relations in Persuasive Essays. In *Proceedings of the the 25th International Conference on Computational Linguistics (COLING 2014)*, pages 1501–1510, Dublin, Ireland.

Christian Stab, Christian Kirschner, Judith Eckle-Kohler, and Iryna Gurevych. 2014. Argumentation Mining in Persuasive Essays and Scientific Articles from the Discourse Structure Perspective. In *Frontiers and Connections between Argumentation Theory and Natural Language Processing*, Bertinoro, Italy.

Pontus Stenetorp, Sampo Pyysalo, Goran Topić, Tomoko Ohta, Sophia Ananiadou, and Jun'ichi Tsujii. 2012. BRAT: a web-based tool for NLP-assisted text annotation. In *Proceedings of the Demonstrations at the 13th Conference of the European Chapter of the Association for Computational Linguistics (EACL)*, pages 102–107, Avignon, France.

Anna Südkamp and Jens Möller. 2009. Referenzgruppeneffekte im Simulierten Klassenraum. *Zeitschrift für Pädagogische Psychologie*, 23(3):161–174.

Simone Teufel and Marc Moens. 2002. Summarizing scientific articles: experiments with relevance and rhetorical status. *Computational linguistics*, 28(4):409–445.

Simone Teufel, Advaith Siddharthan, and Colin Batchelor. 2009. Towards discipline-independent argumentative zoning: evidence from chemistry and computational linguistics. In *Proceedings of the 2009 Conference on Empirical Methods in Natural Language Processing (EMNLP)*, pages 1493–1502, Singapore.

Simone Teufel. 1999. *Argumentative Zoning: Information Extraction from Scientific Text*. Ph.D. thesis, University of Edinburgh.

Stephen E. Toulmin. 1958. *The uses of Argument*. Cambridge University Press.

Lonneke van der Plas, Tanja Samardžić, and Paola Merlo. 2010. Cross-lingual validity of PropBank in the manual annotation of French. In *Proceedings of the Fourth Linguistic Annotation Workshop*, pages 113–117, Uppsala, Sweden.

Douglas Walton, Chris Reed, and Fabrizio Macagno. 2008. *Argumentation Schemes*. Cambridge University Press.

Douglas N Walton. 1996. *Argumentation schemes for presumptive reasoning*. Routledge.

Bonnie Webber, Mark Egg, and Valia Kordoni. 2012. Discourse structure and language technology. *Natural Language Engineering*, 18:437–490.

Mann William and Sandra Thompson. 1988. Rhetorical structure theory: Towards a functional theory of text organization. *Text-Interdisciplinary Journal for the Study of Discourse*, 8(3):243–281.

Antonio Jimeno Yepes, James G. Mork, and Alan R. Aronson. 2013. Using the argumentative structure of scientific literature to improve information access. In *Proceedings of the 2013 Workshop on Biomedical Natural Language Processing (BioNLP)*, pages 102–110, Sofia, Bulgaria.

Seid Muhie Yimam, Iryna Gurevych, Richard Eckart de Castilho, and Chris Biemann. 2013. WebAnno: A Flexible, Web-based and Visually Supported System for Distributed Annotations. In *Proceedings of the 51st Annual Meeting of the Association for Computational Linguistics (System Demonstrations) (ACL 2013)*, pages 1–6, Sofia, Bulgaria.

*** Formatting Issue - Best Available Paper/Graphic ***

Identifying Argumentation Schemes in Genetics Research Articles

Nancy L. Green
Dept. of Computer Science
U. of N. Carolina Greensboro
Greensboro, NC 27402, USA
nlgreen@uncg.edu

Abstract

This paper presents preliminary work on identification of argumentation schemes, i.e., identifying premises, conclusion and name of argumentation scheme, in arguments for scientific claims in genetics research articles. The goal is to develop annotation guidelines for creating corpora for argumentation mining research. This paper gives the specification of ten semantically distinct argumentation schemes based on analysis of argumentation in several journal articles. In addition, it presents an empirical study on readers' ability to recognize some of the argumentation schemes.

1 Introduction

There has been an explosion in the on-line publication of genetics research articles, creating a critical need for information access tools for genetics researchers, biological database curators, and clinicians. Research on biological/biomedical natural language processing (BioNLP) is an active area of research with the goal of developing such tools. Previous research in BioNLP has focused mainly on fundamental text mining challenges such as named entity recognition and relation extraction (Cohen and Demner-Fushman 2014). However, a key feature of scientific writing is the use of argumentation.

It is important for information access tools to recognize argumentation in scientific text. First, argumentation is a level of discourse analysis that provides critical context for interpretation of a text. For example, a text may give an argument against a hypothesis P, so it would be misleading for a text mining program to extract P as a fact stated in that text. Second, a user should be able to access a summary of arguments for and against a particular claim. Also, to evaluate the strength of an argument a user should be able to see the arguments upon which it depends, i.e., arguments supporting or attacking its premises. Third, tools that display citation relationships among documents (Teufel 2010) could provide finer-grained information about relationships between arguments in different documents.

Argumentation mining aims to automatically identify arguments in text, the arguments' premises, conclusion and argumentation scheme (or form of argument), and relationships between arguments in a text or set of texts. Most previous work in argumentation mining has focused on non-scientific text (e.g. Mochales and Moens 2011; Feng and Hirst 2011; Cabrio and Villata 2012). Previous NLP research on scientific discourse (e.g. Mizuta et al. 2005; Teufel 2010; Liakata 2012a) has focused on recognizing information status (hypothesis, background knowledge, new knowledge claim, etc.) but has not addressed deeper argumentation analysis.

This paper presents our preliminary work on identification of argumentation schemes in genetics research articles. We define this subtask, unlike some others, e.g. Feng and Hirst (2011), as identifying the premises and conclusion of an argument together with the name of its argumentation scheme. One contribution of the paper is the specification of ten semantically distinct argumentation schemes based on analysis of argumentation in several genetics journal articles. Our goal is to develop annotation guidelines for creating corpora for argumentation mining research. Most of the schemes do not appear in the principal catalogue of argumentation schemes cited in past argumentation mining studies (Walton et al. 2008). In addition, we present an empirical study on readers' ability to recognize some

Proceedings of the 2nd Workshop on Argumentation Mining, pages 12–21,
Denver, Colorado, June 4, 2015.

of the argumentation schemes. The paper concludes with discussion on plans for annotating debate in this type of discourse.

2 Background and Related Work

An argument consists of a set of *premises* and a *conclusion*. *Enthymemes* are arguments with implicit premises and/or conclusions. *Argumentation schemes* are abstract descriptions of acceptable, but not necessarily deductively valid, forms of argument used in everyday conversation, law, and science (Walton et al. 2008). To illustrate, an abductive argumentation scheme is common in medical diagnosis. The premise is that a certain event E has been observed (e.g. coughing). Another, sometimes implicit, premise is that C-type events often lead to E-type events. The tentative conclusion is that a certain event C has occurred (e.g. a respiratory infection) that caused the event that was observed.

As in this example, the conclusions of many argumentation schemes are considered to be defeasible, and are open to debate by means of *critical questions* associated with each scheme (Walton et al. 2008). For example, one of the critical questions of the above argumentation scheme is whether there is an alternative more plausible explanation for the observed event. Recognition of the argumentation scheme underlying an argument is critical for challenging an argument via critical questions and recognizing answers to those challenges, i.e., in representing and reasoning about scientific debate.

There has been some work on argumentation mining of debate, but none addressing debate in the natural sciences. Teufel et al. (2006) developed a scheme with categories such as support and anti-support for annotating citation function in a corpus of computational linguistics articles. Cabrio and Villata (2012) addressed recognition of support and attack relations between arguments in a corpus of on-line dialogues stating user opinions. Stab and Gurevych (2013) and Stab et al. (2015) are developing guidelines for annotating support-attack relationships between arguments based on a corpus of short persuasive essays written by students and another corpus of 20 full-text articles from the education research domain. Peldszus and Stede (2013) are developing guidelines for annotating relations between arguments which have been applied to the Potsdam Commentary Corpus (Stede 2004). However research on mining debate has not addressed more fine-grained relationships such as asking and responding to particular critical questions of argumentation schemes.

Furthermore, there has been no work on argumentation scheme recognition in scientific text. Feng and Hirst (2011) investigated argumentation scheme recognition using the Araucaria corpus, which contains annotated arguments from newspaper articles, parliamentary records, magazines, and on-line discussion boards (Reed et al. 2010). Taking premises and conclusion as given, Feng and Hirst addressed the problem of recognizing the name of the argumentation scheme for the five most frequently occurring schemes of Walton et al. (2008) in the corpus: *Argument from example* (149), *Argument from cause to effect* (106), *Practical reasoning* (53), *Argument from Consequences* (44), and *Argument from Verbal Classification* (41). (The number of instances of each scheme is given in parentheses.) Classification techniques achieved high accuracy for *Argument from example* and *Practical reasoning*.

Text with genetics content has been the object of study in some previous NLP research. Mizuta et al. (2005) investigated automatic classification of information status of text segments in genetics journal articles. The Colorado Richly Annotated Full Text Corpus (CRAFT) contains 67 full-text articles on the mouse genome that have been linguistically annotated (Verspoor et al. 2012) and annotated with concepts from standard biology ontologies (Bada et al. 2012). The Variome corpus, consisting of 10 journal articles on the relationship of human genetic variation to disease, has been annotated with a set of concepts and relations (Verspoor et al. 2013). None of these corpora have been annotated for argumentation mining.

Finally, Green et al. (2011) identified argumentation schemes in a corpus of letters written by genetic counselors. The argumentation schemes were used by a natural language generation system to generate letters to patients about their case. However, the argumentation in genetics research articles appears more complex than that used in patient communication. Green (2014; 2015) analyzed argumentation in one genetics journal article but did not generalize the results to other articles, nor provide any empirical evaluation.

3 Argumentation Schemes

This section describes ten argumentation schemes that we identified in four research articles on genetic variants/mutations that may cause human disease (Schrauwen et al. 2012; Baumann et al. 2012; Charlesworth et al. 2012; McInerney et al. 2013). The ten schemes are not the only ones we found but they represent major forms of causal argumentation for the scientific claims of the articles. The schemes are semantically distinct in terms of their premises and conclusions. Most of these schemes are not described in the catalogue of argumentation schemes frequently cited by argumentation mining researchers (Walton et al. 2008). None of them are the same as the ones addressed by Feng and Hirst (2011).

To facilitate comparison of the schemes, they are presented in Table 1 in a standardized format highlighting how the schemes vary in terms of two event variables, X and Y. The articles where the schemes were found are identified by the first initial of the surname of the first author, in parentheses next to the name of the scheme. Most scheme names were chosen for mneumonic value. In the table, X and Y are events, such as the existence of a genetic mutation and disease, respectively, in an individual or group. The premises describe (i) whether the X events have been hypothesized, observed, or eliminated from further consideration, (ii) whether the Y events have been observed, and (iii) (the *Causal potential* column) whether a potential causal relation has been previously established between Xs and Ys. The conclusions, which are understood to be defeasible, describe whether an event X is concluded to have possibly occurred and/or to be a/the possible cause of Y.

As a step towards annotating these argumentation schemes in a corpus, we created initial guidelines containing examples and descriptions of the ten schemes. Illustrating some of the challenges in identifying arguments in this literature, Figure 1 shows the guidelines for two schemes (*Effect to Cause* and *Failed to Observe Effect of Hypothesized Cause*). In Figure 1, three text excerpts from an article are presented. The first two excerpts contain general information needed to interpret the arguments, including one premise of each argument. The third excerpt contains an additional premise of each argument, and conveys the conclusion of each argument. The last sentence of the third excerpt, "He was initially suspected to have EDS VIA, but the urinary LP/HP ratio was within the normal range" conveys the conclusion of the first argument: the patient may have EDS VIA. However, by providing evidence conflicting with that conclusion (the LP/HP data), the sentence also implicitly conveys the conclusion of the second argument: it is not likely that the patient has EDS VIA. The only overt signals of this conflict seem to be the qualifier 'initially suspected' and the 'but' construction.

Our guidelines provide a paraphrase of each argument since many of the example arguments have implicit premises or conclusions (i.e. are enthymemes). For example, the conclusion of the *Failed to Observe Effect of Hypothesized Cause* argument shown in Figure 1 is implicit. In some cases a missing premise is supplied from information presented in the article but not in the given excerpts. In other cases, a missing premise is paraphrased by presenting generally accepted background knowledge of the intended reader such as "A mutation of a gene that is expressed in a human tissue or system may cause an abnormality in that tissue or system." In yet other cases, a conclusion of one argument is an implicit premise of another argument.

As illustrated in Figure 1, each paraphrased argument in the guidelines is followed by a more abstract description of the argumentation scheme. Abstract descriptions of each argumentation scheme are presented in Figures 2 and 3. Note that *Effect to Cause, Eliminate Candidates*, and *Failed to Observe Effect of Hypothesized Cause* are similar but not identical to the *Abductive Argumentation Scheme, Argument from Alternatives*, and *Argument from Falsification* of (Walton et al. 2008), respectively. However, none of the descriptions in (Walton et al. 2008) are attributed to arguments found in the science research literature.

4 Pilot Study

A pilot study was performed to determine the effectiveness of the initial guidelines for identifying a subset of the argumentation schemes. For the study, we added a two-page overview of the task to the beginning of the guidelines and a quiz at the end; and, in the interest of reducing the time required to complete the task, removed the five examples from one article (Charlesworth et al. 2012), which repeated three of the argumentation schemes from the other sources. To summarize, the pilot study materials consisted of examples of eight schemes from (Schrauwen et al. 2012) and (Baumann et al. 2012), and a multiple-choice quiz based upon examples from (McInerney et al. 2013).

The quiz consisted of five multi-part problems, each problem concerning one or more excerpts from (McInerney et al. 2013) containing an argument. The quiz did not address the task of determining the presence of an argument and its boundaries within an article. Problems I-III tested participants' ability to recognize premises and/or conclusions and names of four key argumentation schemes: *Effect to Cause, Eliminate Candidates, Causal Agreement and Difference*, and *Joint Method of Agreement and Difference*. Problem I (shown in Figure 4) presented a paraphrase of the conclusion of the argument and asked the participant to identify the excerpts containing the premises; and to identify the name of the argumentation scheme from a list of six names (the four scheme names that begin with *Failed* were omitted, although the participant could have selected *None of the above* for those). Problem II asked the participant to select the premises and conclusion of the argument from a list of paraphrases; and to identify the name of the argumentation scheme from the same list of choices given in problem I.

In problem III, the excerpts contained two arguments for the same conclusion. The participant was given a paraphrase of the conclusion and asked to select the excerpt best expressing the premise of the Causal Agreement and Difference argument and the excerpt best expressing the premise of the Joint Method of Agreement and Difference argument. The purpose of problems IV and V was to evaluate participants' ability to interpret more complex argumentation. The excerpts given in problem IV actually conflated multiple arguments. Rather than ask the participant to tease apart the component arguments, the problem asked the participant to select the paraphrases expressing the (main) conclusion and premise. Problem V asked the participant to select the paraphrase best expressing the conclusion of the excerpts in IV and V together.

The study was performed with two different groups of participants. The first group consisted of university students in an introductory genetics class early in the course. They had not received instruction on argumentation in their biology courses, had covered basic genetics in their first two years of study, and had no experience reading genetics research articles. The students were required to participate in the study but were informed that the quiz results would not influence their course grade and that allowing use of their quiz results in our study was voluntary. The students completed the study in 45 to 60 minutes. The results are shown in Table 2.

To comment, since the students had limited relevant background and may not have been motivated to succeed in the task, some of the class did very poorly. The mean number answered correctly on the 11 problems was 49% (N=23). However, six students scored between 73% and 82% (the highest score). The best performance was on Problem I on an *Effect to Cause* argument. This may be due, at least in part, to the fact that this argumentation scheme appeared first in the guidelines and was also the first problem. The question that the fewest number of students answered correctly was III.1, which was to identify the excerpt containing a premise of a Causal Agreement and Difference argument. Overall, the main lesson we learned from this group of study participants, compared to the other participants (see below), is that training and/or motivation need to be improved before running such a study with a similar group of students.

The second group of participants consisted of researchers at several different universities in North America. No compensation was provided. The researchers came from a variety of backgrounds: (A) computer science with no background in genetics, NLP or argumentation, (B) learning sciences with background in argumentation but none in genetics, (C) biology with extensive background in genetics but none in NLP or argumentation, and (D and E) BioNLP researchers. The results are shown in Table 3. Researchers A, C, and D answered all of the questions correctly; B missed only one (III.1); E missed two (II.3 and IV.1). B commented that B did not have sufficient knowledge of genetics to understand the excerpt. The results from this group confirm that several key schemes could be recognized by other researchers based upon reading the guidelines.

5 Annotating Debate

The guidelines do not yet address annotation of relationships between pairs of arguments within an article. Our plan is to annotate the following types of relationships which we found. First, as illustrated by the two arguments shown in Figure 1, two arguments with conflicting conclusions may be presented. Note that four of the argumentation schemes we have identified (see Table 1) may play a prominent role in annotation of this type of relationship, since they provide a way of supporting the negation of the conclusions of other schemes. Second, multiple evidence may be presented to strengthen the premises of an argument. In the excerpt illustrating *Failed Predicted Effect* in Figure 2, the premise that G is not predicted to have effect P is supported by evidence from three different genetic analysis tools (Mutation Taster, SIFT, or PolyPhen-2).

The third relationship is to preempt an attack by addressing one of the critical questions of an argumentation scheme. One instance of this occurs in (McInerney-Leo et al. 2013), in which a Causal Agreement and Difference argument concludes that a certain variant is the most likely cause of a disease in a certain family, since the occurrence of the variant and the disease is consistent with (the causal mechanism of) autosomal recessive inheritance. Nevertheless, one might ask the critical question whether some other factor could be responsible. Addressing this challenge, a Joint Method of Agreement and Difference argument is given to provide additional support to that claim, since the disease was not found in a control group of individuals who do not have the variant.

6 Conclusion

This paper presented a specification of ten causal argumentation schemes used to make arguments for scientific claims in genetics research journal articles. The specifications and some of the examples from which they were derived were used to create an initial draft of guidelines for annotation of a corpus. The guidelines were evaluated in a pilot study that showed that several key schemes could be recognized by other researchers based upon reading the guidelines.

Acknowledgments

We thank Dr. Malcolm Schug of the UNCG Department of Biology for verifying our interpretation of some of the articles. We also thank the reviewers for their helpful comments.

Argumentation Scheme	X	Y	Causal potential	Conclusion
Effect to Cause (B, M)	Unknown	Observed	Yes	X occurred & caused Y
Failed to Observe Effect of Hypothesized Cause (B)	Hypothesized	Not observed	Yes	X did not occur & not cause of Y
Failed to Observe Expected Cause (S)	Not observed	Observed	Yes	X not cause of Y
Consistent with Predicted Effect (S)	Observed	Observed	Yes	X cause of Y
Failed Predicted Effect (C)	Observed	Observed	No	X not cause of Y
Hypothesize Candidates (S, C)	Observed set of Xs	Observed	Yes	One of Xs cause of Y
Eliminate Candidates (S, C, M)	Observed set of Xs but X_0 can be eliminated	Observed	Yes	All Xs but X_0 cause of Y
Causal Agreement and Difference (S, C, M)	Observed in group 1, not in group 2	Observed in group 1, not in group 2	Yes	X cause of Y
Failed Causal Agreement and Difference (C)	Observed in all of group	Not observed in all of group	Yes	X not cause of Y
Joint Method of Agreement and Difference (S, M)	Observed in all of group	Observed in all of group	No	X cause of Y

Table 1. Semantic distinctions among argumentation schemes identified in genetics articles.

I.1	I.2	I.3	II.1	II.2	II.3	III.1	III.2	IV.1	IV.2	V.
16	12	15	9	14	11	4	10	12	13	8

Table 2. Number of students (N=23) who answered each question correctly.

*** Formatting Issue - Best Available Paper/Graphic ***

I.1	I.2	I.3	II.1	II.2	II.3	III.1	III.2	IV.1	IV.2	V.
5	5	5	5	5	4	4	5	4	5	5

Table 3. Number of researchers (N=5) who answered each question correctly.

Excerpts from (Baumann et al. 2012):
The Ehlers-Danlos syndrome (EDS) comprises a clinically and genetically heterogeneous group of heritable connective tissue disorders that predominantly affect skin, joints, ligaments, blood vessels, and internal organs… The natural history and mode of inheritance differ among the six major types … Among them, the kyphoscoliotic type of EDS (EDS VIA) … is characterized by severe muscle hypotonia at birth, progressive kyphoscoliosis, marked skin hyperelasticity with widened atrophic scars, and joint hypermobility. …

The underlying defect in EDS VIA is a deficiency of the enzyme lysyl hydroxylase 1 … caused by mutations in *PLOD1* … A deficiency of lysyl hydroxyl results in an abnormal urinary excretion pattern of lysyl pyridinoline (LP) and hydroxylysyl pyridinoline (HP) crosslinks with an increased LP/HP ratio, which is diagnostic for EDS VIA.

At 14 years of age, the index person P1 … was referred to the Department of Paediatrics … for the evaluation of severe kyphoscoliosis, joint hypermobility and muscle weakness. He was initially suspected to have EDS VIA, but the urinary LP/HP ratio was within the normal range.

First Argument Paraphrase:
a. Premise: P1 has severe kyphoscoliosis, joint hypermobility and muscle weakness.
b. Premise: EDS VIA is characterized by severe muscle hypotonia at birth, progressive kyphoscoliosis, marked skin hyperelasticity with widened atrophic scars, and joint hypermobility.
c. Conclusion: P1 may have EDS VIA.

The above is an example of this type of argument:
Effect to Cause (Inference to the Best Explanation)
- Premise (a in example): Certain properties P were observed (such as severe kyphoscoliosis) in an individual.
- Premise (b in example): There is a known potential chain of events linking a certain condition G to observation of P.
- Conclusion (c in example): G may be the cause of P in that individual.

Second Argument Paraphrase:
a. Premise: P1's LP/HP ratio was within normal range.
b. Premise: The underlying defect in EDS VIA is a deficiency of the enzyme lysyl hydroxylase 1 caused by mutations in *PLOD1*. A deficiency of lysyl hydroxyl results in an abnormal urinary excretion pattern of lysyl pyridinoline (LP) and hydroxylysyl pyridinoline (HP) crosslinks with an increased LP/HP ratio.
c. Conclusion: It is not likely that P1 has EDS VIA.

The above is an example of this type of argument:
Failed to Observe Effect of Hypothesized Cause
- Premise (a in example): Certain properties P were not observed (such as increased LP/HP ratio) in an individual.
- Premise (b in example): There is a known potential chain of events linking a certain condition G to observation of P.
- Premise (c in example): G may not be present in that individual.

Figure 1. Description of two argumentation schemes in the initial guidelines.

***** Formatting Issue - Best Available Paper/Graphic *****

Effect to Cause
Premise: Certain properties P were observed in an individual.
Premise: There is a potential chain of events linking a condition G to observation of P.
Conclusion: G may be the cause of P in that individual.
Example: See Figure 1.

Failed to Observe Effect of Hypothesized Cause
Premise: Certain properties P were not observed in an individual.
Premise: There is a potential chain of events linking a condition G to observation of P.
Conclusion: G may not be present in that individual (and is not the cause of P in that individual).
Example: See Figure 1.

Failed to Observe Expected Cause
Premise: G is missing from one or more individuals with property P.
Premise: G may be a cause of P in some cases.
Conclusion: G is not likely the cause of P in this case.
Example (Schrauwen): "We screened 24 unrelated affected Belgian and Dutch individuals with a moderate to severe hearing loss for mutations in *CABP2* ..., but we could not identify a clear damaging mutation in any of them."

Consistent with Predicted Effect
Premise: G and P were observed in certain individuals.
Premise: There is a potential chain of events linking G to P.
Conclusion: G may be the cause of certain cases of P.
Example (Schrauwen) : "On the basis of our present findings ... dysregulation of IHC synaptic transmission could be one pathogenic mechanism underlying hearing impairment in DFNB93. ... In IHCs, the c.637+1G>T mutation in *CABP2* would most likely enhance inactivation of synaptic Ca^{2+} influx. This, in turn, could reduce rates of transmitter release and consequently diminish spiral ganglion neuron firing and ascending auditory-pathway activation."
[Note: Earlier in the article, the authors describe finding the c.637+1G>T variant of *CABP2*, which is in the DFNB93 region, in members of a family who were affected with autosomal recessive non-syndromic hearing loss.]

Failed Predicted Effect
Premise: G was (previously considered to be) a candidate cause of P in some individuals.
Premise: G is not predicted to have effect P.
Conclusion: G may not be a cause of P.
Example (Charlesworth): "The second was a heterozygous missense variant ... in exon 2 of *PPM1K* ... on chromosome 4. It was not predicted to be damaging by MutationTaster, SIFT, or PolyPhen-2 ..."

Hypothesize Candidates
Premise: There is a potential causal relationship between a certain type of event and a certain type of effect.
Premise: Some individual(s) has experienced a certain effect of that type
Conclusion: There is a set of candidates, one of which may be the cause of that effect.
Example (Charlesworth): "In order to maximize the chances of isolating the causal variant ... The first strategy involved selecting only those variants that were present in the exome data of both affected family members for analysis."
[Note: Elsewhere in the article two affected family members whose exome data was analyzed are identified as II-2 and III-7. They are members of a family that exhibits autosomal dominant inheritance of cervical dystonia.]

Figure 2: Some Argumentation Scheme Definitions and Examples

***** Formatting Issue - Best Available Paper/Graphic *****

Eliminate Candidates
Premise: There is a set of candidates C, one of which may be the cause of event E.
Premise: Generally accepted statements that explain why some candidates may be eliminated
Premise: One or more members of C can be eliminated as candidates.
Conclusion: One of the remaining members of C may be the cause of E.
Example (Charlesworth): "Homozygous variants, synonymous variants, and variants recorded in dbSNP135 were initially removed. We then filtered out any variant present at a global minor allele frequency (MAF) ≥ 1% in a range of publically available databases of sequence variation (1000 Genomes, Complete Genomic 69 Database, and the National Heart, Lung, and Blood Institute [NHLBI] Exome Sequencing Project database), as well as those found in two or more of our own in-house exomes from individuals (n = 200) with unrelated diseases."

Causal Agreement and Difference
Premise: There is a set of individuals I_present that have a feature F and property P.
Premise: There is a set of individuals I_absent that have neither feature F nor property P.
Premise: There is a plausible causal mechanism that could account for the similarities and differences between I-absent and I-present.
Conclusion: F may be the cause of P in I_present.
Example (Charlesworth): "The third, a missense mutation (c.1480A>T ...) in exon 15 of *ANO3* ... on chromosome 11, segregated perfectly with the disease status in definitely affected and unaffected individuals."

Failed Causal Agreement and Difference
Premise: There is a set of individuals I_present who have feature F and who do not have property P.
Premise: There is a plausible causal link from F to P that could account for the presence of P in I_present if P had occurred.
Conclusion: F may not be a cause of P.
Example (Charlesworth): "This strategy revealed three potentially pathogenic variants. The first, a heterozygous frameshift deletion ... in exon 2 of *TBC1D7* ...., failed to fully segregate, given that individual II-5, who is unaffected at age 61, and individual III-8, who is unaffected at age 32, exhibit the deletion."

Joint Method of Agreement and Difference
Premise: There is a set of individuals I_present that have a feature F and property P.
Premise: There is a set of individuals I_absent that have neither feature F nor property P.
Conclusion: F may be the cause of P in I_present.
Example (Schrauwen): "Next, we checked the inheritance of the *CABP2* variant in the entire Sh10 family (Figure 1) and screened an additional 100 random Iranian controls to ensure that the variant is not a frequent polymorphism. The mutation was not detected in any of the controls..."
[Note: This scheme differs from Causal Agreement and Difference by the absence of the third premise, about a previously known potential causal link from F to P.]

Figure 3: More Argumentation Scheme Definitions and Examples

***** Formatting Issue - Best Available Paper/Graphic *****

Problem I.

Excerpts from (McInerney-Leo et al. 2013):

A. Within the ciliopathies, a subgroup of disorders including short-rib polydactyly syndrome (SRPS), Jeune syndrome … are characterized by skeletal abnormalities including a small rib cage, shortening of the long bones, and in some cases, polydactyly … Among the skeletal ciliopathies, the SRPS subtypes are the most severe and are incompatible with postnatal life.

B. To date many mutations causing skeletal ciliopathies affect genes encoding components of the intraflagellar transport (IFT) machinery, a motor-driven trafficking process responsible for transporting proteins required for cilia assembly and function along the axoneme.

C. The first family [SKDP42] is a nonconsanguineous Australian family of predominantly British but also Maori descent, with healthy parents and two affected individuals with SRPS type III.

D. Individual SKDP42.3 presented with short long bones on ultrasound at 16 weeks' gestation. Follow-up ultrasound at 31 weeks demonstrated polyhydramnios, severe shortening of long bones with bowed femurs, macrocephaly, short ribs, and ambiguous genitalia. The baby was born at 32 weeks' gestation but died at 2 hr of age. Autopsy … revealed postaxial polydactyly of both hands ...

E. None of the above excerpts.

1. What evidence was presented that is consistent with the conclusion that the individual referred to as SKDP42.3 (a member of the family identified as SKDP42) had SRPS? (Choose the best single answer from excerpts A-E above.)

2. What general biomedical knowledge explains the connection between the evidence you selected (in A-E) and the diagnosis that individual SKDP42.3 had SRPS? (Choose the best single answer from excerpts A-E above.)

3. Select the argumentation scheme that best fits the argument for the diagnosis (Choose the best single answer from the following):

- Causal Agreement and Difference
- Consistent with Predicted Effect
- Effect to Cause (Inference to the Best Explanation)
- Eliminate Candidates
- Hypothesize Candidates
- Joint Method of Agreement and Difference
- None of the above.

Figure 4. Part of quiz used in pilot study. The answers are 1-D, 2-A, and 3-Effect to Cause

***** Formatting Issue - Best Available Paper/Graphic *****

References

Bada, M., Eckert, M., Evans, D., et al. 2012. Concept Annotation in the CRAFT corpus. *BMC Bioinformatics* 13:161

Baumann et al. 2012 Mutations in *FKBP14* Cause a Variant of Ehlers-Danlos Syndrome with Progressive Kyphoscoliosis, Myopathy, and Hearing Loss". *Am J Hum Genetics* 90, 201-216

Cabrio, E. and Villata, S. 2012. Generating Abstract Arguments: A Natural Language Approach. In Verheij, B., Szeider, S., and Woltran, S. (eds.) *Computational Models of Argument: Proceedings of COMMA 2012*. Amsterdam, IOS Press, 454-461.

Charlesworth et al. 2012. Mutations in *ANO3* Cause Dominant Craniocervical Dystonia: Ion Channel Implicated in Pathogenesis. *The American Journal of Human Genetics* 91, 1041–1050

Cohen, K.B. and Demner-Fushman, D. 2014 *Biomedical Natural Language Processing*, Amsterdam: John Benjamins Publishing Company

Feng, V.W. and Hirst, G. 2011. Classifying Arguments by Scheme. In *Proceedings of the 49th Annual Meeting of the Association for Computational Linguistics,* Portland, OR, 987-996.

Green, N., Dwight, R., Navoraphan, K., and Stadler, B. 2011. Natural Language Generation of Transparent Arguments for Lay Audiences. *Argument and Computation* 2(1): 23-50.

Green, N. L. 2014. Towards Creation of a Corpus for Argumentation Mining the Biomedical Genetics Research Literature. In *Proc. of the First Workshop on Argumentation Mining*, ACL 2014, Baltimore.

Green, N. L. 2015. Argumentation for Scientific Claims in a Biomedical Research Article. In Cabrio, E., Viallata, S., and Wyner, A. (Eds.) *ArgNLP 2014: Frontiers and Connections between Argumentation Theory and Natural Language Processing*, Forli-Cesena, Italy, July 21-25, 2014, CEUR Workshop Proceedings, Vol-1341.

Liakata, M, et al. 2012. Automatic Recognition of Conceptualization Zones in Scientific Articles and Two Life Science Applications. *Bioinformatics* 28(7).

McInerney-Leo, A.M. et al. 2013. Short-Rib Polydactyly and Jeune Syndromes Are Caused by Mutations in WDR60. *Am J Hum Gen* 93, 515-523, Sept 5, 2013

Mizuta, Y., Korhonen, A., Mullen, T. and Collier, N. 2005. Zone Analysis in Biology Articles as a Basis for Information Extraction. *International Journal of Medical Informatics* 75(6): 468-487.

Mochales, R. and Moens, M. 2011. Argumentation Mining. *Artificial Intelligence and Law* 19, 1-22.

Peldszus, A. and Stede, M. 2013. From Argument Diagrams to Argumentation Mining in Texts: A Survey. *Int. J of Cognitive Informatics and Natural Intelligence* 7(1), 1-31)

Reed, C., Mochales-Palau, R., Moens, M., and Milward, D. 2010. Language Resources for Studying Argument. In *Proceedings of the 6th Conference on Language Resources and Evaluation, LREC2008, ELRA*, 91-100.

Schrauwen et al. 2012. A Mutation in *CABP2*, Expressed in Cochlear Hair Cells, Causes Autosomal-Recessive Hearing Impairment. *The American Journal of Human Genetics* 91, 636-645, October 5, 2012.

Stab, C. and Gurevych, I. 2014. Annotating Argument Components and Relations in Persuasive Essays. In *Proc. COLING 2014*, pp. 1501-1510

Stab, C., Kirschner, C., Eckle-Kohler, J., and Gurevych, I. 2015. Argumentation Mining in Persuasive Essays and Scientific Articles from the Discourse Structure Perspective. In Cabrio, E., Viallata, S., and Wyner, A. (Eds.) *ArgNLP 2014: Frontiers and Connections between Argumentation Theory and Natural Language Processing*, Forli-Cesena, Italy, July 21-25, 2014, CEUR Workshop Proceedings, Vol-1341

Stede, M. 2004. The Potsdam Commentary Corpus. In *Proc. ACL Workshop on Discourse Annotation,* Barcelona, Spain, pp. 96-102.

Teufel, S. 2010. The Structure of Scientific Articles: Applications to Citation Indexing and Summarization. Stanford, CA, CSLI Publications.

Teufel, S., Siddharthan, A., and Tidhar, D. 2006. An Annotation Scheme for Citation Function. In *Proc. of SIGDIAL-06*, Sydney, Australia.

Verspoor, K., Cohen, K.B., Lanfranchi, A., et al. 2012. A Corpus of Full-text Journal Articles is a Robust Evaluation Tool for Revealing Differences in Performance of Biomedical Natural Language Processing Tools. *BMC Bioinformatics* 2012, 13:207

Verspoor, K., Yepes, A.J., Cavedon, L., et al. 2013. Annotating the Biomedical Literature for the Human Variome. *Database*, Vol. 2013, Article ID bat019

Walton, D., Reed, C., and Macagno, F. 2008. *Argumentation Schemes.* Cambridge University Press.

Extracting argument and domain words for identifying argument components in texts

Huy V. Nguyen
Computer Science Department
University of Pittsburgh
Pittsburgh, PA 15260, USA
hvn3@pitt.edu

Diane J. Litman
Computer Science Department & LRDC
University of Pittsburgh
Pittsburgh, PA 15260, USA
litman@cs.pitt.edu

Abstract

Argument mining studies in natural language text often use lexical (e.g. n-grams) and syntactic (e.g. grammatical production rules) features with all possible values. In prior work on a corpus of academic essays, we demonstrated that such large and sparse feature spaces can cause difficulty for feature selection and proposed a method to design a more compact feature space. The proposed feature design is based on post-processing a topic model to extract argument and domain words. In this paper we investigate the generality of this approach, by applying our methodology to a new corpus of persuasive essays. Our experiments show that replacing n-grams and syntactic rules with features and constraints using extracted argument and domain words significantly improves argument mining performance for persuasive essays.

1 Introduction

Argument mining in text involves automatically identifying argument components as well as argumentative relations between components. Argument mining has been studied in a variety of contexts including essay assessment and feedback (Burstein et al., 2003; Stab and Gurevych, 2014b), visualization and search in legal text (Moens et al., 2007), and opinion mining in online reviews and debates (Park and Cardie, 2014; Boltužić and Šnajder, 2014). Problem formulations of argument mining have ranged from argument detection (e.g. does a sentence contain argumentative content?) to argument component (e.g. claims vs. premise) and/or relation (e.g. support vs. attack) classification.

Due to the loosely-organized nature of many types of texts, associated argument mining studies have typically used generic linguistic features, e.g. n-grams and syntactic rules, and counted on feature selection to reduce large and sparse feature spaces. For example, in texts such as student essays and product reviews there are optional titles but typically no section headings, and claims are substantiated by personal experience rather than cited sources. Thus, specialized features as used in scientific articles (Teufel and Moens, 2002) are not available.

While this use of generic linguistic features has been effective, we propose a feature reduction method based on the semi-supervised derivation of lexical signals of argumentative and domain content. Our approach was initially developed to identify argument elements, i.e. hypothesis and findings, in academic essays (written following APA guidelines) of college students (Nguyen and Litman, submitted). In particular, we post-processed a topic model to extract argument words (lexical signals of argumentative content) and domain words (terminologies in argument topics) using seeds from the assignment description and essay prompts. The extracted argument and domain words were then used to create novel features and constraints for argument mining, and significantly outperformed features derived from n-grams and syntactic rules.

In this paper we apply our argument and domain word extraction method to a new corpus of persuasive essays, with the goal of answering: (1) whether our proposed feature design is general and can be

Proceedings of the 2nd Workshop on Argumentation Mining, pages 22–28,
Denver, Colorado, June 4, 2015.

(1) My view is that the [*government should give priorities to invest more money on the basic social welfares such as education and housing instead of subsidizing arts relative programs*]$_{majorClaim}$. ¶
(2) [*Art is not the key determination of quality of life, but education is*]$_{claim}$. (3) [*In order to make people better off, it is more urgent for governments to commit money to some fundamental help such as setting more scholarships in education section for all citizens*]$_{premise}$ ... ¶
(4) To conclude, [*art could play an active role in improving the quality of people's lives*]$_{premise}$, but I think that [*governments should attach heavier weight to other social issues such as education and housing needs*]$_{claim}$ because [*those are the most essential ways enable to make people a decent life*]$_{premise}$.

Figure 1: Excerpt of a persuasive essay with three paragraphs. The title is "*Do arts and music improve the quality of life?*". Sentences are numbered for easy look-up. Argument components are enclosed in square brackets.

adapted easily across different corpora, (2) whether lexical signals of argumentative content (part of our proposed features) learned from one corpus also signal argumentation in a second corpus. For the first question we test whether features based on argument and domain words outperform n-grams and syntactic rules for argument mining in persuasive essays. For the second question, we test whether our originally derived argument word set is useful for argument mining in persuasive essays.

2 Data

Data for our study is an annotated corpus of persuasive essays[1] (Stab and Gurevych, 2014a). Writing prompts of persuasive essays requires students to state their opinions (i.e. major claims) on topics and validate those opinions with convincing arguments (i.e. claim and premise). Figure 1 shows an excerpt of an annotated persuasive essay in the corpus.

The corpus consists of 1673 sentences in 90 essays collected from www.essayforum.com. Essay sentences were annotated for possible argument components of three types: *major claim* – writer's stance towards the topic, *claim* – controversial statement that supports or attacks major claim, and *premise* – underpins the validity of claim. An argument component can be a clause, e.g. premises in sentence (4), or the whole sentence, e.g. claim sentence (2). A sentence can have from zero to multiple argument components (yielding more data instances than corpus sentences). Inter-rater agreement of three annotators was $\alpha_U = 0.72$.

[1] A type of writing response to test questions on standardized tests (cf. (Burstein et al., 2003)).

MajorClaim	Claim	Premise	None
90	429	1033	327

Table 1: Number of instances in each class.

Class distribution of total 1879 instances is shown in Table 1. Except for the *None* class which consists of 327 sentences having no argument component, the other classes contain the exact argument components so their instances can be clauses or sentences (Stab and Gurevych, 2014b).

3 Prediction Models

3.1 Baseline

Stab and Gurevych (2014b) utilized the corpus (Stab and Gurevych, 2014a) for automated argument component identification. We re-implement their features as a baseline to evaluate our approach.

Structural features: #tokens and #punctuations in argument component (AC), in covering sentence, and preceding/following the AC in sentence, token ratio between covering sentence and AC. Two binary features indicate if the token ratio is 1 and if the sentence ends with a question mark. Five position features are sentence's position in essay, whether the AC is in the first/last paragraph, the first/last sentence of a paragraph.

Lexical features: all n-grams of length 1-3 extracted from AC's including preceding text which is not covered by other AC's in sentence, verbs like '*believe*', adverbs like '*also*', and whether the AC has a modal verb.

Syntactic features: #sub-clauses and depth of parse tree of the covering sentence, tense of main verb and production rules (VP → VBG NP) from parse tree of the AC.

Discourse markers: discourse connectives of 3 relations: comparison, contingency, and expansion but not temporal[2] extracted by addDiscourse program (Pitler et al., 2009).

[2] Authors of (Stab and Gurevych, 2014b) manually collected 55 PDTB markers after removing those that do not indicate argumentative discourse, e.g. markers of temporal relations.

First person pronouns: whether each of *I*, *me*, *my*, *mine*, and *myself* is present in the sentence.

Contextual features: #tokens, #punctuations, #sub-clauses, and presence of modal verb in preceding and following sentences.

3.2 Proposed model

Our proposed model is based on the idea of separating argument and domain words (Nguyen and Litman, submitted) to better model argumentative content and argument topics in text. It is common in argumentative text that argument expressions start with an argument shell[3], e.g. "*My view is that*", "*I think*", "*to conclude*" followed by argument content. To model this writing style, we consider features of lexical and structural aspects of the text. As for the *lexical aspect*, we learn a topic model using development data (described below) to separate argument words (e.g. '*view*', '*conclude*', '*think*') from domain words (e.g. '*art*', '*life*'). Compared to n-grams, our argument words provide a much more compact representation. As for the *structural aspect*, instead of production rules, e.g. "*S* $\rightarrow$ *NP VP*", we use dependency parses to extract pairs of subject and main verb of sentences, e.g. "*I.think*", "*view.be*". Dependency relations are minimal syntactic structures compared to production rules. To further make the features topic-independent, we keep only dependency pairs that do not include domain words.

3.2.1 Post-processing a topic model to extract argument and domain words

We define argument words as those playing a role of argument indicators and commonly used in different argument topics, e.g. '*reason*', '*opinion*', '*think*'. In contrast, domain words are specific terminologies commonly used within the topic, e.g. '*art*', '*education*'. Our notions of argument and domain languages share a similarity with the idea of shell language and content in (Madnani et al., 2012) in that we aim to model the lexical signals of argumentative content. However while Madnani et al. (2012) emphasized the boundaries between argument shell and content, we do not require such a physical separation between the two aspects of an argument. Instead we emphasize more the lexical signals themselves and allow argument words to occur in the argument content. For example, the major claim in Figure 1 has two argument words '*should*' and '*instead*' which makes the statement controversial.

To learn argument and domain words, we run the LDA (Blei et al., 2003) algorithm[4] and post-process the output. Our development data to build the topic model are 6794 essays posted on www.essayforum.com excluding those in the corpus. Our post-processing algorithm requires a minimal seeding with predefined argument keywords and essay prompts (i.e. post titles). We examine frequent words (more than 100 occurrences) in prompts of development data and choose 10 words as argument keywords: *agree, disagree, reason, support, advantage, disadvantage, think, conclusion, result* and *opinion*. Seeds of domain words are those in the prompts but not argument or stop words. Each domain seed word is associated with an occurrence frequency f as a ratio of the seed occurrences over total occurrences of all domain seeds in essay prompts. All words including seeds are then stemmed.

We vary the number of LDA topics from 20 to 80; in each run, we return the top 500 words for each topic, then remove words with total occurrence less than 3. For words in multiple LDA topics, we compare every pair of word probability given each of two topics t_1, t_2: $p(w|t_1)$ and $p(w|t_2)$ and remove the word from topic with smaller probability if the ratio $p(w|t_1)/p(w|t_2) > 7$. This allows us to only punish words with very low conditional probability while still keeping a fair amount of multiple-topic words.

For each LDA topic we calculate three weights: argument weight (AW) is the number of unique argument seeds in the topic; domain weight (DW) is the sum of frequencies f of domain seeds in the topic; and combined weight $CW = AW - DW$. To discriminate the LDA topic of argument words from LDA topics of domain words given a number of LDA topics, we compute a relative ratio of the largest over the second largest combined weights (e.g. $(CW_{t1} - CW_{t2})/CW_{t2}$ as in Table 2). These settings prioritize argument seeds and topics with more argument seeds, and less domain seeds. Given the number of LDA topics that has the highest ratio (36 topics given our development data), we select LDA topic with the largest combined weight as the

[3]Cf. shell language (Madnani et al., 2012)

[4]We use GibbsLDA++ (Phan and Nguyen, 2007)

Topic 1 *reason exampl support agre think becaus disagre statement opinion believe therefor idea conclus*	
Topic 2 *citi live big hous place area small apart town build communiti factori urban*	
Topic 3 *children parent school educ teach kid adult grow childhood behavior taught*	

Table 2: Samples of top argument (topic 1), and domain (topics 2 and 3) words. Words are stemmed.

argument word list. Domain words are the top words of other topics, but not argument or stop words.

Table 2 shows examples of top argument and domain words (stemmed) returned by our algorithm. Given 10 argument keywords, our algorithm returns a list of 263 argument words which is a mixture of keyword variants (e.g. *think, believe, viewpoint, opinion, argument, claim*), connectives (e.g. *therefore, however, despite*), and other stop words.

Our proposed model takes all features from the baseline except n-grams and production rules, and adds the following features: *argument words* as unigrams, *filtered dependency pairs* (§3.2) as skipped bigrams, and *numbers* of argument and domain words.[5] Our proposed model is compact with 956 original features compared to 5132 of the baseline[6].

4 Experimental Results

4.1 Proposed vs. baseline models

Our first experiment replicates what was conducted in (Stab and Gurevych, 2014b). We perform 10-fold cross validation; in each run we train models using LibLINEAR (Fan et al., 2008) algorithm with top 100 features returned by the InfoGain feature selection algorithm performed in the training folds. We use LightSIDE (lightsidelabs.com) to extract n-grams and production rules, the Stanford parser (Klein and Manning, 2003) to parse the texts, and Weka (Hall et al., 2009) to conduct the machine learning experiments. Table 3 (left) shows the performances of three models.

We note that there are notable performance disparities between BaseI (our implementation §3.1), and BaseR (reported performance of the model by Stab and Gurevych (2014b)). Particularly, BaseI obtains higher F1:Premise, F1:None, and smaller F1:MajorClaim, F1:Claim than BaseR. The differences may mostly be due to dissimilar feature extraction methods and NLP/ML toolkits. Comparing BaseI and AD (our proposed model using learned **a**rgument and **d**omain words §3.2, §3.2.1) shows that our proposed model AD yields higher Kappa, F1:Claim (significantly) and accuracy (trending).

	BaseR	BaseI	AD	BaseI	AD
#features	100	100	100	130	70
Accuracy	0.77	0.78	0.79+	0.80	0.83*
Kappa	NA	0.63	0.65*	0.64	0.69*
F1	0.73	0.71	0.72	0.71	0.76+
Precision	0.77	0.76	0.76	0.76	0.79
Recall	0.68	0.69	0.70	0.68	0.74+
F1:MajorClaim	0.62	0.54	0.51	0.48	0.59
F1:Claim	0.54	0.47	0.53*	0.49	0.56*
F1:Premise	0.83	0.84	0.84	0.86	0.88*
F1:None	0.88	1.00	1.00	1.00	1.00

Table 3: Model performances with top 100 features (left) and best number of features (right). +, * indicate $p < 0.1, p < 0.05$ respectively in AD vs. BaseI comparison.

To further analyze performance improvement by the AD model, we use 75 randomly-selected essays to train and estimate the best numbers of features of BaseI and AD (w.r.t F1 score) through a 9-fold cross validation, then test on 15 remaining essays. As shown in Table 3 (right), AD's test performance is consistently better with far smaller number of top features (70) than BaseI (130). AD has 6 of 31 argument words not present in BaseI's 34 unigrams: *analyze, controversial, could, debate, discuss, ordinal*. AD keeps only 5 dependency pairs: *I.agree, I.believe, I.conclude, I.think* and *people.believe* while BaseI keeps up to 31 bigrams and 13 trigrams in the top features. These indicate the dominance of our proposed features over generic n-grams and syntactic rules.

4.2 Alternative argument word list

In this experiment, we evaluate the prediction transfer of the actual argument word list across genres. In (Nguyen and Litman, submitted), our LDA post-processing algorithm returned 429 argument words from a development set of 254 academic writings, where the seeds (*hypothesis, support, opposition, finding, study*) were taken from the assignment. To

[5]A model based on seed words without expansion to argument words yields significantly worse performance than the baseline. This shows the necessity of our proposed topic model.

[6]N-grams and production rules of less than 3 occurrences were removed to improve baseline performance.

	AltAD	AD
Accuracy	0.77	0.79*
Kappa	0.62	0.65*
F1:MajorClaim	0.56	0.51
F1:Claim	0.47	0.53*
F1:Premise	0.83	0.84*
F1:None	1.00	1.00

Table 4: Performance with different argument words lists.

build an alternative model (AltAD), we replace the argument words in AD with those 429 argument words, re-filter dependency pairs and update the number of argument words. We follow the same setting in §4.1 to train AD and AltAD using top 100 features. As shown in Table 4, AltAD performs worse than AD, except a higher F1:MajorClaim but not significant. AltAD yields significantly lower accuracy, Kappa, F1:Claim and F1:Premise.

Comparing the two learned argument word lists gives us interesting insights. The lists have 142 common words with 9 discourse connectives (e.g. '*therefore*', '*despite*'), 72 content words (e.g. '*result*', '*support*'), and 61 stop words. 30 of the common argument words appear in top 100 features of AltAD, but only 5 are content words: '*conclusion*', '*topic*', '*analyze*', '*show*', and '*reason*'. This shows that while the two argument word lists have a fair amount of common words, the transferable part is mostly limited to function words, e.g. discourse connectives, stop words. In contrast, 270 of the 285 unique words to AltAD are not selected for top 100 features, and most of those are popular terms in academic writings, e.g. '*research*', '*hypothesis*', '*variable*'. Moreover AD's top 100 features have 20 argument words unique to the model, and 19 of those are content words, e.g. '*believe*', '*agree*', '*discuss*', '*view*'. These non-transferable parts suggest that argument words should be learned from appropriate seeds and development sets for best performance.

5 Related Work

Research in argument mining has explored novel features to model argumentative discourse, e.g pre-defined indicative phrases for argumentation (Mochales and Moens, 2008), headlines and citations (Teufel and Moens, 2002), sentiment clue and speech event (Park and Cardie, 2014). However, the major feature sets were still generic n-grams. We propose to replace generic n-grams with argument words learned using a topic model.

Role-based word separation in texts have been studied in a wide variety of contexts: opinion and topic word separation in opinion mining (see (Liu, 2012) for a survey), domain and review word separation for review visualization (Xiong and Litman, 2013), domain concept word tagging in tutorial dialogue systems (Litman et al., 2009), and dialog act cues for dialog act tagging (Samuel et al., 1998).

Post-processing LDA (Blei et al., 2003) output was studied to identify topics of visual words (Louis and Nenkova, 2013) and representative words of topics (Brody and Elhadad, 2010; Funatsu et al., 2014). Our work is the first of its kind to use topic models to extract argument and domain words from argumentative texts. Our technique has a similarity with (Louis and Nenkova, 2013) in that we use seed words to guide the separation.

6 Conclusions and Future Work

We have shown that our novel method for modeling argumentative content and argument topic in academic writings also applies to argument mining in persuasive essays, with our results outperforming a baseline model from a prior study of this genre.

Our contributions are 2-fold. First, our proposed features are shown to efficiently replace generic n-grams and production rules in argument mining tasks for significantly better performance. The core component of our feature extraction is a novel algorithm that post-processes LDA output to learn argument and domain words with a minimal seeding.

Second, our analysis gives insights into the lexical signals of argumentative content. While argument word lists extracted for different data can have parts in common, there are non-transferable parts which are genre-dependent and necessary for the best performance. Thus such indicators of argumentative content should be learned within genre.

Our next task is argumentative relation classification, i.e. support vs. attack. We would also like to explore sequence labeling to identify argument language, and combine them with topic models.

Acknowledgments. This research is supported by NSF Grant 1122504. We thank Wencan Luo, Zahra Rahimi and the reviewers for their feedback.

References

David M Blei, Andrew Y Ng, and Michael I Jordan. 2003. Latent dirichlet allocation. *the Journal of machine Learning research*, 3:993–1022.

Filip Boltužić and Jan Šnajder. 2014. Back up your Stance: Recognizing Arguments in Online Discussions. In *Proceedings of the First Workshop on Argumentation Mining*, pages 49–58, Baltimore, Maryland, June. Association for Computational Linguistics.

Samuel Brody and Noemie Elhadad. 2010. An unsupervised aspect-sentiment model for online reviews. In *Human Language Technologies: The 2010 Annual Conference of the North American Chapter of the Association for Computational Linguistics*, pages 804–812. Association for Computational Linguistics.

Jill Burstein, Daniel Marcu, and Kevin Knight. 2003. Finding the WRITE Stuff: Automatic Identification of Discourse Structure in Student Essays. *IEEE Intelligent Systems*, 18(1):32–39, January.

Rong-En Fan, Kai-Wei Chang, Cho-Jui Hsieh, Xiang-Rui Wang, and Chih-Jen Lin. 2008. LIBLINEAR: A Library for Large Linear Classification. *J. Mach. Learn. Res.*, 9:1871–1874, June.

Toshiaki Funatsu, Yoichi Tomiura, Emi Ishita, and Kosuke Furusawa. 2014. Extracting Representative Words of a Topic Determined by Latent Dirichlet Allocation. In *eKNOW 2014, The Sixth International Conference on Information, Process, and Knowledge Management*, pages 112–117.

Mark Hall, Eibe Frank, Geoffrey Holmes, Bernhard Pfahringer, Peter Reutemann, and Ian H. Witten. 2009. The WEKA Data Mining Software: An Update. *SIGKDD Explor. Newsl.*, 11(1):10–18, November.

Dan Klein and Christopher D Manning. 2003. Accurate unlexicalized parsing. In *Proceedings of the 41st Annual Meeting on Association for Computational Linguistics-Volume 1*, pages 423–430. Association for Computational Linguistics.

Diane Litman, Johanna Moore, Myroslava O. Dzikovska, and Elaine Farrow. 2009. Using Natural Language Processing to Analyze Tutorial Dialogue Corpora Across Domains Modalities. In *Proceedings of the 2009 Conference on Artificial Intelligence in Education: Building Learning Systems That Care: From Knowledge Representation to Affective Modelling*, pages 149–156, Amsterdam, The Netherlands, The Netherlands. IOS Press.

Bing Liu. 2012. *Sentiment Analysis and Opinion Mining*. Morgan & Claypool.

Annie Louis and Ani Nenkova. 2013. What Makes Writing Great? First Experiments on Article Quality Prediction in the Science Journalism Domain. *Transactions of the Association of Computational Linguistics – Volume 1*, pages 341–352.

Nitin Madnani, Michael Heilman, Joel Tetreault, and Martin Chodorow. 2012. Identifying High-Level Organizational Elements in Argumentative Discourse. In *Proceedings of the 2012 Conference of the North American Chapter of the Association for Computational Linguistics: Human Language Technologies*, pages 20–28, Montreal, Canada. Association for Computational Linguistics.

Raquel Mochales and Marie-Francine Moens. 2008. Study on the Structure of Argumentation in Case Law. In *Proceedings of the 2008 Conference on Legal Knowledge and Information Systems: JURIX 2008: The Twenty-First Annual Conference*, pages 11–20, Amsterdam, The Netherlands, The Netherlands. IOS Press.

Marie-Francine Moens, Erik Boiy, Raquel Mochales Palau, and Chris Reed. 2007. Automatic Detection of Arguments in Legal Texts. In *Proceedings of the 11th International Conference on Artificial Intelligence and Law*, ICAIL '07, pages 225–230, New York, NY, USA. ACM.

Huy Nguyen and Diane Litman. submitted. Identifying argument elements in diagram-based academic writing.

Joonsuk Park and Claire Cardie. 2014. Identifying Appropriate Support for Propositions in Online User Comments. In *Proceedings of the First Workshop on Argumentation Mining*, pages 29–38, Baltimore, Maryland, June. Association for Computational Linguistics.

Xuan-Hieu Phan and Cam-Tu Nguyen. 2007. *GibbsLDA++: A C/C++ implementation of latent Dirichlet allocation (LDA)*. Technical report.

Emily Pitler, Annie Louis, and Ani Nenkova. 2009. Automatic sense prediction for implicit discourse relations in text. In *Proceedings of the Joint Conference of the 47th Annual Meeting of the ACL and the 4th International Joint Conference on Natural Language Processing of the AFNLP: Volume 2-Volume 2*, pages 683–691. Association for Computational Linguistics.

Ken Samuel, Sandra Carberry, and K. Vijay-Shanker. 1998. Dialogue Act Tagging with Transformation-Based Learning. In *Proceedings of the 36th Annual Meeting of the Association for Computational Linguistics and 17th International Conference on Computational Linguistics - Volume 2*, ACL '98, pages 1150–1156, Stroudsburg, PA, USA. Association for Computational Linguistics.

Christian Stab and Iryna Gurevych. 2014a. Annotating Argument Components and Relations in Persuasive Essays. In *Proceedings of COLING 2014, the 25th International Conference on Computational Linguistics: Technical Papers*, pages 1501–1510, Dublin,

Ireland. Dublin City University and Association for Computational Linguistics.

Christian Stab and Iryna Gurevych. 2014b. Identifying Argumentative Discourse Structures in Persuasive Essays. In *Proceedings of the 2014 Conference on Empirical Methods in Natural Language Processing (EMNLP)*, pages 46–56, Doha, Qatar. Association for Computational Linguistics.

Simone Teufel and Marc Moens. 2002. Summarizing Scientific Articles: Experiments with Relevance and Rhetorical Status. *Computational Linguistics, Volume 28, Number 4, December 2002.*

Wenting Xiong and Diane Litman. 2013. Evaluating Topic-Word Review Analysis for Understanding Student Peer Review Performance. pages 200–207, Memphis, TN, July.

Towards relation based Argumentation Mining

Lucas Carstens
Imperial College London
United Kingdom
SW2 7AZ, London
lc1310@imperial.ac.uk

Francesca Toni
Imperial College London
United Kingdom
SW2 7AZ, London
ft@imperial.ac.uk

Abstract

We advocate a relation based approach to Argumentation Mining. Our focus lies on the extraction of argumentative relations instead of the identification of arguments, themselves. By classifying pairs of sentences according to the relation that holds between them we are able to identify sentences that may be factual when considered in isolation, but carry argumentative meaning when read in context. We describe scenarios in which this is useful, as well as a corpus of annotated sentence pairs we are developing to provide a testbed for this approach.

1 Introduction

Arguments form an integral part of human discourse. Whether we argue in dialogue with another person or advocate the merits of a product in a review, arguments are ubiquitous, in real life as much as in the world wide web. The ever increasing amounts of data on the web mean that manual analysis of this content, including debates and arguments, seems to become increasingly infeasible. Among other problems Argumentation Mining addresses this issue by developing solutions that automate, or at least facilitate, the process of building *Argument Frameworks (AFs)* (Amgoud et al., 2008; Dung, 1995) from free text. To build AFs we are generally concerned with two problems, (1) the identification of arguments and (2) the identification of relations between arguments. With this paper we highlight the intricate link between those two tasks and argue that treating them separately raises a number of issues. On the back of this we propose a relation based way of performing Argumentation Mining. Instead of treating the identification of arguments and their relations to each other as two problems we define it as a single task. We do this by classifying sentences according to whether they stand in an *argumentative* relation to other sentences. We consider any sentence which supports or attacks another sentence to be argumentative. This includes cases such as the one shown in section 3.1, where a sentence contains only parts of an arguments (premises or a conclusion) and the remainder of the argument is left implicit for the reader to infer.

The remainder of this paper is organised as follows. We discuss related work in section 2. In section 3 we discuss three issues that arise when trying to decouple the process of identifying arguments and finding relations between them. Following this we describe a relation based approach to perform Argumentation Mining for the creation of AFs in section 4. We discuss an application in section 5.1, as well as a corpus design to help us build such applications in section 5.2. We conclude the paper in section 6.

2 Related work

Work on Argumentation Mining has addressed a number of tasks crucial to the problem, including the automatic construction of *Argument Frameworks (AFs)* (Cabrio and Villata, 2012; Feng and Hirst, 2011) and the creation of resources such as annotated corpora (Mochales and Moens, 2008; Stab and Gurevych, 2014; Walker et al., 2012). Amidst the increasing interest in Argumentation Mining various types of online content have been the target of anal-

Proceedings of the 2nd Workshop on Argumentation Mining, pages 29–34,
Denver, Colorado, June 4, 2015. ©2015 Association for Computational Linguistics

ysis. (Park and Cardie, 2014) use *multi-class Support Vector Machines (SVM)* (Crammer and Singer, 2002) to identify different classes of argumentative propositions in online user comments. (Ghosh et al., 2014) use SVM to analyse multilogue, instead, classifying relations between user comments. (Boltuzic and Šnajder, 2014) use Textual Entailment to identify support relations between posts in discussion fora. Other application areas for Argumentation Mining have been the biomedical (Faiz and Mercer, 2014; Green, 2014; Houngbo and Mercer, 2014) and legal domains, where the well-structured nature of legal text and the development of corpora such as the *ECHR* corpus (Mochales and Moens, 2008) have sparked development in this area (Palau and Moens, 2009; Wyner et al., 2010).

3 Motivation

The separation of identifying arguments and the relations between them raises a number of problems, three of which are highlighted here to motivate our approach.

3.1 This is just a fact - so why does it attack this other sentence?

The context in which a sentence appears can change its meaning significantly, and with it a sentence's *argumentativeness*. Consider the following statement:

> (1) Nigel Farage[1] has attended private school and used to work as a banker in the City.

This is a simple enough fact and, on its own, conveys no particular attitude towards Nigel Farage, his education, or his professional past. If however, we consider the above sentence in relation to the one below, the situation changes:

> (2) Nigel Farage understands the common folks; he is the face of UKIP, the people's army!

It now becomes quite possible that sentence (1) is meant to be an attack on sentence (2) and the notion of Nigel Farage being the leader of a *people's army*. After all, how could someone who went to

[1]Nigel Farage is the leader of the UK Independence Party (UKIP), see www.ukip.org

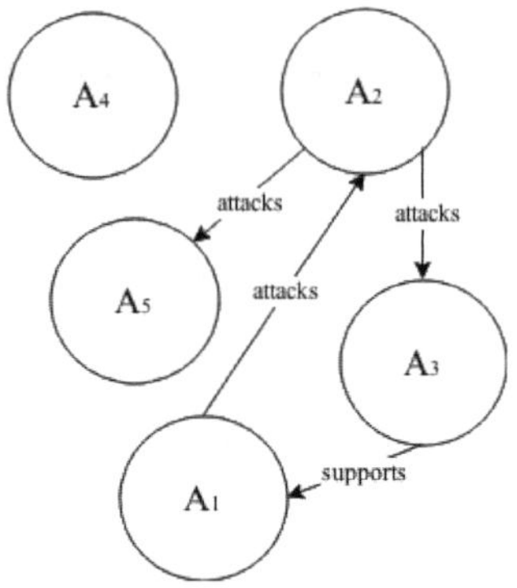

Figure 1: Example Argument Framework.

private school and has a history as a banker possibly understand the common people? This conclusion is not stated explicitly, but one may easily infer it. Trying to identify arguments in isolation may hence lead us to discard factual sentences such as sentence (1), even though, when considered in context with sentence (2), we should arguably consider it to be argumentative.

3.2 I have found the arguments - relating them is still a three-class problem!

Let us consider again the task of identifying a sentence as argumentative or non-argumentative. Say we have built a model that provides us with a good split between the two classes, so that we can reliably discard non-argumentative sentences (though, as discussed in section 3.1, this concept may be questionable, as well). We now need to find relations, i.e. attacks and supports between the sentences that have been classified as argumentative. In spite of our knowledge of all sentences in question being arguments, we are still faced with a three-class problem, as three scenarios need to be accounted for. A sentence may attack another, it may supports another, and, lastly, both sentences may be arguments, but otherwise unrelated. By discarding non-argumentative sentences we thus simply limit the search space for the construction of an AF, the complexity of the problem itself remains unchanged.

3.3 This is an argument - but is it relevant?

While in section 3.1 we argue that, by trying to identify sentences as argumentative or non-argumentative, we may discard potentially valuable input to our AF, we may also end up retaining sentences that are of little use. Though often enough toy examples of AFs contain isolated arguments, as shown in figure 1, such arguments may arguably not be useful in real life applications. In the example AF, argument A_4 does not offer us any insight either as to whether it is viable/acceptable or in what way it may contribute to identifying *good* arguments, by whichever measure this may be.

4 Relation based Argumentation Mining

Based on the issues we describe in section 3 we have set out to offer an alternative, relation based view on Argumentation Mining. We hope that this will offer new ways of building AFs from text that may be useful on their own, but also complementary to other approaches. Instead of identifying sentences or other text snippets as (non)argumentative we classify *pairs* of sentences according to their relation. If this relation is classified as an *attack* or *support* relation we consider *both* sentences to be argumentative, irrespective of their individual quality. Accordingly we classify sentence pairs as belonging to one of three classes, *A* = *Attack*, *S* = *Support*, or *N* = *Neither*, where *Neither* includes both cases where the two sentences are unrelated and those where they are related, but not in an argumentative manner. To construct pairs and build AFs from them we currently consider two options. On the one hand, we create a *root node*, a sentence to be compared to a set of other sentences. Consider, for example, a journalist who is in the process of composing an article on UKIP. To gather insights on the attitude towards UKIP he or she may want to test a claim against an existing body of articles. A claim here is a sentence conveying a hypothesis, such as:

> C = "UKIP's proposed immigration policies effectively discriminate against migrants from specific European countries, thereby undermining the inclusiveness and unity of the European Union."

To evaluate this claim we take a set of relevant sentences $S = \{s_1, s_2, ..., s_n\}$, for example other news articles on UKIP. We then construct a set of sentence pairs $P = \{(C, s_1), (C, s_2), ..., (C, s_n)\}$, where each $p \in P$ needs to be assigned a class label $L \in \{A, S, N\}$. We can then determine which sentences from the articles attack or support the journalist's claim and can iteratively establish further connections between the sentences related to the original claim. On the other hand we may want to create an AF from a single piece of text. If the text is not very large and/or we have the computing power available we can simply create sentence pairs by matching every sentence with every other sentence appearing in the article. This, however, means we have to classify an exponentially growing number of pairs as we consider larger texts. It may hence be prudent to preselect pairs, e.g. by matching sentences containing the same entities. Once we have constructed pairs in some way we need to represent them in a manner that lets us classify them. To achieve this we represent each sentence pair as a single feature vector. The vector is comprised of a set of features, of which some characterise the sentences themselves and others describe the relation between the sentences. We describe preliminary work on building a corpus of such vectors, each annotated with a class label, in section 5.2.

5 Putting theory into practice

Based on the ideas described in section 4 we have defined a number of use cases, one of which we discuss here, and have also developed a first annotated corpus of sentence pairs.

5.1 Application

The first application we are developing following our approach offers a way of evaluating claims against a body of text, as described in section 4. As a first step, this provides us with a gauge of what proportion of a text argues for or against our claim. In a second step we can then discard sentences which do not appear to have an argumentative relation to our claim and try to establish further connections between those sentences that do, giving us a preliminary AF. At this stage the result will not be a fully fledged AF that reflects the argumentative structure of the text itself, simply because it relates to an external claim. To test our approach *in real life* we have teamed up with the BBC News Labs[2] to define a use case, for which figure 2 provides an overview. One

[2] www.BBCNewsLabs.co.uk

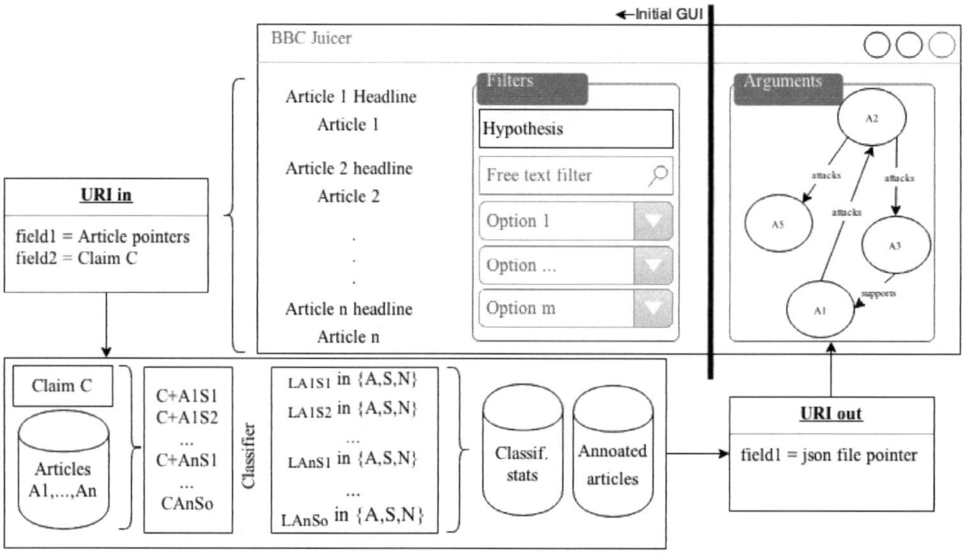

Figure 2: Mock Up of the Juicer, including the way the API interacts with it to retrieve & classify contents and then feed it back to the Juicer. The user enters a Claim and chooses a set of articles via the available filters. Pointers to the articles, as well as the Claim are then processed via an API. The classification output is fed back into the Juicer.

of the applications developed by the News Labs is *The Juicer*[3], a platform used to facilitate the semantic tagging of BBC content. The Juicer provides an interface to a large repository of news articles and social media posts from various sources, such as the BBC websites and Twitter. Each article stored in the repository is assigned to various categories, such as topic and source, and is then semantically tagged for people, places, events, etc. We are currently developing an API to integrate a concrete realisation of relation based Argumentation Mining, to be used as an additional semantic filter in the Juicer. This will allow us to utilise the existing filters of the BBC Juicer to select the articles we want to compare with the claim. Pointers to the articles retrieved using the filters, as well as the provided claim are sent to be processed via the API. The content of the articles are then compared to the provided claim, as described in section 4. We are considering a number of options for how the resulting classifications may be presented to the user:

1. He or she may access simple statistics on the resulting classifications, e.g. the proportion of sentences attacking or supporting the claim.
2. Alternatively the user may access the full articles, with sentences highlighted for argumentative contents.
3. Another option is to just view argumentative sentences directly, without the articles in which they appear. These sentence may be represented in graph form, as shown in figure 2.

5.2 Corpus development

To develop applications such as the one described in section 5.1 we need to build solid classification models. In turn, to build such models, we need a sizeable corpus of labeled examples, in our case sentence pairs that are labeled with $L \in \{A, S, N\}$. To identify the challenges in this we have built a preliminary corpus of 854 annotated sentence pairs[4], examples of which are shown in table 1. Based on the insights gained from annotating a reasonable amount of sentence pairs we are now in the process of building a larger corpus in which each instance will be labeled by at least two annotators. The annotators are either native or fully proficient English speakers. We summarise the main points of the setup below.

Firstly, we do not ask annotators to identify arguments. This is based on the issues this raises, as

[3] www.bbc.co.uk/partnersandsuppliers/connectedstudio/newslabs/projects/juicer.html

[4] Available at www.doc.ic.ac.uk/~lc1310/

Parent	Child	Class
UKIP doesn't understand that young people are, by and large, progressive.	But UKIP claims to be winning support among younger voters and students.	a
It's a protest vote because (most) people know that UKIP will never net in power.	Emma Lewell-Buck made history becoming the constituency's first female MP.	n
It is because of UKIP that we are finally discussing the European question and about immigration and thank goodness for that.	I believe that what UKIP is doing is vital for this country.	s

Table 1: Example sentence pairs, labeled according to the relation pointing from the Child to the Parent

explained in section 3. Instead we ask annotators to focus on the relation, taking into account whatever may be implied in the sentences to then decide whether one attacks or supports the other. We will also ask annotators to provide qualitative feedback on whether they can pinpoint why they have classified pairs the way they have. This will be achieved via free text feedback or the completion of templates and will be used as a basis for further exploration on how we may represent and identify arguments.

This leads to the second challenge in building models that we can use in our applications: We need to decide how to represent the sentence pairs. Here, we have two options. We may either choose a *Bag-of-Words (BOW)* approach or develop a set of features that are representative of a sentence pair. The BOW approach is straight forward and has proven to yield reasonable results for many NLP problems, e.g. (Maas et al., 2011; Sayeedunnissa et al., 2013). We will hence use it as one of two baselines, the other being random classification. To see whether we can improve on both these baselines we have set out to collect a set of features that give us numerical representation of a sentence pair. Most broadly we distinguish two types of features, *Relational features* and *Sentential features*. Relational features will be comprised of any type of features that represent how the two sentences that make up the pair relate to each other. Features we have been experimenting with on our preliminary corpus include WordNet based similarity (Miller, 1995), Edit Distance measures (Navarro, 2001), and Textual Entailment measures (Dagan et al., 2006). The second category includes a set of features that characterise the individual sentences. Here we are considering various word lists, e.g. keeping count of discourse markers, sentiment scores, e.g. using SentiWordNet (Esuli and Sebastiani, 2006) or the Stanford Sentiment library (Socher et al., 2013), and other features. All features are then pooled together to create the feature vector representing a sentence pair. Experiments on the preliminary corpus, representing sentence pairs using all features described, show promising results on our approach, with classification accuracy of up to 77.5% when training Random Forests (Breiman, 2001) on the corpus.

6 Conclusion

We have advocated a relation based approach to performing Argumentation Mining. We focus on the determination of argumentative relations, foregoing the decision on whether an isolated piece of text is an argument. We do this arguing that often times the relation to other text is what lends text its argumentative quality. To illustrate the usefulness of this approach we have described a use case we are developing, as well as a corpus of annotated sentence pairs. Alongside the developments proposed in section 5 we need to conduct experiments to track the quality of data and classification output. For the construction of our corpus this means collecting multiple annotations, not just for a subset of the corpus, but for its entirety. This will allow us to monitor the quality of our annotations more reliably. Next to introducing features to represent sentence pairs we must determine the optimal feature combination at all stages of development. We need to avoid features that are detrimental to performance and those which do not contribute to it and waste computational resources.

References

Leila Amgoud, Claudette Cayrol, Marie-Christine Lagasquie-Schiex, and Pierre Livet. 2008. On bipolarity in argumentation frameworks. *International Journal of Intelligent Systems*, 23(10):1062–1093.

Filip Boltuzic and Jan Šnajder. 2014. Back up your stance: Recognizing arguments in online discussions. In *Proceedings of the First Workshop on Argumentation Mining*, pages 49–58.

Leo Breiman. 2001. Random forests. *Machine learning*, 45(1):5–32.

Elena Cabrio and Serena Villata. 2012. Generating abstract arguments: A natural language approach. In *COMMA*, pages 454–461.

Koby Crammer and Yoram Singer. 2002. On the algorithmic implementation of multiclass kernel-based vector machines. *The Journal of Machine Learning Research*, 2:265–292.

Ido Dagan, Oren Glickman, and Bernardo Magnini. 2006. The pascal recognising textual entailment challenge. In *Machine learning challenges. evaluating predictive uncertainty, visual object classification, and recognising tectual entailment*, pages 177–190. Springer.

Phan Minh Dung. 1995. On the acceptability of arguments and its fundamental role in nonmonotonic reasoning, logic programming and n-person games. *Artificial intelligence*, 77(2):321–357.

Andrea Esuli and Fabrizio Sebastiani. 2006. Sentiwordnet: A publicly available lexical resource for opinion mining. In *Proceedings of LREC*, volume 6, pages 417–422. Citeseer.

Syeed Ibn Faiz and Robert E Mercer. 2014. Extracting higher order relations from biomedical text. *ACL 2014*, page 100.

Vanessa Wei Feng and Graeme Hirst. 2011. Classifying arguments by scheme. In *Proceedings of the 49th Annual Meeting of the Association for Computational Linguistics: Human Language Technologies-Volume 1*, pages 987–996. Association for Computational Linguistics.

Debanjan Ghosh, Smaranda Muresan, Nina Wacholder, Mark Aakhus, and Matthew Mitsui. 2014. Analyzing argumentative discourse units in online interactions. In *Proceedings of the First Workshop on Argumentation Mining*, pages 39–48.

Nancy L Green. 2014. Towards creation of a corpus for argumentation mining the biomedical genetics research literature. *ACL 2014*, page 11.

Hospice Houngbo and Robert E Mercer. 2014. An automated method to build a corpus of rhetorically-classified sentences in biomedical texts. *ACL 2014*, page 19.

Andrew L Maas, Raymond E Daly, Peter T Pham, Dan Huang, Andrew Y Ng, and Christopher Potts. 2011. Learning word vectors for sentiment analysis. In *Proceedings of the 49th Annual Meeting of the Association for Computational Linguistics: Human Language Technologies-Volume 1*, pages 142–150. Association for Computational Linguistics.

George A Miller. 1995. Wordnet: a lexical database for english. *Communications of the ACM*, 38(11):39–41.

Raquel Mochales and Marie-Francine Moens. 2008. Study on the structure of argumentation in case law. *Proceedings of the 2008 Conference on Legal Knowledge and Information Systems*, pages 11–20.

Gonzalo Navarro. 2001. A guided tour to approximate string matching. *ACM computing surveys (CSUR)*, 33(1):31–88.

Raquel Mochales Palau and Marie-Francine Moens. 2009. Argumentation mining: the detection, classification and structure of arguments in text. In *Proceedings of the 12th international conference on artificial intelligence and law*, pages 98–107. ACM.

Joonsuk Park and Claire Cardie. 2014. Identifying appropriate support for propositions in online user comments. *ACL 2014*, page 29.

S Fouzia Sayeedunnissa, Adnan Rashid Hussain, and Mohd Abdul Hameed. 2013. Supervised opinion mining of social network data using a bag-of-words approach on the cloud. In *Proceedings of Seventh International Conference on Bio-Inspired Computing: Theories and Applications (BIC-TA 2012)*, pages 299–309. Springer.

Richard Socher, Alex Perelygin, Jean Y Wu, Jason Chuang, Christopher D Manning, Andrew Y Ng, and Christopher Potts. 2013. Recursive deep models for semantic compositionality over a sentiment treebank. In *Proceedings of the conference on empirical methods in natural language processing (EMNLP)*, volume 1631, page 1642. Citeseer.

Christian Stab and Iryna Gurevych. 2014. Annotating argument components and relations in persuasive essays. In *Proceedings of the 25th International Conference on Computational Linguistics (COLING 2014)*, pages 1501–1510.

Marilyn A Walker, Jean E Fox Tree, Pranav Anand, Rob Abbott, and Joseph King. 2012. A corpus for research on deliberation and debate. In *LREC*, pages 812–817.

Adam Wyner, Raquel Mochales-Palau, Marie-Francine Moens, and David Milward. 2010. *Approaches to text mining arguments from legal cases*. Springer.

A Shared Task on Argumentation Mining in Newspaper Editorials

Johannes Kiesel **Khalid Al-Khatib** **Matthias Hagen** **Benno Stein**
Bauhaus-Universität Weimar
99421 Weimar, Germany
<first name>.<last name>@uni-weimar.de

Abstract

This paper proposes a shared task for the identification of the argumentative structure in newspaper editorials. By the term "argumentative structure" we refer to the sequence of argumentative units in the text along with the relations between them. The main contribution is a large-scale dataset with more than 200 annotated editorials, which shall help argumentation mining researchers to evaluate and compare their systems in a standardized manner. The paper details how we model and manually identify argumentative structures in order to build this evaluation resource. Altogether, we consider the proposed task as a constructive step towards improving writing assistance systems and debating technologies.

1 Introduction

Even though argumentation theories have been studied extensively in many areas (e.g., philosophy), using these theories for mining real world text is a relatively new direction of research. Recently, argumentation mining has attracted many Natural Language Processing (NLP) researchers with papers published in major conferences and even a specialized workshop series.

Argumentation mining typically refers to the tasks of automatically identifying the argumentative units of a given text and the relations between them (i.e., support or attack). The automatic analysis of this discourse structure has several applications, such as supporting writing skills or assisting information-seeking users in constructing a solid personal standpoint on controversial topics.

To further foster the young field of argumentation mining, we propose a respective shared task to evaluate the current state of the art and compare to newly emerging ideas. According to the standard understanding of argumentation mining, we propose two focused sub-tasks: (1) unit identification and (2) relation extraction. The shared task will allow researchers to evaluate their systems in an open but standardized competition, which will help to push forward argumentation mining research.

For the corpus of the shared task, we are currently annotating a collection of newspaper editorials. These articles convey the opinions of their authors towards specific topics and try to persuade the readers of theses opinions. In order to do so, the authors support their opinions by reasons, which leads to an argumentative discourse. We plan to annotate at least 200 editorials from three different online newspapers paragraph-wise. Participants can use about two thirds of this corpus for training while the remainder will be used for evaluation.

The paper is structured as follows. Section 2 describes the argumentative structure that participants have to extract from the corpus that is described in detail in Section 3. Section 4 proposes the general scheme of the two sub-tasks while the task submission is outlined in Section 5. Conclusions are given in Section 6.

2 Argumentation Model

As the basis for the shared task, we employ a dialectical model of argumentation focusing on the conflict of opinions inspired by the definitions found in current research (Apothéloz et al., 1993; Bayer,

Proceedings of the 2nd Workshop on Argumentation Mining, pages 35–38,
Denver, Colorado, June 4, 2015.

1999; Freeman, 2011; Stab and Gurevych, 2014), and especially that of Peldszus and Stede (2013).

The argumentation model consists of two elements: explicit argumentative units and implicit argumentative relations. Argumentative units are (explicitly written) text segments while argumentative relations correspond to inter-unit relationships (i.e., support or attack) that the reader implicitly establishes while comprehending the text. As a side remark, note that factual correctness is not modeled and also not part of our proposed shared task.

Although the argumentation model is primarily focused on dialectical discourse, it is also applicable to monologues in which the author switches roles. For instance authors of editorials often mention possible objections of others which they then attack when they switch back to their original role.

In applying the rather generic dialectical model, our proposed shared task is open for extensions/subtasks in many directions that are currently investigated in argumentation mining.

2.1 Detailed Model Description

An (argumentative) unit in our model is a consecutive segment of text that contains a formulation of at least one complete proposition which is written by the author to discuss, directly or indirectly, one of the main topics of the article.[1] Each proposition consists of an entity and a predicate that is assigned to this entity. For example, the unit "Alice is nasty" contains a predication of "nasty" to the entity "Alice," but note that this also includes implicit entities or predicates like for instance in "He too."[2]

An (argumentative) relation in our model is a directed link from one *base* unit to the *target* unit it *supports* or *attacks* most directly. In support relations, the base argues that the target is valid, relevant, or important. In this case, the base is also often referred to as premise or reason and the target as claim, conclusion or proposal (Mochales and Moens, 2011; Stab and Gurevych, 2014). In attack relations, the base argues that the target is invalid, irrelevant, or unimportant. Our proposed model only considers the most direct link (if any) for each base.

[1]For editorials, the title often introduces (one of) its main topics.

[2]Questions can also be formulations of propositions if the answer is already suggested (i.e., rhetorical questions).

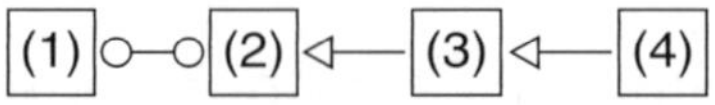

Figure 1. Structure of the example "Even though Eve says that [Alice is nasty]$^{(1)}$, I think [she is nice]$^{(2)}$. [She helps me a lot]$^{(3)}$. [She even taught me how to cook]$^{(4)}$!" Units are depicted as squares, supports by arrows, and an opposition by lines with a circle at each end.

For example, in Figure 1, even though Unit 4 also supports Unit 2, it is only linked to Unit 3 as it supports Unit 3 more directly.

The relations for a given text form one or more trees in our model; with the major claims of the text as their root nodes. Discussions in which a unit directly or indirectly supports or attacks itself can hence not be modeled.

Authors sometimes state the same proposition twice (*restatement*), or the directly contrary proposition if they take their opponents role (*opposition*). We take that into account by modeling special bidirectional support (for restatement) and attack (for opposition) relations. Note that in the case of restatements and oppositions, the tree structure of the text is no longer unambiguous. For example, in an equivalent structure to Figure 1, Unit 3 would attack Unit 1 instead of supporting Unit 2. In the proposed shared task, participants will have to identify restatements as supports and oppositions as attacks respectively, but all equivalent structures are scored as being correct (cf. Section 4 for further details).

2.2 Differences to Other Models

Our proposed model for the shared task does not explicitly categorize argumentative units into premises and claims since such a distinction gets problematic when claims are premises for further claims. Stab and Gurevych (2014) try to handle this problem by introducing so-called major claims—which are supported by claims. However, for longer reasoning chains, in which even these major claims would support further claims, this approach fails. In our model, premises and claims are defined relative to each other by support relations: every base is a premise to the target claim it supports. In this way, we can adequately represent reasoning chains of any length.

Although more fine-grained labels, such as different types of attack and support, will be annotated in our corpus, we will drop this distinction for the task in order to reduce its complexity as well as have a more straightforward evaluation (cf. Section 4 for more details). In comparison to the model of Peldszus and Stede (2013), our model employed in the shared task will subsume the types "basic argument" and "linked support" under support and "rebutting" and "undercutting" under attack.

Unlike Peldszus and Stede (2013), we do not directly distinguish between units from proponent or opponent views since this distinction is difficult for discussions evolving around several topics. In our model, such a distinction is present on a local level: when one unit attacks another.

3 Corpus

In order to acquire high quality opinionated articles, we only consider editorials from newspaper portals which include a separate section for opinion articles and have a high international reputation. For our corpus, we selected the portals of Al Jazeera, Fox News, and The Guardian. From their opinion section we crawled 1415, 1854, and 110 articles, respectively. From each crawl, we exclude particularly short or long articles and select the 75 articles with the most comments. We see the number of comments as an indicator of how controversial the discussed topic is and expect articles with many comments to contain more conflicting arguments.

After the editorials are selected, they are annotated based on our model (cf. Section 2). The annotation process is conducted with three workers from the online platform oDesk.[3] We first annotate ten articles in a pilot study and annotate the remaining ones (or even more) after we inspected the results. Annotation will be carried out in three steps: the identification of (1) the topics, (2) the argumentative units, and (3) the argumentative relations. After each step, the annotations of the workers are manually unified to create a single consistent annotation as foundation for the next step.

4 Task Description

The task of argumentative structure extraction can be divided into two steps: the identification of argumentative units and the identification of the relations between them. Accordingly, we propose two sub-tasks focusing on one of these steps each.

4.1 Argumentative Unit Classification

For each article in the corpus, the participants get a list of the main topics and a list of propositions that they have to classify as argumentative with respect to one of the given topics or not.

Since this is a binary classification task, standard accuracy is an appropriate measure for evaluation purposes. Let P be the set of propositions in the corpus, $\mathrm{c}_S(p)$ be the system's predicted class (argumentative or not) for proposition p, and $\mathrm{c}_G(p)$ be the gold standard class of the proposition p. Moreover, let $\mathrm{C}_G(p, c)$ be 1 if $\mathrm{c}_G(p) = c$ and 0 otherwise. The unit classification accuracy of a system S then is:

$$\mathrm{accuracy}_{\mathrm{C}_G}(S) = \frac{\sum_{p \in P} \mathrm{C}_G(p, \mathrm{c}_S(p))}{|P|},$$

where $|P|$ is the number of propositions.

The participants' results will be compared to several baselines, one natural one being the random guessing of a class based on the class distribution in the training set.

4.2 Argumentative Relation Identification

For each paragraph in the corpus, the participants get the text and the argumentative units as input and have to produce the support and attack relations between the units in the paragraph. The relations extracted from each paragraph have to form one or more trees with the units as nodes. Furthermore, relations always have to be directed towards the root of the tree. If several structures are possible for one paragraph due to restatements and oppositions (cf. Section 2), any of them will get a perfect score. If a restatement (or opposition) occurs in the test corpus, systems are expected to produce a support (or attack) relation between the units in any direction.

This sub-task uses unit-wise accuracy as evaluation measure. Our proposed model states that each base can have only one target (cf. Section 2). The same restriction applies to the systems of the participants. This allows us to define unit-wise accuracy as follows. Let U be the set of units in the corpus and let $\mathrm{r}_S(u)$ be the relation with unit u as a base in the system output or a special no-relation-symbol $\perp$

[3]https://www.odesk.com/

if no such relation exists. Furthermore, let $\mathrm{R}_G(u, r)$ be 1 if r is a correct relation with base u with regard to the gold standard and 0 otherwise. The relation identification accuracy of a system S then is:

$$\mathrm{accuracy}_{\mathrm{R}_G}(S) = \frac{\sum_{u \in U} \mathrm{R}_G(u, \mathrm{r}_S(u))}{|U|},$$

where $|U|$ is the number of units in the corpus. A relation r with base u is correct if the same or an equivalent relation with regard to polarity (support/attack) and target unit exists in the gold standard. Here, equivalence takes into account restatements and oppositions (cf. Section 2). Moreover, if r is $\perp$, then $\mathrm{R}_G(u, r)$ is 1 if and only if there is also no relation with u as a base in the gold standard.

Similar to the first sub-task, we plan to compare the results of the participants to simple baseline approaches. One such baseline is random guessing according to the distributions in the training set. Another approach is a classifier which uses only one feature (e.g., the output of a textual entailment software package).

5 Submission

For the participants' submissions, we want to employ recent advances in reproducible computer science and ask the participants to submit their software instead of submitting their results on the test dataset. In detail, the participants will setup their systems with a unified interface on a remote virtual machine. This machine is then used to evaluate the systems, which makes the experiments directly reproducible in the future.

System submissions are currently becoming increasingly popular in shared tasks. For example, the CoNLL 2015 shared task on shallow discourse parsing[4] applies this technology. We plan to use the same system as the CoNLL task, TIRA (Gollub et al., 2012),[5] which is already successfully applied in the PAN workshops on plagiarism detection.[6]

6 Conclusions

We propose a shared task for mining the argumentative structure in newspaper editorials. This includes modeling the argumentative discourse, creating an annotated corpus, and proposing two sub-tasks for automatic argumentation mining. The sub-tasks are the identification of argumentative units in a text and the identification of relations between the units. We propose appropriate evaluation measures, and suggest to use a new submission approach to increase the reproducibility of the participants' systems.

We believe that it is of great importance for the further development of argumentation mining to establish a shared task in which different systems are evaluated against each other in a standardized and objective manner. Any comments and requests from the research community can still be included in the final task design.

References

Denis Apothéloz, Pierre-Yves Brandt, and Gustavo Quiroz. 1993. The Function of Negation in Argumentation. *Journal of Pragmatics*, 19(1):23–38.

Klaus Bayer. 1999. *Argument und Argumentation: logische Grundlagen der Argumentationsanalyse*, volume 1 of *Studienbücher zur Linguistik*. Westdeutscher Verlag.

J. B. Freeman. 2011. *Argument Structure: Representation and Theory*, volume 18 of *Argumentation Library*. Springer.

Tim Gollub, Benno Stein, and Steven Burrows. 2012. Ousting Ivory Tower Research: Towards a Web Framework for Providing Experiments as a Service. In *35th International ACM Conference on Research and Development in Information Retrieval (SIGIR 12)*, pages 1125–1126. ACM.

Raquel Mochales and Marie-Francine Moens. 2011. Argumentation Mining. *Artificial Intelligence and Law*, 19(1):1–22.

Andreas Peldszus and Manfred Stede. 2013. From Argument Diagrams to Argumentation Mining in Texts: A Survey. *International Journal of Cognitive Informatics and Natural Intelligence (IJCINI)*, 7(1):1–31.

Christian Stab and Iryna Gurevych. 2014. Annotating Argument Components and Relations in Persuasive Essays. In *Proceedings of the the 25th International Conference on Computational Linguistics (COLING 2014)*, pages 1501–1510, August.

[4] `http://www.cs.brandeis.edu/~clp/conll15st/`

[5] `http://www.tira.io/`

[6] `http://www.pan.webis.de`

Conditional Random Fields for Identifying Appropriate Types of Support for Propositions in Online User Comments

Joonsuk Park
Dept. of Computer Science
Cornell University
Ithaca, New York, USA
jpark@cs.cornell.edu

Arzoo Katiyar
Dept. of Computer Science
Cornell University
Ithaca, New York, USA
arzoo@cs.cornell.edu

Bishan Yang
Dept. of Computer Science
Cornell University
Ithaca, New York, USA
bishan@cs.cornell.edu

Abstract

Park and Cardie (2014) proposed a novel task of automatically identifying appropriate types of support for propositions comprising online user comments, as an essential step toward automated analysis of the adequacy of supporting information. While multiclass Support Vector Machines (SVMs) proved to work reasonably well, they do not exploit the sequential nature of the problem: For instance, verifiable experiential propositions tend to appear together, because a personal narrative typically spans multiple propositions. According to our experiments, however, Conditional Random Fields (CRFs) degrade the overall performance, and we discuss potential fixes to this problem. Nonetheless, we observe that the F_1 score with respect to the unverifiable proposition class is increased. Also, semi-supervised CRFs with posterior regularization trained on 75% labeled training data can closely match the performance of a supervised CRF trained on the same training data with the remaining 25% labeled as well.

1 Introduction

The primary domain for argumentation mining has been professionally written text, such as parliamentary records, legal documents and news articles, which contain well-formed arguments consisting of explicitly stated premises and conclusions (Palau and Moens, 2009; Wyner et al., 2010; Feng and Hirst, 2011; Ashley and Walker, 2013). In contrast, online user comments are often comprised of *implicit* arguments, which are conclusions with no explicitly stated premises[1]. For instance, in the following user comment, neither of the two propositions are supported with a reason or evidence. In other words, each of the two propositions is the conclusion of its own argument, with no explicit support provided (thus called *implicit* arguments):

> All airfare costs should include the passenger's right to check at least one standard piece of baggage.$_A$ All fees should be fully disclosed at the time of airfare purchase, regardless of nature.$_B$

When the goal is to extract well-formed arguments from a given text, one may simply disregard such implicit arguments. (Villalba and Saint-Dizier, 2012; Cabrio and Villata, 2012). However, with the accumulation of a large amount of text consisting of implicit arguments, a means of assessing the adequacy of support in arguments has become increasingly desirable. It is not only beneficial for analyzing the strength of arguments, but also for helping commenters to construct better arguments by suggesting the appropriate types of support to be provided.

As an initial step toward automatically assessing the adequacy of support in arguments, Park and Cardie (2014) proposed a novel task of classifying each proposition based on the appropriate type of support: unverifiable (UNVERIF), verifiable non-experiential (VERIF$_{NON}$), or verifiable experiential

[1]Note that implicit arguments are different from so called *enthymemes*, which may contain explicit premises, along with one or more missing premises.

Proceedings of the 2nd Workshop on Argumentation Mining, pages 39–44,
Denver, Colorado, June 4, 2015.

(VERIF$_{EXP}$)[2]. They show that multiclass Support Vector Machines (SVMs) can perform reasonably well on this task.

SVMs, however, do not leverage on the sequential nature of the propositions: For instance, when a commenter writes about his past experience, it typically spans multiple propositions. (In our dataset, VERIF$_{EXP}$ is followed by VERIF$_{EXP}$ with 57% probability, when VERIF$_{EXP}$ constitutes less than 15% of the entire dataset.) Thus, we expect that the probability of a proposition being a verifiable experiential proposition significantly increases when the previous proposition is a verifiable experiential proposition.

In this paper, we test our intuition by employing Conditional Random Field (CRF), a popular approach for building probabilistic models to classify sequence data, for this task (Lafferty et al., 2001). In addition, we experiment with various ways to train CRFs in a semi-supervised fashion.

Unlike our intuition, we find that a CRF performs worse than a multiclass SVM overall. Still, the F_1 score with respect to the UNVERIF class is improved. Also, we show that semi-supervised CRFs with posterior regularization trained on 75% labeled training data can closely match the performance of a supervised CRF trained on the same training data with the remaining 25% labeled as well.

2 Appropriate Support Type Identification

2.1 Task

The task is to classify a given proposition based on the type of appropriate support. In this subsection, we give a brief overview of the target classes[3].

Verifiable Non-experiential (VERIF$_{NON}$). Propositions are verifiable if its validity can be proved/disproved with objective evidence. Thus, it cannot contain subjective expressions, and there should be no room for multiple subjective interpretations. Also, assertions about the future is considered unverifiable, as its truthfulness cannot be confirmed at the present time. As the propositions of this type are verifiable, the appropriate type of support is objective evidence. ("Non-experiential" here means that the given proposition is not about a personal state or experience. The reason for making this distinction is discussed in the next paragraph.)

Verifiable Experiential (VERIF$_{EXP}$). The only difference between this class and VERIF$_{NON}$ is that this type of propositions is about a personal state or experience. Verifiable propositions about a personal state or experience are unique in that it can be inappropriate to evidence for them: People often do not have objective evidence to prove their past experiences, and even if they do, providing it may violate privacy. Thus, the appropriate type of support for this class is still evidence, but optional.

Unverifiable (UNVERIF). Propositions are unverifiable if they contain subjective opinions or judgments, as the subjective nature prevents the propositions from having a single truth value that can be proved or disproved with objecive evidence. Also, assertions about a future event is also unverifiable, because the future has not come yet. As there is no objective evidence for this type of propositions, the appropriate type of support is a *reason*.

Other Statement (OTHER). The remainder of user comments, i.e. text spans that are not part of an argument, falls under this category. Typical examples include questions, greetings, citations and URLs. Among these, only citations and URLs are considered argumentative, as they can be used to provide objective evidence. Luckily they can be accurately identified with regular expressions and thus are excluded from his classification task.

2.2 Conditional Random Fields

We formulate the classification task as a sequence labeling problem. Each user comment consists of a sequence of propositions (in the form of sentences or clauses), and each proposition is classified based on its appropriate support type. Instead of predicting the labels individually, we jointly optimize for the sequence of labels for each comment.

We apply CRFs (Lafferty et al., 2001) to the task as they can capture the sequence patterns of propositions. Denote $\mathbf{x}$ as a sequence of propositions within a user comment and $\mathbf{y}$ as a vector of labels. The CRF

[2] See Section 2 for a more information.

[3] For more details with examples, please refer to the original paper.

models the following conditional probabilities:

$$p_\theta(\mathbf{y}|\mathbf{x}) = \frac{\exp(\theta \cdot f(\mathbf{x}, \mathbf{y}))}{Z_\theta(\mathbf{x})}$$

where $f(\mathbf{x}, \mathbf{y})$ are the model features, θ are the model parameters, and $Z_\theta(\mathbf{x}) = \sum_{\mathbf{y}} \exp(\theta \cdot f(\mathbf{x}, \mathbf{y}))$ is a normalization constant. The objective function for a standard CRF is to maximize the log-likelihood over a collection of labeled documents plus a regularization term:

$$\max_\theta \mathcal{L}(\theta) = \max_\theta \sum_{(\mathbf{x},\mathbf{y})} \log p_\theta(\mathbf{y}|\mathbf{x}) - \frac{||\theta||_2^2}{2\delta^2}$$

Typically CRFs are trained in a supervised fashion. However, as labeled data is very difficult to obtain for the task of support identification, it is important to exploit distant supervision in the data to assist learning. Therefore, we investigate semi-supervised CRFs which train on both labeled and unlabeled data by using the posterior regularization (PR) framework (Ganchev et al., 2010). PR has been successfully applied to many structured NLP tasks such as dependency parsing, information extraction and sentiment analysis tasks (Ganchev et al., 2009; Bellare et al., 2009; Yang and Cardie, 2014).

The training objective for semi-supervised CRFs augments the standard CRF objective with a posterior regularizer:

$$\begin{aligned} \max_\theta & \mathcal{L}(\theta) - \min_{q \in \mathcal{Q}} \{KL(q(\mathbf{Y})||p_\theta(\mathbf{Y}|\mathbf{X})) \\ & + \beta||E_q[\phi(\mathbf{X}, \mathbf{Y})] - \mathbf{b}||_2^2\} \end{aligned} \quad (1)$$

The idea is to find an optimal auxiliary distribution q that is closed to the model distribution $p_\theta(\mathbf{Y}|\mathbf{X})$ (measured by KL divergence) which satisfies a set of posterior constraints. We consider equality constraints which are in the form of $E_q[\phi(\mathbf{X}, \mathbf{Y})] = \mathbf{b}$, where $\mathbf{b}$ is set based on domain knowledge. We can also consider these constraints as features, which encode indicative patterns for a given support type label and prior beliefs on the correlations between the patterns and the true labels.

In this work, we consider two ways of generating constraints. One approach is to manually define constraints, leveraging on our domain knowledge. For instance, the unigram "should" is usually used as part of imperative, meaning it is tightly associated with the UNVERIF class. similarly, having 2 or more occurrences of a strong subjective token is also a distinguishing feature for UNVERIF. We manually define 10 constraints in this way. The other approach is to automatically extract constraints from the given labeled training data using information gain with respect to the classes as a guide.

2.3 Features

As the goal of this work is to test the efficacy of CRFs with respect to this task, most of the features are taken from the best feature combination reported in Park and Cardie (2014) for a fair comparison.

Unigrams and Bigrams. This is a set of binary features capturing whether a given unigram or bigram appears in the given proposition. N-grams are useful, because certain words are highly associated with a class. For instance, sentiment words like *happy* is associated with the UNVERIF class, as propositions bearing emotion are typically unverifiable. Also, verbs in past tense, such as *went*, is likely to appear in VERIF_{EXP} propositions, because action verbs in the past tense form are often used in describing a past event in a non-subjective fashion.

Parts-of-Speech (POS) Count Based on the previous work distinguishing imaginative and informative writing, the conjecture is that the distribution of POS tags can be useful for telling apart UNVERIF from the rest (Rayson et al., 2001).

Dictionary-based Features. Three feature sets leverage on predefined lexicons to capture informative characteristics of propositions. Firstly, the subjectivity clue lexicon is used to recognize occurrences of sentiment bearing words (Wilson, 2005). Secondly, a lexicon made of speech event text anchors from the *MPQA 2.0* corpus are used to identify speech events, which are typically associated with VERIF_{NON} or VERIF_{EXP} (Wilson and Wiebe, 2005). Lastly, imperatives, which forms a subclass of UNVERIF, are recognized with a short lexicon of imperative expressions, such as *must, should, need to*, etc.

Emotion Expression Count The intuition is having much emotion often means the given proposition is subjective and thus unverifiable. Thus, the level of emotion in text is approximated by counting tokens such as "!" and fully capitalized words.

Tense Count The verb tense can provide a crucial information about the type of the proposition. For instance, the future tense is highly correlated with UNVERIF, because propositions about a future event is generally unverifiable at the time the proposition is stated. Also, the past tense is a good indicator of UNVERIF or VERIF$_{EXP}$, since propositions of type VERIF$_{NON}$ are usually factual propositions irrelevant of time, such as "peanut reactions can cause death."

Person Count One example of the grammatical person being useful for classification is that VERIF$_{NON}$ propositions rarely consist of first person narratives. Also, imperatives, instances of UNVERIF, often comes with the second person pronoun.

3 Experiments and Analysis

3.1 Experiment Setup

The experiments were conducted on the dataset from Park and Cardie (2014), which consists of user comments collected from *RegulationRoom.org*, an experimental eRulemaking site. The dataset consists of user comments about rules proposed by government agencies, such as the Department of Transportation. For comparison purposes, we used the same train/test split (See Table 1). On average, roughly 8 propositions constitute a comment in both sets.

The goal of the experiments is two-fold: 1) comparing the overall performance of CRF-based approaches to the prior results from using multiclass SVMs and 2) analyzing how the semi-supervised CRFs perform with different percentages of the training data labeled, under different conditions. To achieve this, a set of repeated experiments were conducted, where gradually increasing portions of the training set were used as labeled data with the remaining portion used as unlabeled data.[4]

For evaluation, we use the macro-averaged F1 score computed over the three classes. Macro-F1 is used in the prior work, as well, to prevent the performance on the majority class[5] from dominating the overall evaluation.

	VERIF$_{NON}$	VERIF$_{EXP}$	UNVERIF	Total
Train	987	900	4459	6346
Test	370	367	1687	2424
Total	1357	1267	6146	8770

Table 1: # of Propositions in Training and Test Set

3.2 Results and Discussion

CRF vs Multiclass SVM As shown in Table 2, the multiclass SVM classifier performs better overall. But at the same time, a clear trend can be observed: With CRF, the precision makes a significant gain at the cost of the recall for both VERIF$_{NON}$ and VERIF$_{EXP}$. And the opposite is the case for VERIF.

One cause for this is the heavy skew in the dataset that can be better handled in SVMs; As mentioned before, the majority class (UNVERIF) comprises about 70% of the dataset. When training the multiclass SVM, it is relatively straight forward to balance the class distribution in the training set, as each proposition is assumed to be independent of others. Thus, Park and Cardie randomly oversample the instances of non-majority classes to construct a balanced trained set. The situation is different for CRF, since the entire sequence of propositions comprising a comment is classified together. Further investigation in resolving this issue is desirable.

Semi-supervised CRF Table 3 reports the average performance of CRFs trained on 25%, 50%, 75% and 100% labeled training data (the same dataset), using various supervised and semi-supervised approaches over 5 rounds. Though, the amount is small, incorporating semi-supervised approaches consistently boosts the performance for the most part. The limited gain in performance is due to the small set of accurate constraints.

As discussed in Section 2.2, one crucial component of training CRFs with Posterior Regularization is designing constraints on features. For a given feature, a respective constraint defines a probability distribution over the possible classes. For the best performance, the distribution needs to be accurate, and the constrained features occur in the unlabeled training set frequently.

[4]Mallet (2002) was used for training the CRFs.

[5]UNVERIF comprises about 70% of the data

Method	UNVERIF vs All			VERIF_{NON} vs All			VERIF_{EXP} vs All			F_1
	Pre.	Rec.	F_1	Pre.	Rec.	F_1	Pre.	Rec.	F_1	(Macro-Ave.)
Multi-SVM (P&C)	**86.86**	83.05	84.91	49.88	**55.14**	**52.37**	66.67	**73.02**	**69.70**	**68.99**
Super-CRF 100%	80.35	**93.30**	**86.34**	**60.34**	28.38	38.60	**74.57**	59.13	65.96	63.63

Table 2: Multi-SVM vs Supervised CRF Classification Results

Method	UNVERIF vs All			VERIF_{NON} vs All			VERIF_{EXP} vs All			F_1
	Pre.	Rec.	F_1	Pre.	Rec.	F_1	Pre.	Rec.	F_1	(Macro-Ave.)
Super-CRF 100%	80.35	93.30	86.34	60.34	28.38	38.60	74.57	59.13	65.96	63.63
Super-CRF 75%	79.57	92.59	85.59	54.33	30.54	39.10	77.08	53.13	62.90	62.53
CRF-PR_H 75%	79.42	93.12	85.73	57.14	31.35	40.49	79.01	52.32	62.95	63.06
CRF-PR_{H+IG} 75%	79.72	94.37	86.43	63.58	27.84	38.72	76.6	55.31	64.24	63.13
Super-CRF 50%	79.16	93.01	85.53	51.92	21.89	30.82	71.68	55.86	62.79	59.71
CRF-PR_H 50%	79.28	92.12	85.17	55.68	26.49	35.92	69.23	53.95	60.64	60.57
CRF-PR_{H+IG} 50%	79.23	92.23	85.24	55.37	26.49	35.83	70.32	54.22	61.23	60.77
Super-CRF 25%	75.93	96.86	85.13	57.89	5.95	10.78	79.06	50.41	61.56	52.49
CRF-PR_H 25%	76.27	96.03	85.02	41.54	7.30	12.41	79.15	50.68	61.79	53.07
CRF-PR_{H+IG} 25%	75.83	96.32	84.86	38.78	5.14	9.07	79.31	50.14	61.44	51.79

Table 3: Supervised vs Semi-Supervised CRF Classification Results

*The percentages refer to the percentages of the labeled data in the training set.

*The methods are as follows: Super-CRF = supervised approach only using the labeled data, CRF-PR_H = CRF with posterior regularization using constraints that are manually selected, CRF-PR_{H+IG} = CRF with posterior regularization using constraints that are manually written and automatically generated using information gain.

*Precision, recall, and F_1 scores are computed with respect to each one-vs-all classification problem for evaluation purposes, though a single model is built for the multi-class classification problem.

Our manual approach resulted in a small set of about 10 constraints on features that are tightly coupled with a class. Examples include the word "should", large number of strong subjective expressions, and imperatives, which are all highly correlated with the UNVERIF. While the constraints are accurate, the coverage is too small to boost the performance. However, it is quite difficult to generate a large set of constraints, because there are not that many features that are indicative of a single class. Also, given that UNVERIF comprises a large percentage of the dataset, and the nature of verifiability[6], it is even more difficult to identify features tightly coupled with VERIF_{NON} and VERIF_{EXP} class. One issue with automatically generated constraints, based on information gain, is that they tend to be inaccurate.

[6]Verifiability does not have many characterizing features, but the lack of any of the characteristics of unverifiability, such as sentiment bearing words, is indicative of verifiability.

4 Conclusions and Future Work

We present an empirical study on employing Conditional Random Fields for identifying appropriate types of support for propositions in user comments. An intuitive extension to Park and Cardie (2014)'s approach is to frame the task as a sequence labeling problem to leverage on the fact that certain types of propositions tend to occur together. While the overall performance is reduced, we find that Conditional Random Fields (CRFs) improves the F_1 score with respect to the UNVERIF class. Also, semi-supervised CRFs with posterior regularization trained on 75% labeled training data can closely match the performance of a supervised CRF trained on the same training data with the remaining 25% labeled as well.

An efficient way to handle the skewed distribution of classes in the training set is needed to boost the performance of CRFs. And a set of efficient constraints is necessary for better performing semi-supervised CRFs with posterior regularization.

References

Kevin D. Ashley and Vern R. Walker. 2013. From information retrieval (ir) to argument retrieval (ar) for legal cases: Report on a baseline study. In *JURIX*, pages 29–38.

Kedar Bellare, Gregory Druck, and Andrew McCallum. 2009. Alternating projections for learning with expectation constraints. In *Proceedings of the Twenty-Fifth Conference on Uncertainty in Artificial Intelligence*, pages 43–50. AUAI Press.

Elena Cabrio and Serena Villata. 2012. Combining textual entailment and argumentation theory for supporting online debates interactions. In *Proceedings of the 50th Annual Meeting of the Association for Computational Linguistics (Volume 2: Short Papers)*, pages 208–212, Jeju Island, Korea, July. Association for Computational Linguistics.

Vanessa Wei Feng and Graeme Hirst. 2011. Classifying arguments by scheme. In *Proceedings of the 49th Annual Meeting of the Association for Computational Linguistics: Human Language Technologies - Volume 1*, HLT '11, pages 987–996, Stroudsburg, PA, USA. Association for Computational Linguistics.

Kuzman Ganchev, Jennifer Gillenwater, and Ben Taskar. 2009. Dependency grammar induction via bitext projection constraints. In *Proceedings of the Joint Conference of the 47th Annual Meeting of the ACL and the 4th International Joint Conference on Natural Language Processing of the AFNLP: Volume 1-Volume 1*, pages 369–377. Association for Computational Linguistics.

Kuzman Ganchev, Joao Graça, Jennifer Gillenwater, and Ben Taskar. 2010. Posterior regularization for structured latent variable models. *The Journal of Machine Learning Research*, 99:2001–2049.

John D. Lafferty, Andrew McCallum, and Fernando C. N. Pereira. 2001. Conditional random fields: Probabilistic models for segmenting and labeling sequence data. In *Proceedings of the Eighteenth International Conference on Machine Learning*, ICML '01, pages 282–289, San Francisco, CA, USA. Morgan Kaufmann Publishers Inc.

Andrew Kachites McCallum. 2002. Mallet: A machine learning for language toolkit. http://www.cs.umass.edu/ mccallum/mallet.

Raquel Mochales Palau and Marie-Francine Moens. 2009. Argumentation mining: The detection, classification and structure of arguments in text. In *Proceedings of the 12th International Conference on Artificial Intelligence and Law*, ICAIL '09, pages 98–107, New York, NY, USA. ACM.

Joonsuk Park and Claire Cardie. 2014. Identifying appropriate support for propositions in online user comments. In *Proceedings of the First Workshop on Argumentation Mining*, pages 29–38, Baltimore, Maryland, June. Association for Computational Linguistics.

Paul Rayson, Andrew Wilson, and Geoffrey Leech. 2001. Grammatical word class variation within the british national corpus sampler. Language and Computers.

Maria Paz Garcia Villalba and Patrick Saint-Dizier. 2012. Some facets of argument mining for opinion analysis. In *COMMA*, pages 23–34.

Theresa Wilson and Janyce Wiebe. 2005. Annotating attributions and private states. In *Proceedings of ACL Workshop on Frontiers in Corpus Annotation II: Pie in the Sky*.

Theresa Wilson. 2005. Recognizing contextual polarity in phrase-level sentiment analysis. In *In Proceedings of HLT-EMNLP*, pages 347–354.

Adam Wyner, Raquel Mochales-Palau, Marie-Francine Moens, and David Milward. 2010. Semantic processing of legal texts. chapter Approaches to Text Mining Arguments from Legal Cases, pages 60–79. Springer-Verlag, Berlin, Heidelberg.

Bishan Yang and Claire Cardie. 2014. Context-aware learning for sentence-level sentiment analysis with posterior regularization. In *Proceedings of ACL*.

A Computational Approach for Generating Toulmin Model Argumentation

Paul Reisert **Naoya Inoue** **Naoaki Okazaki** **Kentaro Inui**

Tohoku University
Graduate School of Information Sciences
6-6 Aramaki Aza Aoba, Aobaku, Sendai, Miyagi 980-8579, Japan
{preisert,naoya-i,okazai,inui}@ecei.tohoku.ac.jp

Abstract

Automatic generation of arguments is an important task that can be useful for many applications. For instance, the ability to generate coherent arguments during a debate can be useful when determining strengths of supporting evidence. However, with limited technologies that automatically generate arguments, the development of computational models for debates, as well as other areas, is becoming increasingly important. For this task, we focused on a promising argumentation model: the Toulmin model. The Toulmin model is both well-structured and general, and has been shown to be useful for policy debates. In this preliminary work we attempted to generate, with a given topic motion keyword or phrase, Toulmin model arguments by developing a computational model for detecting arguments spanned across multiple documents. This paper discusses our subjective results, observations, and future work.

1 Introduction

Given an input motion, or claim, the task of *automatic argumentation generation* is to generate *coherent* and *logically structured* argumentation in various scenarios. In this paper, we examined two extreme types of scenarios: (i) an input claim should be supported, and (ii) a counterclaim should be supported. For example, with *the House should ban alcohol in schools* as an input claim, our goal was to automatically generate supportive output, such as "The input claim is valid *because alcohol causes brain damage. Brain damage loses concentration for study.*"; and with *the House should not ban alcohol in schools* as our counterclaim, our goal, like before, was to generate supportive output, such as "The counterclaim is valid *because alcohol makes people fun. Sociality can be developed by pleasure.*". The automatic generation of arguments is a challenging problem that is not only useful for identifying *evidence* of certain claims but also for *why* the evidence of certain claims is significant.

As a basis for generating logically structured output, we required the utilization of a structured framework ideal for debate arguments. A promising option for accomplishing this goal includes the integration of the Toulmin model [18], which consists of three main components (claim, data, and warrant), where a claim is something an individual believes, data is support or evidence to the claim, and a warrant is the hypothetical link between the claim and data. When considering this structure for debate topic motions, such as *alcohol should be banned*, then data such as *alcohol causes liver disease* and a warrant such as *if alcohol causes liver disease, then it should be banned* can be supportive for the claim, as the data's relevance to the claim is provided by the warrant. Although many possibilities exist for constructing a Toulmin model, we refer to a single possibility as a *Toulmin instantiation*; and due to its promising usefulness in policy debates [1], we explored the Toulmin model for argumentation generation. As such, no previous work has experimented with automatically constructing Toulmin instantiations through computational modeling.

As an information source of argumentation generation, we aggregate statements relevant to the in-

Proceedings of the 2nd Workshop on Argumentation Mining, pages 45–55,
Denver, Colorado, June 4, 2015.

put claim spanned across *multiple* documents on the Web. One can exploit one *single* document that includes the input claim; however, it may not include information sufficient to organize a logically structured answer comprehensively.

The most challenging part of automatic construction of a Toulmin instantiation is to construct a *coherent* and *well-organized* argumentation from the relevant pieces of statements from multiple documents. In this paper, we manually give relations between each Toulmin component in terms of causality and the sentiment polarity of their participants. We focus on two extreme causality relations, namely PROMOTE or SUPPRESS in this paper. By utilizing these relations, our task is reduced to finding relation tuples that can satisfy the definitions. We use our evaluation results as a basis of justification as to whether or not the these relation tuples are sufficient for argumentation construction. To ensure the coherency of overall argumentation, we find contextually similar relations. In future work, we plan to apply state-of-the-art technologies from discourse relation recognition and QAs for generating each Toulmin component, where a significant amount of research has been done [20, 15, 13, 8, 17].

The rest of the paper is as follows. We first describe related work in Section 2 and an overview of the Toulmin model in Section 3. In Section 4, we describe our methodology for generating patterns for Toulmin construction. In Section 5, we experiment with constructing Toulmin instantiations for a given claim and report our findings. In Section 6, we discuss our results. Finally, in Section 7, we conclude our work and describe our future work.

2 Related Work

To the best of our knowledge, no prior work has developed a computation model for automatically constructing Toulmin instantiations. However, various components of the Toulmin model have individually been researched and are discussed below.

The most similar work to ours is the automatic detection of enthymemes using Walton [21]'s argumentation schemes [5]. Similarly, we aim to discover enthymemes in the Toulmin model explicitly through computational modeling in order to assist with generating constructive debate speeches. In future work, we plan to adopt different, less general argumentation theories.

Given a motion-like topic, previous work has found relevant claims to support the topic [8]. Other work has utilized a list of controversial topics in order to find relevant claim and evidence segments utilizing discourse markers [17]. Previous Why-QA work [20, 15, 13] has dealt with finding answers for questions such as *Why should alcohol be banned?*. In this case, a passage such as *Alcohol causes heart disease* can be retrieved; however, the passage is not necessarily concerned with *Why is heart disease negative?* which can act as a link between the question and answer. In this work, in addition to a claim and it data, or evidence, we explore finding the link, or warrant, and its backing, in order to strengthen the relationship between the claim and data, one of the aspects of the Toulmin model.

In terms of determining stance, previous work has utilized attack or support claims in user comments as a method for determining stance [3]. Inspired by Hashimoto et al. [6]'s excitatory and inhibitory templates, in this work, we similarly compose a manual list of PROMOTE(X,Y) and SUPPRESS(X,Y) relations and rely on these relations, coupled with positive and negative sentiment values, as a means to signify stance. Simultaneously, not only does this assist with stance, but it is an important feature for argument construction in our first round of constructing automatic Toulmin instantiations.

Finally, we generate arguments spanned across multiple documents using the PROMOTE(X,Y) and SUPPRESS(X,Y) relations. Previous work such as Cross Document Structure theory [16] has organized information from multiple documents via relations.

Furthermore, the Statement Map [14] project, for a given query, has detected agreeing and conflicting support which are spanned across multiple documents. In this work, we attempt to construct an implicit Warrant and generate its Backing for a Claim (query) and its Data (support).

3 Toulmin Model

Toulmin was the first to believe that most arguments could simply be modeled using the following six components: claim, data, warrant, backing, qualifier, and rebuttal [18]. This model is referred to as the Toulmin model and is shown in Figure 1, along with an instantiation. In this work, we focus on constructing an argument consisting of a claim, data, warrant, as these three components make up the bare minimum of the Toulmin model. The claim consists of the argument an individual wishes for others to believe. Data consists of evidence to support the claim. However, in the event the data is considered unrelated to the claim by another individual, such as a member of a negative team in a policy debate, the warrant, although typically implicit, can explicitly be mentioned to state the relevance of the data with the claim.

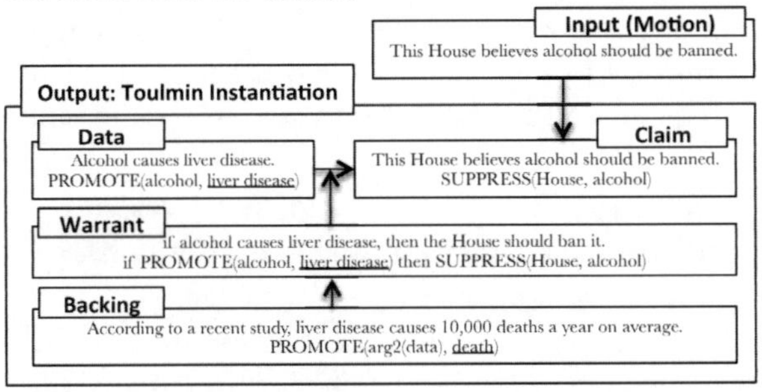

Figure 1: An Instantiation of the Toulmin Model. The underlined word represents negative sentiment.

In addition to the basic components, one individual may require more information to support the warrant. This component is referred to as backing, and we attempt to generate backing as evidence to the warrant. By generating a warrant and its backing, we can strengthen the data in relation to the claim which can be important for determining the relevancy of the data in a debate. Additional Toulmin components consist of a rebuttal, which is an exception to a claim, and a qualifier, which is a component, such as a sentence or word, in which affects the degree of the claim.

4 Methodology

As shown in Figure 1, our task consists of the following: given a topic motion in the form PROMOTE(House,Y) or SUPPRESS(House, Y), where Y is a topic motion keyword, we instantiate a Toulmin model by first recognizing the topic motion as a Toulmin model claim, and through computational modeling, we generate the remaining Toulmin model arguments.

For instantiating a Toulmin model through computational modeling given a motion, or claim in the Toulmin model, we need to recognize the semantic relation between sentences in a corpus. For example, to find data of the claim, we need find a set of sentences that can serve as the evidence of the claim. However, as described in Section 1, there are still a lot of challenging problems in this research area.

Therefore, our idea is to focus on the sentences that can be represented by an excitation relation, namely PROMOTE(X, Y) or SUPPRESS(X, Y), which is inspired by [6]. Focusing on such sentences, we can recast the problem of semantic relation recognition between sentences as a simple pattern matching problem. For example, suppose we are given the claim SUPPRESS(government, riot). Then, we can find the supporting evidence of this claim by searching for sentences that match PROMOTE(riot, Z), where the sentiment polarity of Z is negative.

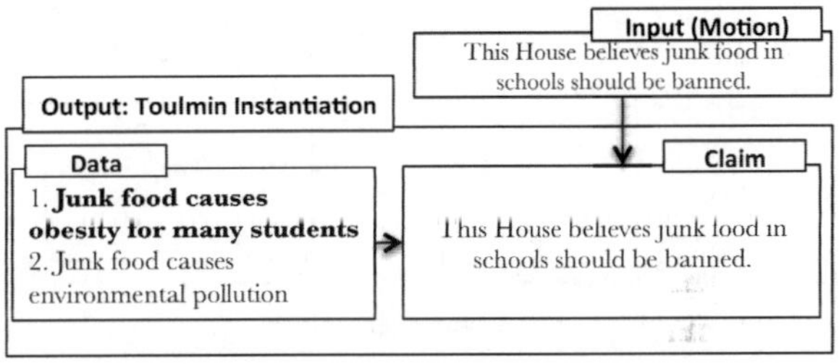

Figure 2: An example of contextual information for argument generation. The selected data is shown in bold.

One of the challenges of argument generation is the ability to produce coherent arguments. Figure 2 shows an example of this challenge. In the claim in Figure 2, one can see that opposed to banning all junk food in the world, the claim is limited to banning junk food in schools only. If we were to discover that *junk food causes obesity for many students* and *junk food causes environmental pollution* as data, then we would like to choose the data which is most likely related to the claim. Therefore, we also account for contextual similarity when generating arguments. In the case of Figure 2, we would prefer the first data over the second, given the similarity between *student* and *school*. More details regarding our contextual similarity calculation method are described in Section 4.3.

4.1 Overview

We develop a two-staged framework for the automatic construction of Toulmin instantiations. First, we extract a set of claims represented by two-place predicates (e.g., *cause(alcohol, cancer)*) from a text corpus and generalize them into an excitation relation, namely either PROMOTE(X, Y) or SUPPRESS(X, Y). We then store the generalized relations into a database, which we call a *knowledge base*. In addition to the PROMOTE(X, Y) and SUPPRESS(X, Y) relation extraction, we also append direct object sentiment and first-order dependency information for our relations. This is further elaborated in Section 4.2.

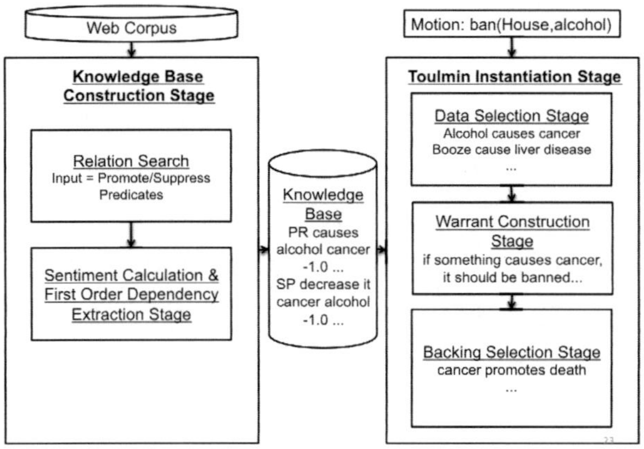

Figure 3: Overall framework

Second, given the motion claim that is also represented by a two-place predicate (e.g., *ban(house, alcohol)*) by the user, we find relevant relations from the knowledge base to generate data, warrant, and backing for the input motion claim. For counter-claims, we apply a simple hypothesis for reversing an original input motion (*ban(house, alcohol)* to *not ban(house, alcohol)*) and repeat the Toulmin construction stage for the new input. In the rest of this section, we elaborate on the two processes one by one.

4.2 Knowledge Base Construction

For constructing a knowledge base of PROMOTE(X,Y) and SUPPRESS(X,Y) relations, we rely on a manually created list of verbs representing PROMOTE/SUPPRESS relations and parsed dependency output. Similar to Open Information Extraction systems [23, 4, 10, etc.], we extract a set of triples (A_1, R, A_2), where R is a verb matching a PROMOTE/SUPPRESS-denoting verb, A_1 is a noun phrase (NP) serving as the surface subject of R, and A_2 is an NP serving as the surface object of R.

In our experiment, we used a collection of web pages extracted from ClueWeb12 as a source corpus of knowledge base construction. ClueWeb12[1] consists of roughly 733 million Web documents ranging from blogs to news articles. All web pages containing less than 30 words were filtered out which resulted in 222 million total web pages. From these web pages, we extract 22,973,104 relations using a manually composed list of 40 PROMOTE (e.g. *increase, cause, raise*) and 76 SUPPRESS (e.g. *harm, kill, prevent*) predicates. We parse each document using Stanford CoreNLP [9] in order to acquire both dependency, named entity, and coreference resolution features. In the case of coreference resolution, in order to reduce parsing time, the search distance was restricted to the previous two sentences.

At this time, we limit our extraction on a simple noun subject/direct objects opposed to passive sentences (e.g. *cancer is caused by smoking*). In future work, we will integrate more state of the art relation extraction methods for handling such cases.

4.2.1 Sentiment Polarity Calculation

For calculating the sentiment of each argument's head noun, we use SentiWordNet [2], Takamura et al. [19]'s sentiment corpus, and the Subjectivity Lexicon [22]. For each corpus, we assign a value of 1.0 if the sentiment is positive, -1.0 if negative, or otherwise neutral. We base positive and negative as a value greater than 0 and less than 0, respectively. In the case of SentiWordNet, we focus only on the top-ranked synset polarity value for each noun. Afterwards, we combine the values per noun and calculate sentiment using the following:

$$sp(w)=\left\{\begin{array}{l} pos \text{ if } num\_pos\_votes(w) \geq 2 \\ neg \text{ if } num\_neg\_votes(w) \leq -2 \\ neutral \text{ otherwise} \end{array}\right\},$$

where w is the head noun of the direct object in each PROMOTE and SUPPRESS relation. The functions $num\_pos\_votes(w)$ and $num\_neg\_votes(w)$ refer to the total number of positive sentiment votes and the total number of negative sentiment votes,

[1] http://www.lemurproject.org/clueweb12.php/

respectively, for w.

The results of our knowledge base construction are shown in Table 1. *Positive*, *Negative*, and *Neutral* refer to the number of relations in which a relation's A_2 sentiment is positive, negative, and neutral, respectively.

Table 1: PROMOTE (PR) and SUPPRESS (SP) relations from our data set.

Type	Positive	Negative	Neutral	Total
PR	2,039,644	755,695	17,504,201	20,299,540
SP	115,895	163,408	2,394,261	2,673,564
Total	2,155,539	919,103	19,898,462	22,973,104

From Table 1, we recognize an abundance of PROMOTE(X,Y) relations opposed to SUPPRESS(X,Y) relations. In addition, there are a considerable amount of neutral sentiment values. In our future work, we will focus on generating arguments with relations containing neutral direct object. For now, we limit our argument generation on relations with positive or negative direct object sentiment only.

4.3 Contextual Similarity

For calculating the contextual similarity between two sentences, we use first-order dependency tree information for an extracted relation's arguments' head and predicate. In the event a first-order node is a named entity, we also extract any of its children with named entity information attached.

We then calculate the average pairwise similarity between each relation between sentences using the cosine similarity of word vectors.

We adopt the following hypotheses for contextual similarity for our full model:

- if determining contextual similarity between claim and data, we calculate similarity between a claim's predicate first-order dependency information with data's predicate first-order dependency information, and claims's A_2 first-order dependency information with data's A_1 first-order dependency information
- if determining contextual similarity between data and backing, we calculate similarity between a data's A_2 first-order dependency information with backing's A_1 first-order dependency information, and data's predicate first-order dependency information with backing's predicate first-order dependency information

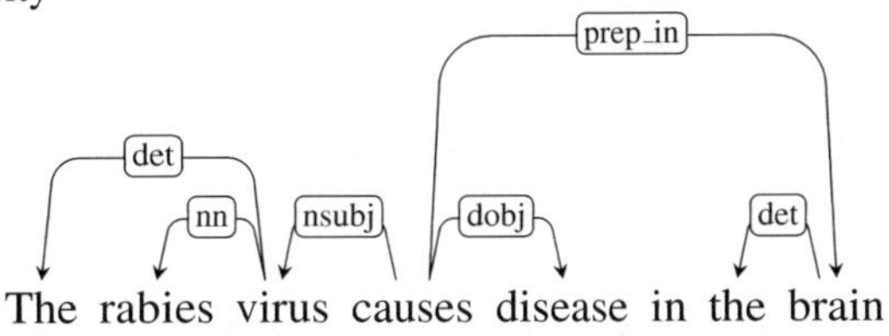

Figure 4: A dependency graph used for contextual similarity

An example is as follows. In the case of the sentence *the rabies virus causes disease in the brain*, the following first-order dependency extractions will be produced for subject (*rabies virus*), object (*disease*), and predicate (*cause*), respectively: {det: the, nn: rabies}, {}, {nsubj: virus, prep_in: brain, dobj: disease}.

4.4 Finding Toulmin Arguments

Below we present our hypotheses for generating claim, data, warrant, and backing.

4.4.1 Data

Given the motion in the form of a triplet $I = (A_1, R, A_2)$, we first extract a set D of candidate triplets of data for the input motion I from the constructed knowledge base. As described in Section 3, data is defined as a statement that supports the input motion, otherwise known as the claim. We find a set of data triplets based on the following hypotheses:

- if the input motion is PROMOTE(X, Y), the supporting data can be in the following two forms: (i) PROMOTE(Y', Z), where the sentiment polarity of Z (henceforth, *sp*(Z)) is positive, or (ii) SUPPRESS(Y', Z), where *sp*(Z) is negative. Y' may also be a full hyponym[2] of Y or Y itself.
- if the input motion is SUPPRESS(X, Y), the supporting data can be either (i) PROMOTE(Y', Z), where *sp*(Z) is negative, or (ii) SUPPRESS(Y', Z), where *sp*(Z) is positive. Y' may also be a full hyponym of Y or Y itself.

[2]We limit hyponyms to the top 10 most similar hyponyms to Y (Z in the case of backing)

For example, given the input motion *ban(house, alcohol)*, where *ban* is a SUPPRESS relation, we extract (i) all PROMOTE relations in which its A_1 is *alcohol*, or a full hyponym of *alcohol*, and $sp(A_2)$ is negative (e.g., *cause(alcohol, liver disease)*), and (ii) SUPPRESS relations in which its A_1 is *alcohol*, or a full hyponym of *alcohol*, and $sp(A_2)$ is positive (e.g., *decrease(alcohol, life expectancy)*).

After we collect a set of candidate triplets, we then cluster by the head noun of each relation's Z which is represented as $\mathcal{D} = D_{n_1}, D_{n_2}, ..., D_{n_m}$, where n_i is the head noun and m is the total size of unique Z. This is in order to diversify our arguments by different topics.

4.4.2 Warrant and Backing

Given that warrant is a hypothetical, bridgelike statement [18], we use a simple combination of a data relation and a claim using an *if...then* construct. Therefore, with the claim *this House should ban alcohol* and a data of *alcohol causes liver disease*, we generate a warrant of *if alcohol causes liver disease, then the House should ban it.* In future work, we will work on expanding this rule.

For each $d \in D, D \in \mathcal{D}$, we extract a set B_d of candidate backings using the similar hypotheses in the data extraction step. As described in Section 3, backing serves as the supporting evidence of the warrant. For example, we would like to find a statement that further provides reason to a warrant of *if alcohol promotes lung cancer, then it should be banned* (in this case, a statement such as *lung cancer causes death* can be a backing).

To capture backing of a warrant, we apply the following hypotheses if the input motion I is PROMOTE(X, Y) and data is d:

- if d is PROMOTE(Y, Z), where *sp*(Z) is positive, the backing can be either: (i) PROMOTE(Z', V), where $sp(V)$ is positive, or (ii) SUPPRESS(Z', V), where $sp(V)$ is negative. Z' may also be a full hyponym of Z or Z itself.
- if d is SUPPRESS(Y, Z), where *sp*(Z) is negative, the backing can be either: (i) PROMOTE(Z', V), where $sp(V)$ is negative, or (ii) SUPPRESS(Z', V), where $sp(V)$ is positive. Z' may also be a full hyponym of Z or Z itself.

Similarly, if the input motion I is SUPPRESS(X, Y), the following rules are applied:

- if d is PROMOTE(Y, Z), where *sp*(Z) is negative, the backing can be either: (i) PROMOTE(Z', V), where $sp(V)$ is negative, or (ii) SUPPRESS(Z', V), where $sp(V)$ is positive. Z' may also be a full hyponym of Z or Z itself.
- if d is SUPPRESS(Y, Z), where *sp*(Z) is positive, the backing can be either: (i) PROMOTE(Z', V), where $sp(V)$ is positive, or (ii) SUPPRESS(Z', V), where $sp(V)$ is negative. Z' may also be a full hyponym of Z or Z itself.

For example, for the input motion *ban(house, alcohol)* and data *cause(alcohol, liver disease)*, we would have as a result *cause(liver disease, death)* and *suppress(liver disease, metabolism)* as a backing.

After we collect a set of candidate triplets, we then cluster by the head noun of each relation's V which is represented as $\mathcal{W} = W_{n_1}, W_{n_2}, ..., W_{n_m}$, where n_i is the head noun and m is the total size of unique V. Similar to data, this is in order to diversify our generated arguments by topic.

4.4.3 Counterclaim

For the purpose of debating, we would like to create a Toulmin instantiation which conflicts with the original claim; that is, which is initialized with a counterclaim. For example, if the original input motion, and thus claim, is *ban(house, alcohol)*, then we would ideally like to construct an independent Toulmin instantiation with the following counterclaim: *not ban(house, alcohol)*. As such, the following two hypotheses are applied:

- if the original input motion is PROMOTE(X, Y), then the claim will be the new input motion SUPPRESS(X,Y)
- if the original input motion is SUPPRESS(X, Y), then the claim will be the new input motion PROMOTE(X,Y)

4.4.4 Toulmin Instantiation

So far, we have a set $\mathcal{D}$ of candidate data clusters, and for each $d \in D, D \in \mathcal{D}$, we have a set $\mathcal{B}_d$ of backing clusters. For generating argumentation, we first select representative data candidate

$repr(D)$ for each $D \in \mathcal{D}$ based on the following score function:

$$repr(D) = \arg\max_{d \in D} score(d; c) \quad (1)$$

$$\begin{aligned} score(x; y) = w_1 \cdot (cs(arg_0(x), arg_1(y)) \\ + cs(pred(x), pred(c))) \\ + w_2 \cdot as(arg_0(x), arg_1(y)) \\ + w_3 \cdot rel(clust(x)) - w_4 \cdot spec(x), \end{aligned} \quad (2)$$

where $cs(x, y)$ and $as(x, y)$ are functions representing contextual similarity and relation argument similarity, respectively. $rel(clust(x))$ determines the reliability of cluster $clust(x)$ based on its total number of items. $spec(x)$ determines the specificity of a given entry x. Both are defined as follows:

$$spec(e) = \frac{e_{ne\_size}}{e_{tokens}} + \log e_{sent\_len} \quad (3)$$

$$rel(X) = \log X_{num\_items} \quad (4)$$

, where e_{ne_size} is the total number of named entities in entry e, e_{tokens} is the total number of tokens, e_{sent_len} is the sentence length of entry e, and X_{num_items} is the number of entries in cluster X.

Contextual similarity is described in Section 4.3. For relation argument similarity, we simply calculate the average between relation argument surfaces using word vectors. We utilize the Google News dataset created by Mikolov et al. [11], which consists of 300-dimensional vectors for 3 million words and phrases. For each representative data candidate $d \in \mathcal{R}$, we select the most likely backing from $B \in \mathcal{B}_d$ based on the following:

$$backing(B) = \arg\max_{b \in B} score(b; d) \quad (5)$$

In order to determine appropriate weights for our ranking function, we create a development set for the motion *ban(House,alcohol in America)* and tune the weights until we discover a suitable value for our results. We determine the following empirical weights for our scoring function which we utilize in our experiment section: $w_1 = .5$, $w_2 = .15$, $w_3 = .3$, *and* $w_4 = .5$. We choose the relation with the highest score for our data selection stage and, similarly, our backing selection stage. Finally, we would like to mention that Equation 2 represents our ranking function for our full model which accounts for predicate similarity between our target argument (data or backing) and original claim. Our baseline model does not include predicate similarity between the targeted argument and original claim.

5 Experiment and Discussion

Given the five topic motion phrases *animal testing, death penalty, cosmetic surgery, smoking in public places, and junk food from schools* that were randomly selected from the iDebate, a popular, well-structured online debate platform, Top 100 Debate list[3], we construct 5 Toulmin instantations for the topic motion *ban(House, Y))*, where *Y* is a topic motion phrase. Similarly, we construct 5 Toulmin instantations for the topic motion *not ban(House, Y))*, which serves as a counterclaim.

For each topic motion, we use WordNet [12] to collect the full hyponyms and lemmas of the topic motion keyword. Next, we calculate the surface similarity between the keyword and its hypoynms, and we use the top 10 most similar hyponyms in order to collect more relations with subjects similar to the main keyword. After hyponym expansion, we filter out passages containing a question mark to avoid non-factual arguments , and we cluster by a relation's direct object head noun. This is in order to diversify our generated arguments by unique topics. Furthermore, we use the Lesk algorithm [7] to disambiguate a sentence using the hyponym synset or original motion topic synset in order to obtain sentences with similar semantic meaning. For instance, for the hypoynm *face lift* of *cosmetic surgery*, we filter out sentences referring to a *renovation face lift* opposed to a *cosmetic face lift*.

For each cluster, we use the appropriate scoring function shown in Section 4.4.4 to rank the relations. After each cluster item is scored, we collect 10 clusters, if available, with the top scores each to represent data. However, as shown from our results in Tables 2 and 3, some topics generated less than 10 data. For each data argument we generate, we repeat our hyponym expansion step for each direct object in our data relation, generate clusters and use the appropriate equations from Section 4.4.4 for generating backing for the constructed hypothetical warrant.

[3]http://idebate.org/view/top_100_debates

Table 2: Precision of baseline model consistency

ban(A_1, A_2)	Data	Backing
A_2=animal testing	-	-
A_2=cosmetic surgery	0.20 (1/5)	0.00 (0/4)
A_2=death penalty	0.20 (1/5)	0.00 (0/5)
A_2=junk food in schools	0.75 (6/8)	0.25 (2/8)
A_2=smoking in public places	1.00 (2/2)	0.00 (0/1)
Average	0.50	0.11
not ban(A_1, A_2)	Data	Backing
A_2=animal testing	0.33 (1/3)	0.00 (0/3)
A_2=cosmetic surgery	0.83 (5/6)	0.00 (0/6)
A_2=death penalty	0.67 (4/6)	0.17 (1/6)
A_2=junk food in schools	-	-
A_2=smoking in public places	-	-
Average	0.67	0.07

5.1 Results

We subjectively evaluate our output based on the following criteria: *i*) Does data support the claim?, and *ii*) Does the backing properly support the warrant? In Tables 2 and 3, we represent *i* and *ii* as data and backing, respectively.

Table 3: Precision of full model consistency

ban(A_1, A_2)	Data	Backing
A_2=animal testing	-	-
A_2=cosmetic surgery	0.20 (1/5)	0.00 (0/4)
A_2=death penalty	0.20 (1/5)	0.00 (0/5)
A_2=junk food in schools	0.75 (6/8)	0.25 (2/8)
A_2=smoking in public places	1.00 (2/2)	0.00 (0/1)
Average	0.50	0.11
not ban(A_1, A_2)	Data	Backing
A_2=animal testing	0.33 (1/3)	0.00 (0/3)
A_2=cosmetic surgery	0.83 (5/6)	0.00 (0/6)
A_2=death penalty	0.67 (4/6)	0.00 (0/6)
A_2=junk food in schools	-	-
A_2=smoking in public places	-	-
Average	0.67	0.00

We achieved almost identical results for our baseline model and full model; however, for the claim *the death penalty should not be banned*, our baseline model generated *death penalty will eliminate sins* and *sin makes men accomplices of one another and causes concupiscence, violence, and injustice to reign among them* as data and backing, respectively. On the other hand, our full model generated the same data argument, but generated the incorrect backing of *any bloggers promoted this, not me, giving people the idea it was making them money and they too should join.*

Overall, our low precision signifies that many issues still remain with our computational model.

Table 4: Sample of one valid Toulmin instantiation constructed by our model

Argument	Sentence
Claim	This House should ban junk food in schools.
Data	Junk food will cause acne.
Warrant	If junk food causes acne, then it should be banned.
Backing	Although acne developing in other parts of body is more severe than facial acne , facial acne greatly hurts ones self esteem due to ugly facial complexion.

Shown in Table 4 is an example of a valid Toulmin instantiation generated by our model. For the claim *this house should ban junk food in schools*, the data *junk food will cause acne* was generated. Using the claim and data, the warrant *if junk food causes acne, then it should be banned* was generated. Finally, to support the warrant, the backing above was generated, thus generating a full Toulmin instantiation.

Table 5: Sample of incorrect output. In the second example, backing only is incorrect.

Argument	Sentence
Data	Smoking causes bad health and it is very deadly .
Data	Capital punishment gives peace of mind to the victim 's family and friends .
Backing	But let us also be prepared to point out , as McGowan does , that peace can make claims on pragmatists at least as compelling as war .

From the output in Table 5, we recognized further improvements must be made to our knowledge base. For instance, for the generated data *smoking causes bad health and it is very deadly*, the object *health*'s sentiment polarity was labeled as positive; however, the phrase *bad health* implies negative sentiment. In future work, we must consider an object's adjective modifiers in our sentiment polarity calculation algorithm.

The second example in Table 5 demonstrates the difficulty in generating backing. In this example, the relation *PR(capital punishment, peace)* generated the data; however, searching for relations in our knowledge base with a subject of *peace* resulted in several unrelated sentences. Therefore, our model generated an unrelated backing. In our future work, we will address this issue, as this accounted for most of errors in backing.

6 Discussion

From our results in the previous section, it is apparent that we must make significant effort for improving our generated output precision in our future work. We learned that while our current knowledge base looks promising for argument generation, we must further modify its construction. In addition to the errors discussed in the previous section, we recognize that another consideration when generating arguments is the credibility of the source of information. As our measure of reliability was based on the frequency of relation occurrences, we also need to incorporate the source of information into our model. For example, if we find a passage such as *researchers mention that cancer causes pain*, then it is important to extract the source of information (e.g. news article, personal blog, etc) as well as the entity stating the fact (e.g. *researchers*). This can be especially important when determining for strengthening an argument's persuasiveness in a debate.

7 Conclusion and Future Work

In this work, we conducted a preliminary study for the development a computational model for the instantiation of a Toulmin model given a debate motion. We constructed a knowledge base of PROMOTE(X,Y) and SUPPRESS(X,Y) relations and created a set of rules for generating Toulmin data, warrant, and backing. From our results, we determined that our model requires significant improvement for the task of argument generation.

7.1 Future Work

As this work is a preliminary study for Toulmin instantiations by taking a computational approach, we recognize several areas for improvement. For example, we are aware that a claim and its respective arguments can come in forms other than PROMOTE(X,Y) and SUPPRESS(X,Y), such as a claim in the form of *the sky is blue*.

We would also like to adopt previous strategies, such as rhetorical structure theory for finding claim and data within one document. We believe that while not all Toulmin arguments may be explicitly mentioned in a single document, we may be able to detect multiple arguments for which we can utilize for discovering the implicit arguments in another document. For example, if one document states *drinking is dangerous because it can lead to liver disease*, then we can extract *drinking is dangerous* as a claim and *it can lead to liver disease* as a data from a single document, and, similarly to the strategies in this work, find the remaining arguments from other documents.

Credibility is also another important integration we must account for in our future work. As we only rely on frequency of relations for the reliability of a relation, we ignore the source of information and any entities stating facts containing our extracted relations. Integrating credibility can help strengthen the arguments our system generates which is beneficial for policy debates.

Finally, we will expand upon our PROMOTE and SUPPRESS keyword list, and we will experiment with state-of-the-art relation extraction technologies, as our current implementation is based on simple extraction rules.

Acknowledgments

The authors would like to give a special thanks to Kohsuke Yanai and Toshihiko Yanase of Central Research Laboratory, Hitachi, Limited. They would also like to thank the workshop reviewers for their invaluable comments. This work was supported by the MEXT Research Student Scholarship and by the JSPS KAKENHI Grant Numbers 15H05318 and 23240018.

References

[1] I. D. E. Association and R. Trapp. *The Debatabase Book: A Must-have Guide for Successful Debate*. International Debate Education Association, 2009.

[2] S. Baccianella, A. Esuli, and F. Sebastiani. Sentiwordnet 3.0: An enhanced lexical resource for sentiment analysis and opinion mining. In *in Proc. of LREC*, 2010.

[3] F. Boltužić and J. Šnajder. Back up your stance: Recognizing arguments in online discussions. In *Proc. of the First Workshop on Argumentation Mining*, pages 49–58, 2014.

[4] A. Fader, S. Soderland, and O. Etzioni. Identifying relations for open information extraction. In *Proc. of EMNLP*, EMNLP '11, pages 1535–1545, 2011.

[5] V. W. Feng and G. Hirst. Classifying arguments by scheme. In *Proc. of ACL: HLT - Volume 1*, HLT '11, pages 987–996, 2011.

[6] C. Hashimoto, K. Torisawa, S. De Saeger, J.-H. Oh, and J. Kazama. Excitatory or inhibitory: A new semantic orientation extracts contradiction and causality from the web. In *Proc. of Joint Conference on EMNLP and CoNLL*, EMNLP-CoNLL '12, pages 619–630, 2012.

[7] M. Lesk. Automatic sense disambiguation using machine readable dictionaries: how to tell a pine cone from an ice cream cone. In *SIGDOC '86: Proceedings of the 5th annual international conference on Systems documentation*, pages 24–26. ACM, 1986.

[8] R. Levy, Y. Bilu, D. Hershcovich, E. Aharoni, and N. Slonim. *Proc. of COLING 2014: Technical Papers*, chapter Context Dependent Claim Detection, pages 1489–1500. 2014.

[9] C. D. Manning, M. Surdeanu, J. Bauer, J. Finkel, S. J. Bethard, and D. McClosky. The Stanford CoreNLP natural language processing toolkit. In *Proc. of 52nd Annual Meeting of the Association for Computational Linguistics: System Demonstrations*, pages 55–60, 2014.

[10] Mausam, M. Schmitz, R. Bart, S. Soderland, and O. Etzioni. Open language learning for information extraction. In *Proc. of the 2012 Joint Conference on EMNLP and CoNLL*, EMNLP-CoNLL '12, pages 523–534, 2012.

[11] T. Mikolov, I. Sutskever, K. Chen, G. Corrado, and J. Dean. Distributed representations of words and phrases and their compositionality. *CoRR*, 2013.

[12] G. A. Miller. Wordnet: A lexical database for english. *Commun. ACM*, pages 39–41, 1995.

[13] J. Mrozinski, E. Whittaker, and S. Furui. Collecting a why-question corpus for development and evaluation of an automatic QA-system. In *Proc. of ACL: HLT*, pages 443–451, 2008.

[14] K. Murakami, E. Nichols, S. Matsuyoshi, A. Sumida, S. Masuda, K. Inui, and Y. Matsumoto. Statement map: Assisting information credibility analysis by visualizing arguments. In *3rd Workshop on Information Credibility on the Web*, 2008.

[15] J.-H. Oh, K. Torisawa, C. Hashimoto, M. Sano, S. De Saeger, and K. Ohtake. Why-question answering using intra- and inter-sentential causal relations. In *Proc. of ACL: long papers*, pages 1733–1743, 2013.

[16] D. R. Radev. A common theory of information fusion from multiple text sources step one: Cross-document structure. In *Proceedings of the 1st SIGdial Workshop on Discourse and Dialogue - Volume 10*, pages 74–83. Association for Computational Linguistics, 2000.

[17] P. Reisert, J. Mizuno, M. Kanno, N. Okazaki, and K. Inui. A corpus study for identifying evidence on microblogs. In *Proc. of LAW VIII*, pages 70–74, 2014.

[18] S. E. Toulmin. *The Uses of Argument*. Cambridge University Press, 1958.

[19] H. Takamura, T. Inui, and M. Okumura. Extracting semantic orientations of words using spin model. In *Proc. of the 43rd Annual Meeting on Association for Computational Linguistics*, ACL '05, pages 133–140, 2005.

[20] S. Verberne. Developing an approach for why-question answering. In *Proc. of EACL: Student Research Workshop*, EACL '06, pages 39–46, 2006.

[21] D. Walton, C. Reed, and F. Macagno. *Argumentation Schemes*. Cambridge University Press, 2008.

[22] T. Wilson, J. Wiebe, and P. Hoffmann. Recognizing contextual polarity in phrase-level sentiment analysis. In *Proc. of HLT and EMNLP*, HLT '05, pages 347–354. Association for Computational Linguistics, 2005.

[23] A. Yates, M. Cafarella, M. Banko, O. Etzioni, M. Broadhead, and S. Soderland. Textrunner: Open information extraction on the web. In *Proc. of HLT: NAACL: Demonstrations*, NAACL-Demonstrations '07, pages 25–26, 2007.

Argument Extraction from News

Christos Sardianos
Dept. of Informatics and Telematics
Harokopio University of Athens
Omirou 9, Tavros, Athens, Greece
sardianos@hua.gr

Ioannis Manousos Katakis and **Georgios Petasis** and **Vangelis Karkaletsis**
Institute of Informatics and Telecommunications
National Centre for Scientific Research (N.C.S.R.) "Demokritos"
GR-153 10, P.O. BOX 60228, Aghia Paraskevi, Athens, Greece
{gkatakis, petasis, vangelis}@iit.demokritos.gr

Abstract

Argument extraction is the task of identifying arguments, along with their components in text. Arguments can be usually decomposed into a claim and one or more premises justifying it. The proposed approach tries to identify segments that represent argument elements (claims and premises) on social Web texts (mainly news and blogs) in the Greek language, for a small set of thematic domains, including articles on politics, economics, culture, various social issues, and sports. The proposed approach exploits distributed representations of words, extracted from a large non-annotated corpus. Among the novel aspects of this work is the thematic domain itself which relates to social Web, in contrast to traditional research in the area, which concentrates mainly on law documents and scientific publications. The huge increase of social web communities, along with their user tendency to debate, makes the identification of arguments in these texts a necessity. In addition, a new manually annotated corpus has been constructed that can be used freely for research purposes. Evaluation results are quite promising, suggesting that distributed representations can contribute positively to the task of argument extraction.

1 Introduction

Argumentation is a branch of philosophy that studies the act or process of forming reasons and of drawing conclusions in the context of a discussion, dialogue, or conversation. Being an important element of human communication, its use is very frequent in texts, as a means to convey meaning to the reader. As a result, argumentation has attracted significant research focus from many disciplines, ranging from philosophy to artificial intelligence. Central to argumentation is the notion of argument, which according to [Besnard and Hunter, 2008] is a set of assumptions (i.e. information from which conclusions can be drawn), together with a conclusion that can be obtained by one or more reasoning steps (i.e. steps of deduction). The conclusion of the argument is often called the claim, or equivalently the consequent or the conclusion of the argument, while the assumptions are called the support, or equivalently the premises of the argument, which provide the reason (or equivalently the justification) for the claim of the argument. The process of extracting conclusions/claims along with their supporting premises, both of which compose an argument, is known as argument extraction [Goudas et al., 2014] and constitutes an emerging research field.

Nowadays, people have the ability to express their opinion with many different ways, using services of the social Web, such as comments on news, fora, blogs, micro-blogs and social networks. Social Web is a domain that contains a massive volume of information on every possible subject, from religion to health and products, and it is a prosperous place for exchanging opinions. Its nature is based on debating, so there already is plenty of useful information that waits to be identified and extracted [Kiomourtzis et al., 2014].

Consequently, there is a large amount of data that can be further explored. A common form for mining useful information from these texts, is by applying sentiment analysis techniques. Sentiment analysis can be proven as a quick way to capture sentiment polarity of people about a specific topic. Two of the domains

Proceedings of the 2nd Workshop on Argumentation Mining, pages 56–66,
Denver, Colorado, June 4, 2015. ©2015 Association for Computational Linguistics

where capturing public opinion is of great importance, are e-Government and policy making. In this way, politicians and policy makers can refine their plans, laws and public consultations prior to their publication or implementation. Additionally, it could help the voters in deciding which policies and political parties suit them better. However, a more fine-grained analysis is required in order to detect in which specific aspects of a policy, a citizen is in favour or against. Such analysis can be achieved through argument extraction: once a document that relates to a policy is located, it is examined in order to identify segments that contain argument elements, such as premises that are against or in support of a claim or an entity (such as nuclear energy or renewable energy sources). The main idea behind this filtering of public opinion as found on the social Web, is that citizens that try to justify their opinion with arguments may be more important or influential than the less justified ones.

Motivated by this need, in this paper we propose a supervised approach for argument extraction from relevant media, based on Conditional Random Fields [Lafferty et al., 2001]. Following the state of the art (i.e. [Goudas et al., 2014; Hou et al., 2013]), our approach studies the applicability of existing approaches on the domain of social Web, mainly news and blogs, although the evaluation focuses only on news, due to copyright issues[1]. Assuming that we know whether a sentence contains an argument element or not (i.e. by applying an approach similar to the one described in [Goudas et al., 2014]), our approach tries to detect the exact segments that represent these elements (i.e. claims and premises) through the use of a CRF classifier [Lafferty et al., 2001]. Targeting a set of thematic domains and languages as wide as possible, we have tried to minimise the use of domain and language depended resources. Thus our approach exploits features such as words, part-of-speech tags, small lists of language-dependent cue words, and distributed representations of words [Mikolov et al., 2013a,b,c], that can be easily extracted from unannotated large corpora. Our approach has been evaluated on manually annotated news in the Greek language, containing news from various thematic domains, including sports, politics, economics, culture, and various social problems, while the evaluation results are quite promising, suggesting that distributed representations can contribute positively to this task.

The rest of the paper is organized as follows: Section 2 refers to the related work on argument extraction, section 3 describes the proposed methodology and the corresponding features used for our approach. Section 4 presents the experimental results and the tools we utilized and finally, section 5 concludes the paper and proposes some future directions.

2 Related Work

A plethora of argument extraction methods consider the identification of sentences containing arguments or not as a key step of the whole process. More specifically, the above approaches face the process of argument extraction as a two-class classification problem. However, there are approaches which try to solve the argument extraction problem in a completely different way. [Lawrence et al., 2014] combined a machine learning algorithm to extract propositions from philosophical text, with a topic model to determine argument structure, without considering whether a piece of text is part of an argument. Hence, the machine learning algorithm was used in order to define the boundaries and afterwards classify each word as the beginning or end of a proposition. Once the identification of the beginning and the ending of the argument propositions has finished, the text is marked from each starting point till the next ending word. An interesting approach was proposed by [Graves et al., 2014], who explored potential sources of claims in scientific articles based on their title. They suggested that if titles contain a tensed verb, then it is most likely (actually almost certain) to announce the argument claim. In contrast, when titles do not contain tensed verbs, they have varied announcements. According to their analysis, they have identified three basic types in which articles can be classified according to genre, purpose and structure. If the title has verbs then the claim is repeated in the abstract, introduction and discussion, whereas if the title does not have verbs, then the claim does not appear in the title or introduction but appears in the abstract and discussion sections.

Another field of argument extraction that has recently attracted the attention of the research community, is the field of argument extraction from online

[1] Although we have created a manually annotated corpus concerning both news and blogs, only the corpus containing news can be redistributed for research purposes.

discourses. As in the most cases of argument extraction, the factor that makes the specific task such challenging, is the lack of annotated corpora. In that direction, [Houngbo and Mercer, 2014], [Aharoni et al., 2014] and [Green, 2014] focused on providing corpora, that could be widely used for the evaluation of the argument extraction techniques. In this context, [Boltužić and Šnajder, 2014] collected comments from online discussions about two specific topics and created a manually annotated corpus for argument extraction. Afterwards they used a supervised model to match user-created comments to a set of predefined topic-based arguments, which can be either attacked or supported in the comment. In order to achieve this, they used textual entailment (TE) features, semantic text similarity (STS) features, and one "stance alignment" (SA) feature. One step further, [Trevisan et al., 2014] described an approach for the analysis of German public discourses, exploring semi-automated argument identification by combining discourse analysis methods with Natural Language Processing methods. They focused on identifying conclusive connectors, substantially adverbs (i.e. hence, thus, therefore), using a multi-level annotation on linguistic means. Their methodological approach consists of three steps, which are performed iteratively (manual discourse linguistic argumentation analysis, semi-automatic Text Mining (PoS-tagging and linguistic multi-level annotation) and data merge) and their results show the argument-conclusion relationship is most often indicated by the conjunction because followed by since, therefore and so. [Ghosh et al., 2014] attempted to identify the argumentative segments of texts in online threads. They trained expert annotators to recognize argumentative features in full-length threads. The annotation task consisted of three subtasks. In the first subtask, annotators had to identify the Argumentative Discourse Units (ADUs) along with their starting and ending points. Secondly, they had to classify the ADUs according to the Pragmatic Argumentation Theory (PAT) into Callouts and Targets. As a final step, they indicated the link between the Callouts and Targets. Apart from that, they proposed a hierarchical clustering technique that assess how difficult it is to identify individual text segments as Callouts. [Levy et al., 2014] defined the task of automatic claim detection in a given context and outlined a preliminary solution. Their supervised learning approach relied on a cascade of classifiers designed to handle the skewed data. Defining their task, they made the assumption that the articles given are relatively small set of relevant free-text articles, provided either manually or by automatic retrieval methods. More specifically, the first step of their task was to identify sentences containing context dependent claims (CDCs) in each article. Afterwards they used a classifier in order to find the exact boundaries of the CDCs detected. As a final step, the ranked each CDC in order to isolate the most relevant to the corresponding topic CDCs. That said, their goal is to automatically pinpoint CDCs within topic-related documents.

3 Proposed Approach

The work presented in this paper is motivated mainly by needs in the area of e-Government and policy making, aiming at performing argument extraction on large corpora collected from the social Web, targeting mainly on-line newspapers and blogs. Through a process that identifies segments that correspond to argument elements (claims and premises), performs aspect-based sentiment analyses, matches arguments to policy elements, and aggregates results from multiple sources, policy makers have the ability to receive the necessary feedback for ongoing public consultations, laws, issues that concern citizens, and captures the public opinion towards various issues. In this context, identified opinions are classified according to the contained argumentation that supports each opinion: Apparently, argument extraction can be a powerful tool for any decision making procedure. For example, it would be extremely useful for a government to be in position of knowing the public opinion about a law that is intended to be presented. Apart from that, it is of great value to detect the arguments against or in favour used in public discussions about the specific issue, in order to end up with a law which would be acceptable from a larger percentage of citizens.

The requirements for an argument extraction approach operating in such a context are several, including the ability to process as many thematic domains as possible, to be as accurate as possible regarding the identified argument elements, and utilise as fewer linguistic resources as possible, as it needs to operate also in less-resourced languages, such as Greek. Of course, it should be able to extract arguments from documents that influence the public opinion (such as news) or documents where citizens express their opinions and views (such as blogs). The goal of this research is to develop an approach for the task of argument extraction, based on machine learning, that will fulfill these requirements and will be applicable to the Greek language.

Our approach is based on Conditional random fields (CRFs) [Lafferty et al., 2001], a probabilistic framework for labeling and segmenting structured data such as sequences, which has been applied to a wide range of segmenting tasks, from named-entity recognition [McCallum and Li, 2003] and shallow parsing [Sha and Pereira, 2003], to aspect-based sentiment analysis [Patra et al., 2014]. Beyond features such as words and part-of-speech tags, our approach exploits a small lexicon of cue words, which usually signal the presence of a premise segment, and distributed representations of words [Mikolov et al., 2013a,b,c]. These map words to vectors of a high-dimensional space (usually more than 100 dimensions), which are created without human intervention from observing the usage of words on large (non-annotated) corpora. More specifically, our approach exploits the "word2vec"[2] tool [Mikolov et al., 2013a,b,c], which can make highly accurate guesses about a word's meaning based on its usage, provided enough data, usage and context for each word are available. The "word2vec" approach tries to arrange words with similar meaning close to each other, and interesting feature that we want to exploit in our approach in order to widen the "word space" beyond the words observed during the training phase.

3.1 Expansion of word feature space

Trying to provide an approach for argument extraction supporting multiple thematic domains, we exploit word similarities for expanding the word feature space. As already discussed, "word2vec" is a tool that computes similarities between words from large corpora and generates a real-valued feature vector for each word. It actually trains a recurrent neural network and maximizes the probability for a word to appear in a specific context.

As shown in figure 1, each word comes as input to the first layer $w(t)$ of the recurrent neural network, representing an input word at time t. As a result, matrix u holds the word representations, with each column representing the words. The hidden layer $s(t)$ maintains a representation of the sentence history by having a recursive connection z^{-1} to the previous word $s(t-1)$. Finally, $y(t)$ produces a probability distribution over words, from which a list of similar words is generated as output. In practice, "word2vec" takes as input a continuous stream of words from a corpus and generates a ranking including the k (defined by the user) most similar words for each word appeared in the input stream. As an example, the most similar words for the word "ορειβασία" ("climbing") according to our "word2vec" generated model for Greek are shown in Table 1, while Table 2 shows the 40 most similar words to the Greek word "λιγνίτης" ("lignite"), selected from the domain of renewable energy sources. As can be seen from Table 2, all suggested words according to cosine similarity over the word feature vectors are relevant to the thematic domain where lignite belongs, with 4 most similar words being either inflected forms of lignite in Greek, or other forms of carbon-related substances.

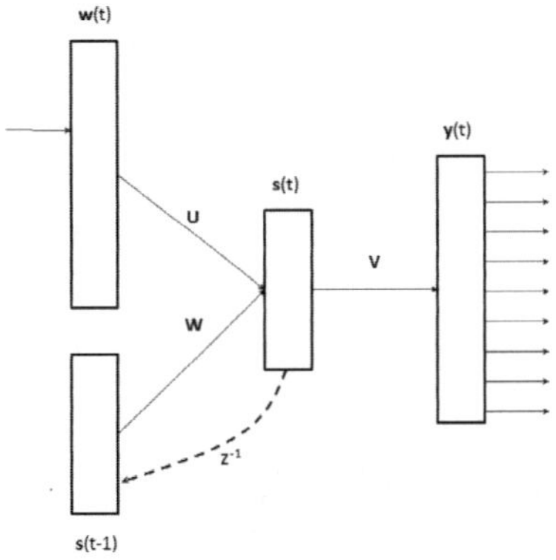

Figure 1: Recurrent Neural Network Language Model (Mikolov et al., 2013)

Five Most Similar Words	Cosine Similarity
ιππασία (horse-riding)	0.748
ποδηλασία (cycling)	0.721
πεζοπορία (hiking)	0.683
ιστιοπλοΐα (sailing)	0.681
καγιάκ (kayak)	0.674

Table 1: *"Word2vec"* sample output (most similar words to the Greek word "ορειβασία" ("climbing")).

[2] `https://code.google.com/p/word2vec/`

Similar Words	Cosine Similarity	Similar Words	Cosine Similarity
λιγνίτη (lignite)	0.694903	ρυπογόνο (polluting)	0.493400
λιθάνθρακας (coal)	0.665466	βιοαιθανόλη (bioethanol)	0.489851
άνθρακας (carbon)	0.644011	βιοαέριο (biogas)	0.481461
λιθάνθρακα (coal)	0.631198	ανανεώσιμα (renewable)	0.481460
ηλεκτροπαραγωγή (electricity production)	0.621633	μαζούτ (fuel)	0.478094
λιγνίτες (lignite)	0.580237	υδροηλεκτρικά (hydropower)	0.473288
ηλεκτρισμός (electricity)	0.555800	ζεόλιθος (zeolite)	0.473254
καύσιμο (fuel)	0.541152	βιομάζας (biomass)	0.473129
ορυκτά (fossil)	0.536743	ορυκτός (fossil)	0.472967
ηλεκτροπαραγωγής (electricity production)	0.532764	παραγόμενη (produced)	0.467192
βιομάζα (biomass)	0.532644	λιγνιτική (lignitic)	0.467016
γαιάνθρακες (coal)	0.509080	γεωθερμία (geothermal)	0.464868
ανανεώσιμη (reniewable)	0.508831	λιγνιτικών (lignitic)	0.464730
υδρογόνο (hydrogen)	0.503391	μεταλλεύματα (ores)	0.456796
αντλησιοταμίευση (pumped storage)	0.500784	ορυκτό (mineral)	0.456025
υ/η (hydropower)	0.499954	υδροηλεκτρική (hydropower)	0.454693
κάρβουνο (charcoal)	0.498860	ρυπογόνος (polluting)	0.451683
αιολική (wind)	0.498321	εξορύσσεται (mined)	0.450633
πλούτος (wealth)	0.496383	λιγνιτικές (lignitic)	0.449569
χάλυβας (steel)	0.494852	καυστήρας (burner, boiler)	0.447930

Table 2: *"Word2vec"* sample output (40 most similar words to the Greek word "λιγνίτης" ("lignite")). Model extracted from documents originating from news and Blogs.

Cosine similarity can also be computed at phrase-level, which means that the model tries to match words or phrases to a specific phrase. However, the size of the phrase vector file is more than twice size of the word vector file produced from the same corpus. Thus, using a phrase model requires a lot more computational resources than a word model.

3.2 Semi-supervised approach for extracting argument components

Concerning our approach for extracting argument components, we decided to extend the approach proposed by [Goudas et al., 2014], which also addressed a less-resourced language, such as Greek. [Goudas et al., 2014] suggested a two-step technique in order to extract arguments from news, blogs and social web. In the first phase of their method, they attempted to identify the argumentative sentences, employing classifiers such as Logistic Regression [Colosimo, 2006], Random Forest [Leo, 2001], Support Vector Machines [Cortes and Vapnik, 1995], Naive Bayes [Nir Friedman and Goldszmidt, 1997], etc. The features used in the classification were divided into features selected from the state of the art approaches and new features that were chosen for the domain of their application. Specifically, the state of the art features chosen, supply information about the position of the sentence inside the document as well as the number of commas and connectives inside the sentence. Moreover they examined the number of verbs (active and passive voice) in the sentence, the existence and number of cue words and entities, the number of words and adverbs in the context of a sentence, and finally the average length in characters of the words in the sentence. Regarding the new features added, this includes the number of adjectives in the sentence, the number of entities in the nth previous sentence and the total number of entities from the previous n sentences. In addition to the previous features, they also examined the ratio of distributions (language models) over unigrams, bigrams, trigrams of words and POS tags.

After the extraction of the argumentative sentences, they proceeded to the process of argument components (claims and premises) identification. In this stage, they applied a CRF classifier on a manually corpus. The features required for this task were the words of the sentences, gazetteer lists of known entities for the thematic domain, gazetteer lists of cue words and lexica of verbs and adjectives that appear most frequently in argumentative sentences of the training data.

In the approach proposed by [Goudas et al., 2014],

gazetteers are core features of the argument extraction process. In our approach, we want to reduce this dependency on gazetteers, by exploiting distributed representation for words, using the proposed method described in subsection 3.1. This will help us widen the spectrum of words that can be handled by our classifier and thus, manage to create a more fine-grained CRF model.

4 Empirical Evaluation

In this section the performance of the proposed approach will be examined. The performance metrics that will be used in order to evaluate our approach is accuracy, precision, recall and F1-measure. The empirical evaluation involves two experiments: The first experiment concerns that use of the "word2vec" tool, in order to obtain a suitable model for Greek, while the second experiment involves the evaluation of our approach for argument extraction on a manually annotated corpus.

4.1 Obtaining a "word2vec" model for Greek

In this section the steps performed for acquiring a "word2vec" model for the Greek language will be described, while the performance of the acquired model regarding word similarities will be examined. The performance metric that will be used in order to evaluate our word similarity model is accuracy. Accuracy denotes the number of words that are strictly related to the word given divided by the total number of words suggested as similar.

4.1.1 Experimental Setup

Dealing with semantic similarities, requires large volumes of data. As a result, in order to extract the distributed representation of words with the "word2vec" tool, we used a corpus that included around 77 million documents. These documents were written in Greek, and originated from news, blogs, Facebook[3] and Twitter[4] postings. Table 3 presents some properties of the utilised corpus. All documents were converted to lower-case before processed with the "word2vec" tool.

The evaluation task for this experiment related to the ability to extend a gazetteer (lexicon) of cue words or domain-specific entities with new entries, by exploiting the "word2vec" generated models to detect similar words. In order to evaluate this task, a seed list of cue words/entities was manually constructed. For each word in the seed list, the five more similar words were identified with the obtained "word2vec" model, and used to augment the list. Then, these new entries to the lists were manually examined, in order to identify which of these additions were correct or not (i.e. new entries were also cue words or entities from the same thematic domain).

	News	Blogs	Facebook	Twitter
Sentences	23.4	42.9	17.6	166
Words	492.8	853.2	197.3	1400

Table 3: Corpus Properties (in millions of documents).

4.1.2 Evaluation Results

Since the documents in our corpus were divided in four large categories (according to their source of origin), we started with the creation of four different "word2vec" models. Evaluation of the acquired models showed that news and blogs provide more fine-grained models in comparison to the models obtained from Facebook and Twitter. This happens because the Facebook and Twitter postings are usually less formal, many words are used with different senses than in news/blogs, postings may not have proper syntax or spelling and often contain abbreviations. As a result, a lot of noise has been inserted in the corresponding output models.

The authors of [Goudas et al., 2014] have made available to us the cue word and entity lists they have used in their experiments, which concern the thematic domain of renewable energy sources. Their list of cue words was manually extracted from their corpus by the researches, while the list of entities was provided by domain experts and policy makers.

Trying to expand these lists, we randomly selected twenty cue words and twenty entities from these, as a seed. For each seed word, the five more similar words were examined. Evaluation results suggest that there was a large variation on the similarities drawn for the same words from the news/blogs corpora and the Facebook/Twitter corpora. As it was expected, the models produced from the Facebook and Twitter corpora were worse than the others.

[3] `http://www.facebook.com/`

[4] `http://www.twitter.com/`. Each "tweet" was considered as a document.

Table 4 shows sample results for the word "λιγνίτης" ("lignite"), from the "word2vec" models of the news and blogs corpora. As we can see, the obtained similar words both for news and blogs corpora belong to the same domain, thus they can all be used to expand our word feature space and gazetteers for this specific domain.

News Corpus	Blogs Corpus
υγροποιημένο (liquefied)	λιγνίτη (lignite)
γαιάνθρακας (coal)	ηλεκτρισμός (electricity)
αέριο (gas)	ηλεκτρισμός (electricity)
σχιστολιθικό (shale)	ηλεκτροπαραγωγή (electricity production)
λιγνίτη (lignite)	λιθάνθρακα (bituminous coal)
ηλεκτρισμός (electricity)	βιοαέριο (biogas)
Σχιστολιθικό (Shale)	υδροηλεκτρικά (hydropower)
σχιστών (slit)	λιθάνθρακας (bituminous coal)
ηλεκτροπαραγωγής (electricity production's)	υδροηλεκτρισμό (hydroelectricity)
ηλεκτροπαραγωγή (electricity production)	βιομάζα (biomass)

Table 4: Similar words according to the News/Blogs "word2vec" model.

On the other hand, as shown in Table 5, the results from Facebook and Twitter for the same word ("λιγνίτης") are completely irrelevant. After examining the results, we observed that the sense of many words varies between news/blogs and facebook/twitter corpora. For example, the word "attractive", in Twitter and Facebook is used in most cases as "handsome" (i.e. attractive person), while in news and blogs is usually referred as "interesting" (i.e. attractive investment). One reason for this, is clearly the irrelevance of the topics discussed in social media and the use of language used in these discussion. In addition, the vocabulary normally used in social media is not as specialized as in news sites. This means that the similarity results from social media are not expected to be efficient for using in domain independent models. A noted fact that supports the above findings is the frequency of appearance of the word "λιγνίτης" ("lignite") in the corpora. Specifically, the word "λιγνίτης", appeared 5087 times in the news/blogs corpora, unlike the Facebook/Twitter corpora that appeared 1615 times.

Even the union of Facebook/Twitter corpora did not improve the performance of the generated model. On the other hand, the merge of the blogs and news corpora showed a significant increase on the performance of the "word2vec" model produced. The final evaluation of the "word2vec" models was conducted by two human annotators. Annotators were supplemented with a set of 20 randomly selected words which did not belong to a specific domain. The analogy between entities and cue words remained the same. Along with each word, a list with the five most similar words, as produced from the "word2vec" model, was provided. The evaluation results are shown in Table 6. According to these results, we can conclude to the fact that "word2vec" can be used for the expansion of the cue word lexicons. In addition, it can be proven a valuable resource as regards to the enrichment of the entities provided by the policy makers.

Facebook Corpus	Twitter Corpus
φόρτος (load)	αντιευρωπαϊσμός (anti-Europeanism)
δανειστής (loaner)	αριθμητής (numerator)
κιτρινισμός (yellowing)	εθνικισμός (nationalism)
εκτιμώμενος (estimated)	ιχνηλάτης (tracker)
αποκαθήλωση (pieta)	τ'αγοράζει (buys)
εισέπρατε (received)	εφοπλισμός (fitting)
τερματοφύλακας (goalkeeper)	Μπερλουσκονισμός (Berlusconism)
ψυχισμός (psyche)	περιπατητικός (ambulatory)
πεισμωμένος (stubborn)	κορπορατισμός (corporatism)
δανειολήπτης (borrower)	μονοπωλιακός (monopolistic)

Table 5: Similar words according to the Facebook/Twitter "word2vec" model.

4.2 CRFs for argument extraction

In this section, the proposed approach based on CRFs and distributed representations of words will be evaluated, with the help of a manually annotated corpus, containing annotated segments that correspond to argument elements (claims and premises).

4.2.1 Experimental Setup

Unfortunately, the corpus used in [Goudas et al., 2014] was not available due to licensing limitations. As a result, we had to create a new manually annotated corpus in order to evaluate our approach. We collected 300 news articles written in Greek from

	Entities			Cue Words		
	Annot. A	**Annot. B**	**A+B**	**Annot. A**	**Annot. B**	**A+B**
Five most similar	0.810	0.840	0.825	0.830	0.870	0.850

Table 6: Evaluation Results: Accuracy of 5 most similar words.

the Greek newspaper "Αυγή"[5]. According to their site, articles can be used without restriction for non-commercial purposes. The thematic domain of the articles varies from politics and economics to culture, various social issues and sports. The documents were manually annotated by two post-graduate students with moderate experience on the annotation process. Prior to the beginning of the annotation task, the annotators were supplied with guidelines describing the identification of arguments, while a QA session was carried out afterwards. The guidelines contained text examples of premises *in favor* or *against* the central claim stated by the articles' author. In these terms, the annotators were initially called to identify the central claims stated from the author of each article. Subsequently, they looked for text segments attacking or supporting every claim respectively. These segments may sometimes start with cue words such as "διότι" ("because"), "για να" ("in order to"), "αλλά" ("but"), or may just follow the usual sentence structure. Each annotator annotated 150 documents with argument components (premises and claims).

Once each annotator has annotated half of the corpus, pre-annotation has been applied, as a proven way to obtain significant gains in both annotation time and quality of annotation [Fort and Sagot, 2010; Marcus et al., 1993; Rehbein et al., 2009]. Since we were targeting errors of omission (segments missed by the annotators), an "overly-general" CRF model was trained on all 300 documents, and applied on the corpus. The CRF model is characterised as "overly-general", as it was derived only from sentences that contained claims and premises. Sentences not containing argument elements were omitted from training. The CRF model detected 4524 segments, significantly more than the 1172 segments annotated by the two annotators. A second round of annotation was performed, where both layers of annotations were visible (both the manual and the segments obtained through machine learning), and each annotator was asked to revise his own annotations, having two goals: *a*) examine whether any of the segments detected by the CRF model is either a claim or a premise, and *b*) exploit their experience from annotating 150 documents, to revise their annotations, especially the ones done during the early stages of annotation. During this second annotation step, a small number of errors was corrected and 19 new segments were added as argument elements, producing the "final" version of the manually annotated corpus[6], which has been used for evaluating our approach. The final version of the corpus contains 1191 segments annotated as argument elements.

Although the production of the corpus is still an ongoing process, we measured the inter-annotation agreement between of the two annotators over a fraction of the entire corpus. For this reason, we asked each annotator to annotate eighty articles already annotated by the other annotator, leading to 170 documents (out of 300) annotated by both annotators. Annotator A has annotated 918 argument elements, while annotator B has annotated 735 argument elements, out of which 624 were common between the two annotators, leading to a precision of 84.90%, a recall of 67.97%, with an F1 measure of 75.50%.

The manually annotated corpus containing 300 documents was used in order to evaluate our approach. For all evaluations, 10-fold cross validation was used, along with precision, recall, and F1 measure as the evaluation metrics. In order to measure the increase in performance, we have used a base case. Our base case was a CRF model, using as features the words and pos tags.

Our approach for argument extraction seeks to detect the boundaries of a text fragment that encloses a claim or a premise of an argument. One way to achieve this task, is to classify each word (token) of a sentence as a "boundary" token, i.e. as a token that "starts" or "ends" an argumentative segment. Using such a representation, the task can be converted into a

[5] `http://www.avgi.gr`

[6] The corpus that has been used in this evaluation is publicly available for research purposes from the authors. A revised (second) version of the corpus may be also available in the future.

classification task on each token. The "BILOU" representation seeks to classify each token with a single tag, which can be any tag from the following set: *a*) **B**: This tag represents the start/begin of a segment. It must be applied on the first token of a segment. *b*) **I**: This tag marks a token as being inside a segment. It must be applied on any token inside a segment, except the first and last ones. *c*) **L**: This tag represents the end of a segment. It must be applied on the last token of a segment. *d*) **O**: This tag marks a token as being outside a segment. It must be applied on any token that is not contained inside a segment. *e*) **U**: This tag correspond to "unit" segments, which are segments that contain a single token. It is a special case that marks a token that is the beginning and end of a segment simultaneously. For example the BILOU representation of the sentence "Wind turbines generate noise in the summer" is presented in Table 7.

BILOU tag	**word**	**prev. word**	**next word**	**...**
B-premise	Wind	-	turbines	...
I-premise	turbines	Wind	generate	...
I-premise	generate	turbines	noise	...
L-premise	noise	generate	in	...
O	in	noise	the	...
O	the	in	summer	...
O	summer	the	-	...

Table 7: Example of the BILOU representation of a sentence.

4.2.2 Results

The base case evaluation is shown in table 8. The features utilized in the base-case evaluation are: a) the words in these sentences, b) the part of speech of the words. We have performed evaluation with various words as context (0, ± 2, and ± 5 words before and after the word in concern). As seen from the results, the experiment which the context-5 was applied shows a slight improvement from the context-2 experiment, while the difference is larger in the case of zero context.

Context	Precision	Recall	F1
0	16.80% ±5.52	7.55% ±2.80	10.39% ±3.69
±2	34.00% ±3.19	22.33% ±2.73	26.93% ±2.85
±5	33.08% ±3.45	22.92% ±3.99	27.04% ±3.89

Table 8: CRF base case evaluation: words + pos tags.

After the evaluation of the base case, we examined the impact of our gazetteer on the results. As seen in the table 9, the addition of the gazetteer provides a slight boost in out results. The most important difference in relationship with the performance of the base case is shown when no context words were used. Unlike to the previous experimental setup, when two words were used as context has better performance results instead of using five.

Context	Precision	Recall	F1
0	20.22% ±4.43	11.95% ±3.32	14.90% ±3.65
±2	35.61% ±3.75	24.36% ±3.34	28.85% ±3.19
±5	34.06% ±3.85	24.96% ±4.18	28.76% ±4.06

Table 9: CRF base case evaluation: words + pos tags + context 2/5.

Afterwards, we examined the case in which word embeddings were used for the expansion of our gazetteer. In this case, we measured in what manner the extended gazetteer created using "word2vec" could affect the performance of our model. Table 10 shows the evaluation results according to the different number of words used as context. The overall performance of our model was improved when two or five words were used as context, whereas the performance of our model decreased in the zero context configuration. As seen below the best result performed by the configuration of two word context.

Context	Precision	Recall	F1
0	20.74% ±2.63	11.29% ±1.88	14.60% ±2.20
±2	39.70% ±4.55	27.59% ±3.54	32.53% ±3.90
±5	38.72% ±5.29	27.60% ±3.36	32.21% ±4.06

Table 10: CRF base case evaluation: words + pos tags + context 2/5.

5 Conclusion

In this research paper we propose an approach for argument extraction that exploits distributed representations of words in order to be applicable on multiple thematic domains, without requiring any other linguistic resource beyond a part-of-speech tagger and a small list of cue words. Our goal was to suggest a semi-supervised method, applicable from traditional news and blogs documents to corpora from social web, mainly written in the Greek language. The proposed approach is based on previous research performed on this domain and attempts to extend its existing functionality. As gazetteer lists of entities and cue words play an important role to the argument extraction process, we suggest the expansion of the above gazetteer list which are usually provided by domain experts (in our case policy makers), using semantic similarities.

Regarding the future work of this research, we are going to examine the impact of applying bootstrapping techniques on the development of CRF models for the identification of argument components. In addition, it would be interesting to explore different classification algorithms for the extraction of premises and claims on argumentative sentences. Moreover, we would like to extract patterns based on verbs and POS and to examine if these patterns can be generalized through a grammatical inference algorithm.

Acknowledgments

The research leading to these results has received funding from the European Union's Seventh Framework Programme (FP7/2007-2013) under grant agreement no 288513, and from Greek national funding (CLARIN-EL). For more details, please see the NOMAD project's website, `http://www.nomad-project.eu`, and CLARIN-EL project's website, `http://www.clarin.gr/`.

References

Ehud Aharoni, Anatoly Polnarov, Tamar Lavee, Daniel Hershcovich, Ran Levy, Ruty Rinott, Dan Gutfreund, and Noam Slonim. A benchmark dataset for automatic detection of claims and evidence in the context of controversial topics. In *Proceedings of the First Workshop on Argumentation Mining*, pages 64–68, Baltimore, Maryland, June 2014. Association for Computational Linguistics.

Philippe Besnard and Anthony Hunter. *Elements of argumentation*, volume 47. MIT press Cambridge, 2008.

Filip Boltužić and Jan Šnajder. Back up your stance: Recognizing arguments in online discussions. In *Proceedings of the First Workshop on Argumentation Mining*, pages 49–58, Baltimore, Maryland, June 2014. Association for Computational Linguistics.

M. Strano; B.M. Colosimo. Logistic regression analysis for experimental determination of forming limit diagrams. *International Journal of Machine Tools and Manufacture*, 46(6):673–682, 2006.

Corinna Cortes and Vladimir Vapnik. Support-vector networks. *Machine Learning*, 20(3):273–297, 1995. ISSN 0885-6125.

Karën Fort and Benoît Sagot. Influence of pre-annotation on pos-tagged corpus development. In *Proceedings of the Fourth Linguistic Annotation Workshop*, LAW IV '10, pages 56–63, Stroudsburg, PA, USA, 2010. Association for Computational Linguistics. ISBN 978-1-932432-72-5.

Debanjan Ghosh, Smaranda Muresan, Nina Wacholder, Mark Aakhus, and Matthew Mitsui. Analyzing argumentative discourse units in online interactions. In *Proceedings of the First Workshop on Argumentation Mining*, pages 39–48, Baltimore, Maryland, June 2014. Association for Computational Linguistics.

Theodosis Goudas, Christos Louizos, Georgios Petasis, and Vangelis Karkaletsis. Argument extraction from news, blogs, and social media. In Aristidis Likas, Konstantinos Blekas, and Dimitris Kalles, editors, *Artificial Intelligence: Methods and Applications*, volume 8445 of *Lecture Notes in Computer Science*, pages 287–299. Springer, 2014.

Heather Graves, Roger Graves, Robert Mercer, and Mahzereen Akter. Titles that announce argumentative claims in biomedical research articles. In *Proceedings of the First Workshop on Argumentation Mining*, pages 98–99, Baltimore, Maryland, June 2014. Association for Computational Linguistics.

Nancy Green. Towards creation of a corpus for argumentation mining the biomedical genetics research literature. In *Proceedings of the First Workshop on Argumentation Mining*, pages 11–18, Baltimore, Maryland, June 2014. Association for Computational Linguistics.

Libin Hou, Peifeng Li, Qiaoming Zhu, and Yuan Cao. Event argument extraction based on crf. In Donghong Ji and Guozheng Xiao, editors, *Chinese Lexical Semantics*, volume 7717 of *Lecture Notes in Computer Science*, pages 32–39. Springer Berlin Heidelberg, 2013.

Hospice Houngbo and Robert Mercer. An automated method to build a corpus of rhetorically-classified sentences in biomedical texts. In *Proceedings of the First Workshop on Argumentation Mining*, pages 19–23, Baltimore, Maryland, June 2014. Association for Computational Linguistics.

George Kiomourtzis, George Giannakopoulos, Georgios Petasis, Pythagoras Karampiperis, and Vangelis Karkaletsis. Nomad: Linguistic resources and tools aimed at policy formulation and validation. In *Proceedings of the* 9th *International Conference on Language Resources and Evaluation (LREC'14)*, Reykjavik, Iceland, May 2014.

John Lafferty, Andrew McCallum, and Fernando CN Pereira. Conditional random fields: Probabilistic models for segmenting and labeling sequence data. 2001.

John Lawrence, Chris Reed, Colin Allen, Simon McAlister, and Andrew Ravenscroft. Mining arguments from 19th century philosophical texts using topic based modelling. In *Proceedings of the First Workshop on Argumentation Mining*, pages 79–87, Baltimore, Maryland, June 2014. Association for Computational Linguistics.

Breiman Leo. Random forests. *Machine Learning*, 45 (1):5–32, 2001.

Ran Levy, Yonatan Bilu, Daniel Hershcovich, Ehud Aharoni, and Noam Slonim. Context dependent claim detection. In *Proceedings of COLING 2014, the 25th International Conference on Computational Linguistics: Technical Papers*, pages 1489–1500. Dublin City University and Association for Computational Linguistics, 2014.

Mitchell P. Marcus, Mary Ann Marcinkiewicz, and Beatrice Santorini. Building a large annotated corpus of english: The penn treebank. *Comput. Linguist.*, 19(2):313–330, June 1993. ISSN 0891-2017.

Andrew McCallum and Wei Li. Early results for named entity recognition with conditional random fields, feature induction and web-enhanced lexicons. In *Proceedings of the Seventh Conference on Natural Language Learning at HLT-NAACL 2003 - Volume 4*, CONLL '03, pages 188–191, Stroudsburg, PA, USA, 2003. Association for Computational Linguistics.

Tomas Mikolov, Kai Chen, Greg Corrado, and Jeffrey Dean. Efficient estimation of word representations in vector space. *arXiv preprint arXiv:1301.3781*, 2013a.

Tomas Mikolov, Ilya Sutskever, Kai Chen, Greg S Corrado, and Jeff Dean. Distributed representations of words and phrases and their compositionality. In *Advances in Neural Information Processing Systems*, pages 3111–3119, 2013b.

Tomas Mikolov, Wen tau Yih, and Geoffrey Zweig. Linguistic regularities in continuous space word representations. In *Proceedings of the 2013 Conference of the North American Chapter of the Association for Computational Linguistics: Human Language Technologies (NAACL-HLT-2013)*. Association for Computational Linguistics, May 2013c.

Dan Geiger Nir Friedman and Moises Goldszmidt. Bayesian network classifiers. *Machine Learning*, 29:131–163, 1997.

Braja Gopal Patra, Soumik Mandal, Dipankar Das, and Sivaji Bandyopadhyay. Ju_cse: A conditional random field (crf) based approach to aspect based sentiment analysis. In *Proceedings of the 8th International Workshop on Semantic Evaluation (SemEval 2014)*, pages 370–374, Dublin, Ireland, August 2014. Association for Computational Linguistics and Dublin City University.

Ines Rehbein, Josef Ruppenhofer, and Caroline Sporleder. Assessing the benefits of partial automatic pre-labeling for frame-semantic annotation. In *Proceedings of the Third Linguistic Annotation Workshop*, ACL-IJCNLP '09, pages 19–26, Stroudsburg, PA, USA, 2009. Association for Computational Linguistics. ISBN 978-1-932432-52-7.

Fei Sha and Fernando Pereira. Shallow parsing with conditional random fields. In *Proceedings of the 2003 Conference of the North American Chapter of the Association for Computational Linguistics on Human Language Technology - Volume 1*, NAACL '03, pages 134–141, Stroudsburg, PA, USA, 2003. Association for Computational Linguistics.

Bianka Trevisan, Eva Dickmeis, Eva-Maria Jakobs, and Thomas Niehr. Indicators of argument-conclusion relationships. an approach for argumentation mining in german discourses. In *Proceedings of the First Workshop on Argumentation Mining*, pages 104–105, Baltimore, Maryland, June 2014. Association for Computational Linguistics.

From Argumentation Mining to Stance Classification

Parinaz Sobhani[1], **Diana Inkpen**[1], **Stan Matwin**[2]
[1] School of Electrical Engineering and Computer Science, University of Ottawa
[2] Faculty of Computer Science, Dalhousie University
[2] Institute of Computer Science, Polish Academy of Sciences
psobh090@uottawa.ca, diana.Inkpen@uottawa.ca, stan@cs.dal.ca

Abstract

Argumentation mining and stance classification were recently introduced as interesting tasks in text mining. In this paper, a novel framework for argument tagging based on topic modeling is proposed. Unlike other machine learning approaches for argument tagging which often require large set of labeled data, the proposed model is minimally supervised and merely a one-to-one mapping between the pre-defined argument set and the extracted topics is required. These extracted arguments are subsequently exploited for stance classification. Additionally, a manually-annotated corpus for stance classification and argument tagging of online news comments is introduced and made available. Experiments on our collected corpus demonstrate the benefits of using topic-modeling for argument tagging. We show that using Non-Negative Matrix Factorization instead of Latent Dirichlet Allocation achieves better results for argument classification, close to the results of a supervised classifier. Furthermore, the statistical model that leverages automatically-extracted arguments as features for stance classification shows promising results.

1 Introduction

In the past, people were only the consumers of information on the web. With the advent of Web 2.0, new tools for producing User Generated Content (UGC) were provided. Consequently, huge amounts of text data is generate every day on the web. As the volume of this unstructured data increases, the request for automatically processing UGC grows significantly. Moreover, this new source of information and opinions contains valuable feedback about products, services, policies, and news and can play an important role in decision making for marketers, politicians, policy makers and even for ordinary people.

So far, there has been a great effort toward subjectivity analysis of sentiment and opinion mining of reviews on concrete entities such as product or movies (Pang et al., 2002), (Dave et al., 2003), (Pang and Lee, 2005); however, this line of research does not fit online discussions opinion mining where comments not only contain the sentiment/stance of the commenter toward the target, but also convey personal beliefs about what is true or what action should be taken. This kind of subjectivity is called argumentation (Wilson and Wiebe, 2005). Argumentation analysis is more focused on the reason for author's overall position.

Stance has been defined as the overall position toward an idea, object or proposition (Somasundaran and Wiebe, 2010). There has been growing interest in stance classification particularly for online debates (Walker et al., 2012a), (Hasan and Ng, 2013). To the best of our knowledge, our paper is the first work for stance classification of the news comments considering particular news as target to investigate the overall position toward it.

Argument tagging was first introduced as a task in (Boltuzic and Šnajder, 2014) in which the arguments were identified from a domain-dependent predefined list of arguments. An argument tag is a controversial aspect in the domain that is abstracted by a representative phrase/sentence (Conrad et al., 2012).

In our paper, a new framework for argument tag-

Proceedings of the 2nd Workshop on Argumentation Mining, pages 67–77,
Denver, Colorado, June 4, 2015.

ging at document-level based on topic modeling, mainly Non-Negative Matrix Factorization, is proposed. The main advantage of this framework is that it is minimally supervised and no labeled data is required.

The correlation between stance labels and argument tags has been addressed in different studies (Boltuzic and Šnajder, 2014) (Hasan and Ng, 2014). In our research, a statistical model for stance classification based on the extracted arguments is suggested, while in previous research stance labels were exploited for argument tagging.

Nowadays, several popular news websites like CNN and BBC allow their readers to express their opinion by commenting; these kinds of commentspheres can be considered as type of social media. Consequently, visualizing and summarizing the content of these data can play a significant role in public opinion mining and decision making. Considering the huge volume of the news comments that are generated every day, manual analysis of these data may be unfeasible. In our research, a corpus of news comments is collected and annotated and is made available to be deployed as a benchmark in this field [1]. Hence, it provides opportunities to further investigate automatic analysis of such types of UGC.

2 Related Work

In (Somasundaran et al., 2007), two types of opinions are considered: sentiment and arguments. While sentiment mainly includes emotions, evaluations, feelings and stances, arguments are focused on convictions and persuasion.

Stance Classification One of the first works related to stance classification is perspective identification (Lin et al., 2006), where this task was defined as subjective evaluation of points of view. Supervised learning has been used in almost all of the current approaches for stance classification, in which a large set of data has been collected and annotated in order to be used as training data for classifiers. In (Somasundaran and Wiebe, 2010), a lexicon for detecting argument trigger expressions was created and subsequently leveraged to identify arguments. These extracted arguments together with sentiment expressions and their targets were employed in a supervised learner as features for stance classification. In (Anand et al., 2011), several features were deployed in their rule-based classifier, such as unigrams, bigrams, punctuation marks, syntactic dependencies and the dialogic structure of the posts. The dialogic relations of agreement and disagreements between posts were exploited in (Walker et al., 2012b),(Ghosh et al., 2014), likewise; while in this paper our aim is to investigate stance without considering the conversational structure which is not always available.

Argument Tagging In (Albert et al., 2011), argument mining for reviews was introduced in order to extract the reasons for positive or negative opinions. Argumentation analysis can be applied at different text granularities. In (Conrad et al., 2012), a model for argument detection and tagging at sentence-level was suggested. In our research, argument tags were organized in a hierarchical structure inspired by a related field in political science "Arguing Dimension" (Baumgartner et al., 2008). In (Hasan and Ng, 2014), a reason classifier for online ideological debates is proposed. In this method document-level reason classification is leveraged by aggregating all sentence-level reasons of a post. Our proposed method tags arguments at document-level and unlike previous works is minimally supervised.

Topic Modeling Topic modeling in more informal documents is more challenging due to the less organized and unedited style of these documents. Topic-modeling has been used in sentimental analysis and opinion mining to simultaneous investigate the topics and the sentiments in a text (Titov and McDonald, 2008a), (Mei et al., 2007). One of the most popular approaches for topic modeling is Latent Dirichlet allocation (LDA) (Blei et al., 2003). This probabilistic model has been extended in (Titov and McDonald, 2008b) to jointly model sentiments and topics in an unsupervised approach. LDA topic modeling was also employed for automatic identification of argument structure in formal documents of 19th century philosophical texts (Lawrence et al., 2014). LDA was applied on the target corpus and the resulting topics were exploited to find similarities between the different propositions. Non-Negative Matrix Factorization (NMF) (Lee and Seung, 2001)

[1] https://github.com/parinaz1366/News-Comments-Breast-Cancer-Screening-v1

has also been extensively used for text clustering and topic modeling (Xu et al., 2003) (Shahnaz et al., 2006).

Online News Comment Analysis Automatic analysis of online news comments has been investigated in (Potthast et al., 2012), (Tsagkias et al., 2010). In (Zhou et al., 2010), different feature sets for sentiment analysis of news comments were compared. In (Chardon et al., 2013), the effect of using discourse structure for predicting news reactions was explored. In (Zhang et al., 2012), a supervised method for predicting emotions toward news such as sadness, surprise, and anger was proposed. Our paper is the first work toward stance classification of news comments which is particularly different from sentiment and emotion classification as stance is not necessary expressed by affective words and determining the polarity of the text is not sufficient since the system should detect favorability toward a specified target that may be different from the opinion target.

3 Dataset

Important results of health-related studies, reported in the scientific medical journals, are often popularized and broadcasted by media. Such media stories are often followed by online discussions in the social media. For our research, we chose to focus on a controversial study published in the British Medical Journal (BMJ) in February 2014, about breast cancer screening (Miller et al., 2014). Subsequently, a set of news articles that broadcasted or discussed about this study was selected and their corresponding comments were collected. There are two Yahoo news articles[2], three CNN[3] and three New York Times articles[4].

[2] 1.http://news.yahoo.com/mammograms-not-reduce-breast-cancer-deaths-study-finds-001906555.html 2.https://news.yahoo.com/why-recent-mammography-study-deeply-flawed-op-ed-170524117.html

[3] 1. http://www.cnn.com/2014/02/12/health/mammogram-screening-benefits/index.html 2.http://www.cnn.com/2014/02/19/opinion/welch-mammograms-canada/index.html 3.http://www.cnn.com/2014/03/18/opinion/sulik-spanier-mammograms/index.html

[4] 1.http://www.nytimes.com/2014/02/12/health/study-adds-new-doubts-about-value-of-mammograms.html, 2.http://www.nytimes.com/2014/02/15/opinion/why-i-never-got-a-mammogram.html, 3.http://well.blogs.nytimes.com/2014/02/17/a-fresh-case-for-breast-self-exams/

Comments were harvested from news websites or their corresponding social media. CNN commentsphere is provided by DISQUS[5]. Only root comments were kept and the rest (reply to the other comments) was discarded since they mostly contain user interactions and their opinion targets are not the study in which we are interested in for this research. A total number of 1063 posts were collected from all the sources and cleaned by removing HTML tags and links.

3.1 Annotation

Our annotation scheme consisted of two tasks: stance classification and argument tagging for each comment. For stance classification, we are interested in the overall position of the commenter toward the target medical research that is the BMJ article about breast cancer screening (Miller et al., 2014). Two possible positions toward this health-related study were considered:

- For/Agree/Support: those comments that are supporting the target study by arguing its pros or showing positive sentiments toward the target research or expressing their agreement. In other words, those commenters that react positively to the target research study.
- Against/Disagree/Opposition: those comments that are opposing the target study by arguing its cons or showing negative sentiments toward the target research or expressing their disagreement. In other words, those commenters that react negatively to the target research study.

In addition to the overall stance (for or against), we are interested in the strength of the position of commenters toward the target research. Thus, the annotators had five options to choose from: "Strongly For", "For", "Other", "Against", and "Strongly Against". Here, "Other" may correspond to neutral, ambiguous, or irrelevant comments. In opinion mining and sentiment analysis, it is essential to recognize what the opinion is about, which is called "opinion target". Irrelevant opinions may

[5] https://disqus.com

not be directly related to our target study. In this case study, we are interested in comments for which their opinion target is mammography/ breast cancer screening/the BMJ article. For instance, if the comment is about the reporter and the way she reports the research, it does not give us any information about the overall stance of the commenter toward the study. For some comments, it is impossible to judge the overall stance of commenters due to the lack of evidence/information about his/her position. This may also be due to a mixture of "for" and "against" arguments without any clear overall position. The annotator has labeled such comments as "Other", as they may be ambiguous or neutral.

We are not only interested in the overall position of commenter, but also in the reasons behind it. Commenters usually back up their stances with arguments. Our second annotation task was argument tagging in which the annotator identified which arguments have been used in a comment, from a predefined list of arguments. These tags are organized in a hierarchical tree-structured order, as some of them may be related. This structure is represented in figure 1. The annotators were instructed to choose leaf arguments (the most specific one) rather than more general ones, when possible. Commenters may use more than one argument to support their position. For this corpus, the annotators were asked to select at most two arguments based on the emphasis of the author on them. In other words, if the comment had more than two arguments, the ones with more emphasis were selected (because more than two arguments appeared in very few comments in our corpus). The predefined list of arguments was manually extracted and the annotators had chosen appropriate tags from this list, for each post.

Inter-annotator Agreement Our annotation consisted of two separate tasks. For each task, a different numbers of annotators have been used and the annotation was evaluated independently. Stance annotation was carried out by three annotators. To measure inter-annotator agreement, the average of weighted Kappa between each pair of annotators was calculated. As the labels have ordinal value and Fleiss' Kappa and Cohen's Kappa are mainly designed for categorical data, we did not use them to assess stance classification annotation. The major difference between weighted Kappa and Cohen's Kappa is that weighted Kappa considers the degree of disagreement.

	Weighted Kappa	Cohen's Kappa
Stance Classification (3-class)	0.62	-
Stance Classification (5-class)	0.54	-
Argument Tagging	-	0.56

Table 1: Inter-annotator agreement for argument tagging and stance classification

One annotator labelled the arguments for each post. However, to evaluate the quality of annotation, a subset of our corpus (220 comments) were selected and independently annotated by the second annotator. The annotations were compared without considering the hierarchical structure of the tags from figure 1. To measure inter-annotator agreement Cohen's Kappa was deployed. It is also possible to consider hierarchical structure of arguments and to calculate a weighted Kappa based on their distance in the tree.

Table 1 shows the inter-annotation agreement results for both tasks. The agreements are in the range of reported agreement in similar tasks and for similar data (Boltuzic and Šnajder, 2014) (Walker et al., 2012c). The values show the difficulty of the task, even for humans. Eventually, those comments for which at least two annotators agreed about the overall position (stance label) were kept and the rest, labeled as "Other" were discarded, as they may be truly ambiguous.

3.2 Corpus Analysis

As described earlier, our corpus has 1063 comments in total. After discarding those comments with stance label of "Other", 781 comments remained. Table 2 provides an overview of the stance labels in the corpus. The distribution of different argument tags over different stance labels is illustrated in table 3. Additionally, this table shows the number of occurrences of each argument in the corpus. As each comment has been annotated by two argument tags, the total is two times the number of comments. The number of "Other/None" labels is high because it was used as the second argument label for com-

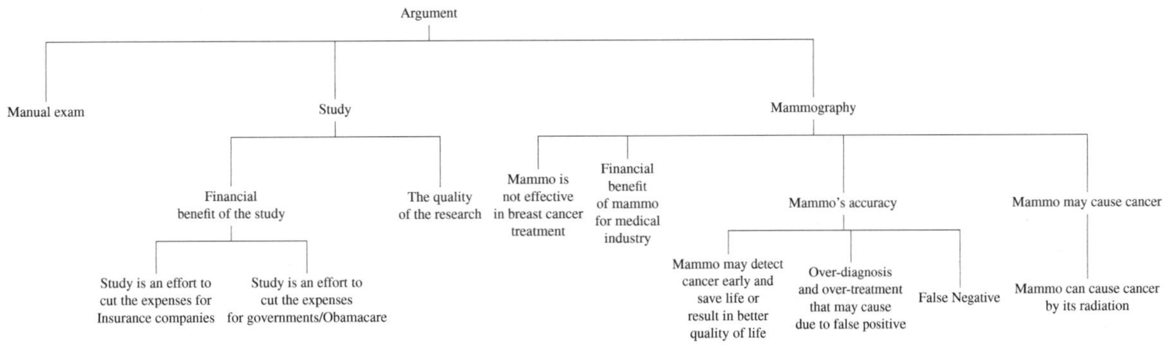

Figure 1: Hierarchical structure of arguments in our corpus

	Strongly For	For	Against	Strongly Against
Post	157	200	172	252

Table 2: Distribution of stance labels in the corpus

ments for which only one argument could be identified by the annotators. Because there are not sufficient instances in the corpus for some of the tags, and the data would be too imbalanced, we decided to remove tags that have less than five percent representatives in the corpus and replace them with the "Other/None" label.

4 Proposed Framework

In this paper, a framework for argument tagging is introduced. The main advantage of this framework is that labeled data is not required. In this approach, NMF is first applied on unlabeled data to extract topics. Subsequently, data are clustered based on these topics. Each post may belong to that topic cluster if its probability of generating from that topic is more than a certain threshold. Later, these clusters are labeled to match a predefined list of argument tags by an annotator. In summary, NMF can cluster comments based on their arguments and these clusters can be labeled by considering top keywords of each cluster topic.

To label each cluster, the top keywords of that topic and the list of arguments were given to the annotators. An annotator who is relatively familiar with comments can easily match topics with arguments, for any domain. The suggested framework for annotation is considerably less tedious and time consuming compared to annotating all posts one by one and leveraging them for training a supervised statistical learner. For our corpus, annotating all comments took 30 hour from for an annotator, while matching topics with argument tags took less than one hour. This illustrates the efficiency of the proposed framework.

In this framework, these extracted argument tags for each comment are subsequently leveraged for stance classification using an SVM classifier. Exploiting argument tags for predicting stance is beneficial, as an argument is often used to back up a single stance, either for or against.

5 Experiments and Results

In this section, first, the experimental setting is reviewed and the evaluation process and metrics are described. Subsequently, the results of applying our proposed framework on our corpus are presented for both argument tagging and stance classification.

5.1 Experimental Setup

After removing those arguments which did not have sufficient representatives, eight argument tags remained. We treated argument tagging as a multiclass multi-label classification problem. Each post can have one or more of those eight labels or none of them.

Each post was represented by using the Term Frequency-Inverse Document Frequency (TF-IDF) weighting scheme over its bag of words. Standard English stopwords were removed. Additionally, we removed corpus specific stopwords by discarding

Argument	Strongly For	For	Against	Strongly Against	Total
Argument about the study	0	1	1	1	3
The quality of the study	5	7	35	43	90
Financial benefit of the study	0	0	4	6	10
Study is an effort to cut the expenses for Insurance companies	0	2	22	26	50
Study is an effort to cut the expenses for governments/Obamacare	0	2	26	41	69
Argument about the mammography	2	1	0	0	3
Mammo is not effective in breast cancer treatment	5	9	1	2	17
Mammo may cause cancer	9	1	0	0	10
Mammo can cause cancer by its radiation	42	23	1	1	67
Mammo's accuracy	2	7	0	2	11
Over-diagnosis and over-treatment that may cause because of false positive	51	36	0	0	87
False Negative	13	17	1	0	31
Mammo may detect cancer early and save life or result in better quality of life	0	8	63	175	246
Financial benefit of mammo for medical industry	47	53	1	0	101
Argument about manual exam	20	29	10	9	68
Other/None	118	204	179	168	699
Total	314	400	344	504	1562

Table 3: Distribution of argument tags for different stance labels in our corpus

terms that have been appeared in more than twenty percent of the documents.

For evaluation, separate test and training data were deployed. Data was randomly divided into test and training sets. Seventy percent of the data was used for training and the rest was used for testing. As mentioned earlier, for our proposed framework, the labels of training are not leveraged and topic models are applied on unlabeled training data. Like similar researches in text classification, precision, recall and f1-score are used as evaluation metrics.

5.2 Argumentation Mining Results

In this section, the results of applying our proposed framework are described and compared to a supervised classifier that uses the same features (TF-IDF). As a supervised classifier, a linear multi-label Support Vector Machine (SVM) is employed using the one-versus-all training scheme. Additionally, in our framework instead of NMF, LDA was used for topic modeling and the results are compared between the two approaches.

The number of topics for our topic models is set to the number of argument tags. As mentioned earlier, after removing those tags with insufficient data, eight arguments remained. These topics, represented by their top keywords, were given to two annotators and we asked them to match them with the list of arguments. Another advantage of the NMF topics is that in this case, both annotators were agreed on all labels. The topics extracted by LDA were difficult for annotators to label, as they were vague. The annotators agreed on fifty percent of labels (4 out of 8 labels). To be able to make a decision in the cases of disagreement, we asked a third annotator to choose one of the suggested labels by two other annotators. Table 4 shows the eight argument tags and their matched NMF and LDA topics, as represented by their top keywords.

Argument	NMF Topic	LDA Topic
1) The quality of the study	study, death, mammography, group, rate, survival, canadian, quality, woman, data, result, question, poor, medical, used, better, trial	insurance, want, company, age, test, early, treatment, screen, write, doctor, thing, benefit, need, unnecessary, group, family, earlier, stage
2) Study is an effort to cut the expenses for insurance companies	insurance, company, pay, cover, sure, way, funded, maybe, wait, ploy, wonder, procedure, benefit, provide, expensive, worth, make, money	saved, insurance, health, care, screening, save, company, money, healthcare, doctor, mammography, exam, self, like, responsible, expensive
3) Study is an effort to cut the expenses for governments/Obamacare	obamacare, drop, test, past, paid, cut, obama, change, socialized, waste, ordered, future, routine, bad supposed, trying, notice, lady, cost	think, test, early, better, obamacare, money, self, treatment, screening, insurance, exam, article, medical, detect, make, told, decision, yearly
4) Mammo can cause cancer by its radiation	radiation, lumpectomy, expose, need, colonoscopy, surgery, chemo, cause, radiologist, machine, treatment, exposure, safe, thermography	know, radiation, mammography, cut, data, radiologist, tumor, need, surgery, medical, early, maybe, really, time, getting, exam, waited, way
5) Over-diagnosis and over-treatment that may cause due to false positive	medical, false, psa, risk, needle, biopsy, screening, prostate, positive, research, surgery, factor, best, painful, over, diagnosis, needed, died	treatment, think, radiation, stage, like, make, yearly, time, article, came, test, doctor, biopsy, self, mother, screening, psa, survivor, lump
6) Mammo may detect cancer early and save life or result in better quality of life	saved, stage, diagnosed, routine, early, today, discovered, mother, believe, alive, friend, annual, detect, late, aggressive, regular	stage, radiation, saved, doctor, early, later, screening, result, want, stop, treatment, like, invasive, happy, routine, mammography, patient, diagnostic
7) Financial benefit of mammo for medical industry	money, care, healthcare, medicine, people, cost, screening, preventive, responsible, administration, way, let, control, doctor expensive, industry	medicine, doctor, treatment, radiation, death, early, catching, money, save, needle, detection, test, making, saved, u, canada, mammography, form
8) Argument about manual exam	exam, self, lump, tumor, physical, manual, regular, examination, time, malignant, trained, nurse, rely, survivor, fast, yes, detecting change	know, people, hope, health, let, need, want, tumor, pay, radiation, like, death, dci, test, alive, exam, age, look, saved, doctor, evidence, say, human

Table 4: Extracted topic by NMF and LDA models represented by their top keywords

	Precision	Recall	F1-score
Linear-SVM	0.76	0.33	0.43
Cluster-LDA	0.26	0.32	0.28
Cluster-NMF	0.58	0.53	**0.49**

Table 5: Results of argument tagging on our corpus

	Precision	Recall	F1-score
Baseline	0.16	0.40	0.23
TF-IDF	0.43	0.45	0.37
TF-IDF+Args	0.48	0.48	**0.47**

Table 6: Results of stance classification in the case of 4-classes (the strength and the overall stance)

Table 5 presents the precision, recall and f1-score of the argument tagging task on our corpus. Our model based on NMF outperforms the other two approaches significantly in term of f1-score and recall, while it is considerably more efficient in terms of the required annotation.

5.3 Stance Classification Results

For stance classification, the predicted argument tags from the previous section were leveraged for stance classification. Our proposed stance classifier deploys the same set of TF-IDF features; in addition, it uses the predicted argument tags as features and as a classification method, linear SVM is employed. These methods are compared with two other classifiers: a linear SVM with TF-IDF as features, and a simple majority class classifier as a baseline. The results are shown in two settings.

Table 6 presents the results of predicting both the stance and its strength (4-class), while table 7 shows the result of stance classification (for or against). Comments with the label of "Other" have been already removed from data. In both settings, the performance is improved when adding the predicted arguments as features.

6 User Generated Content Visualization

In this section, one of the applications of automatic analysis of news comments is illustrated. Following the extraction of arguments from news comments, they can be visualized. In figure 2, the distribution of main arguments in the corpus based on the human annotation are represented, while in figure 3 the distribution based on the automatically-predicted arguments is demonstrated. The figures visualize the relative importance of the arguments. Such visualizations could be really useful to decision makers, even if the arguments were automatically predicted, therefore not all the predictions are correct, because their relative importance was correctly detected. Most importantly, the predictions can be obtained for any domain by using our method, without

	Precision	Recall	F1-score
Baseline	0.32	0.56	0.41
TF-IDF	0.79	0.76	0.74
TF-IDF+Args	0.77	0.77	**0.77**

Table 7: Results of stance classification in the case of 2-classes

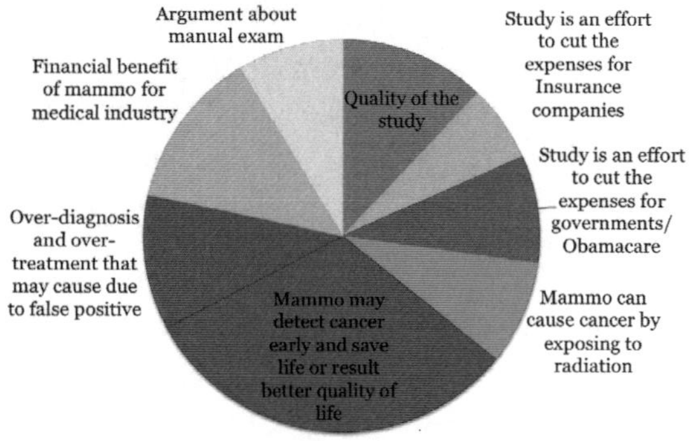

Figure 2: The summary of arguments based on annotated data

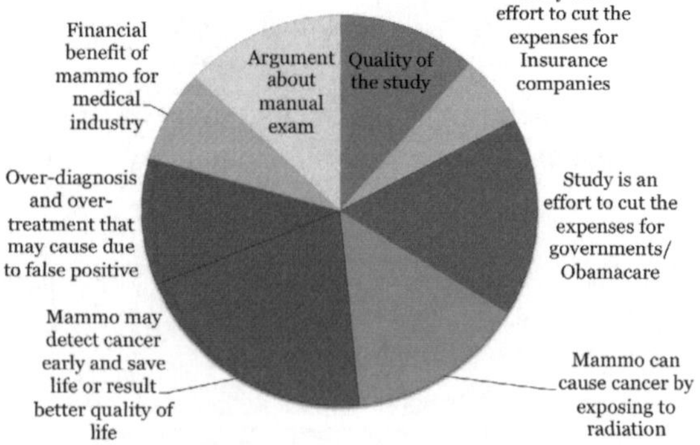

Figure 3: The summary of arguments based on predicted data

the need to label large amounts of data.

7 Discussion

In this section, we further investigate and analyze the results presented earlier. In the previous section, it was shown that using NMF for clustering comments based on their arguments is significantly better than employing LDA. This can be observed in the extracted top keywords of the topics. NMF topics can be matched to the arguments considerably more easily. This is also supported by the evaluation results, as clustering based on NMF has significantly better precision, recall, and f1-score than clustering using LDA. We speculate that the reason for this is the shortness of the comments, since LDA normally works better for longer texts. The other reason may be the fact that all of these data are about the same general topic, breast cancer screening, and LDA cannot distinguish between subtopics (different arguments).

Table 6 demonstrates that stance prediction is significantly improved by leveraging the predicted argument tags. The reason for this can be simply explained by referring to table 3. This table shows that most of the arguments have been leveraged mainly to back up a single stance. Hence, by predicting the correct argument, the stance can be guessed with high probability. The correlation between stance labels and argument tags has been also observed in (Boltuzic and Šnajder, 2014), but they have exploited manually-annotated stance labels for argument classification.

To explore in more details the results of our proposed framework, precision, recall and f1-score for each class (argument tag) is illustrated in table 8. Better precision is achieved for argument classes that are more explicitly expressed and similar sentences are used to convey them. The argument "Mammo may detect cancer early and save life or result in better quality of life" (class 6) has the best precision, as it is mostly expressed by sentences like "Mammography saved my/my mother/ my friend life". On the contrary, our method has better recall for those arguments referred more implicitly in the corpus. For instance, the argument class "Study is an effort to cut the expenses for governments/Obamacare" (class 4) has low precision and high recall, due to several posts such as " Step in the direction of limited health care. You know, hope and change." that implicitly express this argument. Another reason for low precision of some classes, such as "Argument about manual exam" (class 8), is that the corpus is imbalanced and they have less representative data compared to others.

Class	Cluster-NMF		
	Precision	Recall	F1-score
1	0.34	0.61	0.44
2	0.56	0.83	0.67
3	0.57	0.24	0.33
4	0.33	0.68	0.44
5	0.40	0.50	0.44
6	0.91	0.38	0.54
7	0.44	0.65	0.52
8	0.39	0.71	0.51

Table 8: The summary of the performance of proposed framework for each argument (the class numbers match argument tag numbers in table 4)

8 Conclusion and Future Work

Stance classification and argumentation mining were recently introduced as important tasks in opinion mining. There has been a growing interest in these fields, as they can be advantageous particularly for decision making. In this paper, a novel framework for argument tagging was proposed. In our approach, news comments were clustered based on their topics extracted by NMF. These clusters were subsequently labeled by considering the top keywords of each cluster.

The main advantage of the proposed framework is its significant efficiency in annotation. Most of the previous works required a large set of annotated data for training supervised classifiers, and the annotation process is tedious and time-consuming, while in our approach there is no need for labeled training data for the argument detection task. The annotation needed for the argument detection task is minimal: we only need to map the automatically-detected topics to the arguments. This mapping can be easily done for new subjects. Considering the huge amount of news comments that are generated every day for various subjects, this advantage is significant.

Several lines of research can be investigated in the future. First, we plan to apply our framework on available datasets for argument tagging and stance classification of ideological debates. to study its performance in other domains. Furthermore, we intend to concentrate more on the hierarchical structure of the argument tags, by exploiting hierarchical topic modeling to extract arguments with different levels of abstractness. Another area that can be explored is automatic extraction of the set of argument tags, in a similar way to the automatic aspect extraction of product reviews.

Acknowledgments

This research was supported by the Natural Sciences and Engineering Research Council of Canada under the CREATE program, and of the Polish National Scientific Centre NCN grant UMO-2013/09/B/ST6/01549. We thank Kenton White for motivating us to employ NMF for topic modeling. We thank our annotators Raluca Tanasescu and Nasren Musa Elsageyer.

References

Camille Albert, Leila Amgoud, Florence Dupin de Saint-Cyr, Patrick Saint-Dizier, and Charlotte Costedoat. 2011. Introducing argumention in opinion analysis: Language and reasoning challenges. *Sentiment Analysis where AI meets Psychology (SAAIP)*, page 28.

Pranav Anand, Marilyn Walker, Rob Abbott, Jean E Fox Tree, Robeson Bowmani, and Michael Minor. 2011. Cats rule and dogs drool!: Classifying stance in online debate. In *Proceedings of the 2nd workshop on computational approaches to subjectivity and sentiment analysis*, pages 1–9. Association for Computational Linguistics.

Frank R Baumgartner, Suzanna L De Boef, and Amber E Boydstun. 2008. *The decline of the death penalty and the discovery of innocence*. Cambridge University Press.

David M Blei, Andrew Y Ng, and Michael I Jordan. 2003. Latent dirichlet allocation. *the Journal of machine Learning research*, 3:993–1022.

Filip Boltuzic and Jan Šnajder. 2014. Back up your stance: Recognizing arguments in online discussions. In *Proceedings of the First Workshop on Argumentation Mining*, pages 49–58.

Baptiste Chardon, Farah Benamara, Yannick Mathieu, Vladimir Popescu, and Nicholas Asher. 2013. Measuring the effect of discourse structure on sentiment analysis. In *Computational Linguistics and Intelligent Text Processing*, pages 25–37. Springer.

Alexander Conrad, Janyce Wiebe, et al. 2012. Recognizing arguing subjectivity and argument tags. In *Proceedings of the Workshop on Extra-Propositional Aspects of Meaning in Computational Linguistics*, pages 80–88. Association for Computational Linguistics.

Kushal Dave, Steve Lawrence, and David M Pennock. 2003. Mining the peanut gallery: Opinion extraction and semantic classification of product reviews. In *Proceedings of the 12th international conference on World Wide Web*, pages 519–528. ACM.

Debanjan Ghosh, Smaranda Muresan, Nina Wacholder, Mark Aakhus, and Matthew Mitsui. 2014. Analyzing argumentative discourse units in online interactions. In *Proceedings of the First Workshop on Argumentation Mining*, pages 39–48.

Kazi Saidul Hasan and Vincent Ng. 2013. Frame semantics for stance classification. *CoNLL-2013*, 124.

Kazi Saidul Hasan and Vincent Ng. 2014. Why are you taking this stance? identifying and classifying reasons in ideological debates. *EMNLP 2014*.

John Lawrence, Chris Reed, Colin Allen, Simon McAlister, Andrew Ravenscroft, and David Bourget. 2014. Mining arguments from 19th century philosophical texts using topic based modelling. *ACL 2014*, page 79.

Daniel D Lee and H Sebastian Seung. 2001. Algorithms for non-negative matrix factorization. In *Advances in neural information processing systems*, pages 556–562.

Wei-Hao Lin, Theresa Wilson, Janyce Wiebe, and Alexander Hauptmann. 2006. Which side are you on? identifying perspectives at the document and sentence levels. In *Proceedings of the Tenth Conference on Computational Natural Language Learning*, pages 109–116. Association for Computational Linguistics.

Qiaozhu Mei, Xu Ling, Matthew Wondra, Hang Su, and ChengXiang Zhai. 2007. Topic sentiment mixture: modeling facets and opinions in weblogs. In *Proceedings of the 16th international conference on World Wide Web*, pages 171–180. ACM.

Anthony B Miller, Claus Wall, Cornelia J Baines, Ping Sun, Teresa To, Steven A Narod, et al. 2014. Twenty five year follow-up for breast cancer incidence and mortality of the canadian national breast screening study: randomised screening trial. *Bmj*, 348.

Bo Pang and Lillian Lee. 2005. Seeing stars: Exploiting class relationships for sentiment categorization with respect to rating scales. In *Proceedings of the 43rd Annual Meeting on Association for Computational Linguistics*, pages 115–124. Association for Computational Linguistics.

Bo Pang, Lillian Lee, and Shivakumar Vaithyanathan. 2002. Thumbs up?: sentiment classification using machine learning techniques. In *Proceedings of the ACL-02 conference on Empirical methods in natural language processing-Volume 10*, pages 79–86. Association for Computational Linguistics.

Martin Potthast, Benno Stein, Fabian Loose, and Steffen Becker. 2012. Information retrieval in the commentsphere. *ACM Transactions on Intelligent Systems and Technology (TIST)*, 3(4):68.

Farial Shahnaz, Michael W Berry, V Paul Pauca, and Robert J Plemmons. 2006. Document clustering using nonnegative matrix factorization. *Information Processing & Management*, 42(2):373–386.

Swapna Somasundaran and Janyce Wiebe. 2010. Recognizing stances in ideological on-line debates. In *Proceedings of the NAACL HLT 2010 Workshop on Computational Approaches to Analysis and Generation of Emotion in Text*, pages 116–124. Association for Computational Linguistics.

Swapna Somasundaran, Josef Ruppenhofer, and Janyce Wiebe. 2007. Detecting arguing and sentiment in meetings. In *Proceedings of the SIGdial Workshop on Discourse and Dialogue*, volume 6.

Ivan Titov and Ryan McDonald. 2008a. Modeling online reviews with multi-grain topic models. In *Proceedings of the 17th international conference on World Wide Web*, pages 111–120. ACM.

Ivan Titov and Ryan T McDonald. 2008b. A joint model of text and aspect ratings for sentiment summarization. In *ACL*, volume 8, pages 308–316. Citeseer.

Manos Tsagkias, Wouter Weerkamp, and Maarten De Rijke. 2010. News comments: Exploring, modeling, and online prediction. *Advances in Information Retrieval*, pages 191–203.

Marilyn A Walker, Pranav Anand, Rob Abbott, Jean E Fox Tree, Craig Martell, and Joseph King. 2012a. That is your evidence?: Classifying stance in online political debate. *Decision Support Systems*, 53(4):719–729.

Marilyn A Walker, Pranav Anand, Robert Abbott, and Ricky Grant. 2012b. Stance classification using dialogic properties of persuasion. In *Proceedings of the 2012 Conference of the North American Chapter of the Association for Computational Linguistics: Human Language Technologies*, pages 592–596. Association for Computational Linguistics.

Marilyn A Walker, Jean E Fox Tree, Pranav Anand, Rob Abbott, and Joseph King. 2012c. A corpus for research on deliberation and debate. In *LREC*, pages 812–817.

Theresa Wilson and Janyce Wiebe. 2005. Annotating attributions and private states. In *Proceedings of the Workshop on Frontiers in Corpus Annotations II: Pie in the Sky*, pages 53–60. Association for Computational Linguistics.

Wei Xu, Xin Liu, and Yihong Gong. 2003. Document clustering based on non-negative matrix factorization. In *Proceedings of the 26th annual international ACM SIGIR conference on Research and development in informaion retrieval*, pages 267–273. ACM.

Ying Zhang, Yi Fang, Xiaojun Quan, Lin Dai, Luo Si, and Xiaojie Yuan. 2012. Emotion tagging for comments of online news by meta classification with heterogeneous information sources. In *Proceedings of the 35th international ACM SIGIR conference on Research and development in information retrieval*, pages 1059–1060. ACM.

Jie Zhou, Chen Lin, and Bi-cheng Li. 2010. Research of sentiment classification for net news comments by machine learning. *Journal of Computer Applications*, 30(4):1011–1014.

Argument Discovery and Extraction with the Argument Workbench

Adam Wyner
Computing Science
University of Aberdeen
Aberdeen, United Kingdom
azwyner@abdn.ac.uk

Wim Peters
Computer Science
University of Sheffield
Sheffield, United Kingdom
w.peters@sheffield.ac.uk

David Price
DebateGraph
United Kingdom
david@debategraph.org

Abstract

The paper discusses the architecture and development of an Argument Workbench, which is a interactive, integrated, modular tool set to extract, reconstruct, and visualise arguments. We consider a corpora with dispersed information across texts, making it essential to conceptually search for argument elements, topics, and terminology. The Argument Workbench is a processing cascade, developed in collaboration with DebateGraph. The tool supports an argument engineer to reconstruct arguments from textual sources, using information processed at one stage as input to a subsequent stage of analysis, and then building an argument graph. We harvest and preprocess comments; highlight argument indicators, speech act and epistemic terminology; model topics; and identify domain terminology. We use conceptual semantic search over the corpus to extract sentences relative to argument and domain terminology. The argument engineer uses the extracts for the construction of arguments in DebateGraph.

1 Introduction

Argumentative text is rich, multidimensional, and fine-grained, consisting of (among others): a range of (explicit and implicit) discourse relations between statements in the corpus, including indicators for conclusions and premises; speech acts and propositional attitudes; contrasting sentiment terminology; and domain terminology. Moreover, linguistic expression is various, given alternative syntactic or lexical forms for related semantic meaning. It is difficult for humans to reconstruct argument from text, let alone for a computer. This is especially the case where arguments are dispersed across unstructured textual corpora. In our view, the most productive scenario is one in which a human argument engineer is maximally assisted in her work by computational means in the form of automated text filtering and annotation. This enables the engineer to focus on text that matters and further explore the argumentation structure on the basis of the added metadata. The Argument WorkBench (AWB) captures this process of incremental refinement and extension of the argument structure, which the engineer then produces as a structured object with a visual representation.

Given the abundance of textual source data available for argumentation analysis there is a real need for automated filtering and interpretation. Current social media platforms provide an unprecedented source of user-contributed content on most any topic. Reader-contributed comments to a comment forum, e.g. for a news article, are a source of arguments for and against issues raised in the article, where an argument is a claim with justifications and exceptions. It is difficult to coherently understand the overall, integrated meaning of the comments.

To reconstruct the arguments sensibly and reusably, we build on a prototype Argument Workbench (AWB) (Wyner et al.(2012); Wyner(2015)), which is a semi-automated, interactive, integrated, modular tool set to extract, reconstruct, and visualise arguments. The workbench is a processing cascade, developed in collaboration with an industrial partner

Proceedings of the 2nd Workshop on Argumentation Mining, pages 78–83,
Denver, Colorado, June 4, 2015. ©2015 Association for Computational Linguistics

DebateGraph and used by an Argumentation Engineer, where information processed at one stage gives greater structure for the subsequent stage. In particular, we: harvest and pre-process comments; highlight argument indicators, speech act terminology, epistemic terminology; model topics; and identify domain terminology and relationships. We use conceptual semantic search over the corpus to extract sentences relative to argument and domain terminology. The argument engineer analyses the output and then inputs extracts into the DebateGraph visualisation tool. The novelty of the work presented in this paper is the addition of terminology (domain topics and key words, speech act, and epistemic) along with the workflow analysis provided by our industrial partner. For this paper, we worked with a corpus of texts bearing on the Scottish Independence vote in 2014; however, the tool is neutral with respect to domain, since the domain terminology is derived using automatic tools.

In this short paper, we briefly outline the AWB workflow, sketch tool components, provide sample query results, discuss related work in the area, and close with a brief discussion.

2 The Argument WorkBench Workflow

The main user of the Argument WorkBench (AWB) is Argumentation Engineer, an expert in argumentation modeling who uses the Workbench to select and interpret the text material. Although the AWB automates some of the subtasks involved, the ultimate modeler is the argumentation engineer. The AWB distinguishes between the selection and modeling tasks, where selection is computer-assisted and semi-automatic, whereas the modeling is performed manually in DebateGraph (see Figure 1).

The AWB encompasses a flexible methodology that provides a workflow and an associated set of modules that together form a flexible and extendable methodology for the detection of argument in text. Automated techniques provide textually grounded information about conceptual nature of the domain and the argument structure by means of the detection of argument indicators. This information, in the form of textual metadata, enable the argumentation engineer to filter out potentially interesting text for eventual manual analysis, validation and evaluation.

Figure 1 shows the overall workflow. Document collection is not taken into account. In the first stage, text analysis such as topic, term and named entity extraction provides a first thematic grouping and semantic classification of relevant domain elements. This combination of topics, named entities and terms automatically provides the first version of a domain model, which assists the engineer in the conceptual interpretation and subsequent exploration. The texts filtered in this thematic way can then be filtered further with respect to argument indicators (discourse terminology, speech acts, epistemic terminology) as well as sentiment (positive and negative terminology). At each stage, the Argumentation Engineer is able to query the corpus with respect to the metadata (which we also refer to as the conceptual annotations). This complex filtering of information from across a corpus helps the Argumentation Engineer consolidate her understanding of the argumentative role of information.

3 AWB Components

3.1 Text Analysis

To identify and extract the textual elements from the source material, we use the GATE framework (Cunningham et al.(2002)) for the production of semantic metadata in the form of annotations.

GATE is a framework for language engineering applications, which supports efficient and robust text processing including functionality for both manual and automatic annotation (Cunningham et al.(2002)); it is highly scalable and has been applied in many large text processing projects; it is an open source desktop application written in Java that provides a user interface for professional linguists and text engineers to bring together a wide variety of natural language processing tools and apply them to a set of documents. The tools are concatenated into a pipeline of natural language processing modules. The main modules we are using in our bottom-up and incremental tool development (Wyner and Peters(2011)) perform the following functionalities:

- linguistic pre-processing. Texts are segmented into tokens and sentences; words are assigned Part-of-Speech (POS).
- gazetteer lookup. A gazetteer is a list of words

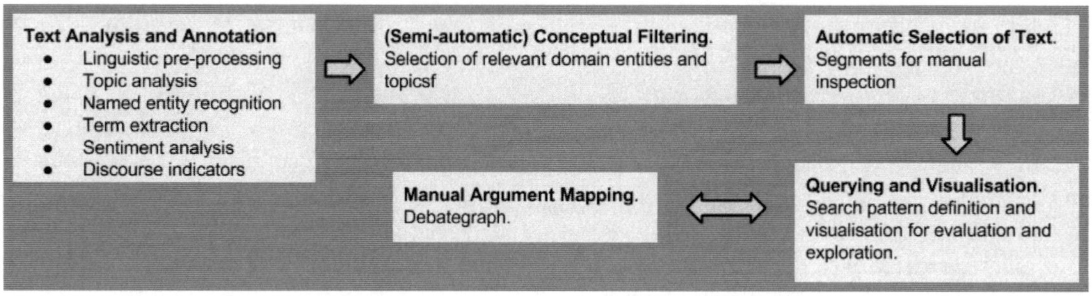

Figure 1: Overview of the Argument WorkBench Workflow

associated with a central concept. In the lookup phase, text in the corpus is matched with terms on the lists, then assigned an annotation.

- annotation assignment through rule-based grammars, where rules take annotations and regular expressions as input and produce annotations as output.

Once a GATE pipeline has been applied, the argument engineer views the annotations *in situ* or using GATE's ANNIC (ANNotations In Context) corpus indexing and querying tool (see section 4), which enables semantic search for annotation patterns across a distributed corpus.

3.2 Term and Topic Extraction

In the current version of the AWB, we used two automatic approches to developing terminology, allowing the tool to be domain independent and rapidly developed. We used the *TermRaider* tool in GATE to identify relevant terminology (Maynard et al.(2008)). TermRaider automatically provides domain-specific noun phrase term candidates from a text corpus together with a statistically derived termhood score. Possible terms are filtered by means of a multi-word-unit grammar that defines the possible sequences of part of speech tags constituting noun phrases. It computes term frequency/inverted document frequency (TF/IDF), which takes into account term frequency and the number of documents in the collection, yielding a score that indicates the salience of each term candidate for each document in the corpus. All term candidates with a TF/IDF score higher than an manually determined threshold are then selected and presented as candidate relevant terms, annotated as such in the corpus. In addition to TermRaider, we have used a tool to model topics, identifying clusters of terminology that are taken to statistically "cohere" around a topic; for this, we have used a tool based on *Latent Dirichlet Allocation* (Blei et al.(2008)). Each word in a topic is used to annotate every sentence in the corpus that contains that word. Thus, with term and topic annotation, the Argumentation Engineer is able to query the corpus for relevant, candidate passages.

3.3 DebateGraph

DebateGraph is a free, cloud-based platform that enables communities of any size to build and share dynamic interactive visualizations of all the ideas, arguments, evidence, options and actions that anyone in the community believes relevant to the issues under consideration, and to ensure that all perspectives are represented transparently, fairly, and fully in a meaningful, structured and iterative dialogue. It supports formal argumentation as well as structured dialogue, and has been used by, amongst others, CNN, The Independent newspaper, the White House Office of Science and Technology Policy, the European Commission, and the UK's Prime Minister's Office as well as the Foreign and Commonwealth Office.

4 Viewing and Querying

The AWB enriches the manual, close reading oriented method of argument map creation in DebateGraph with automated analysis, which filters relevant text segments with respect to a certain topic of interest, and provides initial argument structure information to the text by means of annotations.

Once the corpus is annotated, we can view the annotations in the documents themselves. In Figure 2, we have a text that has been highlighted with

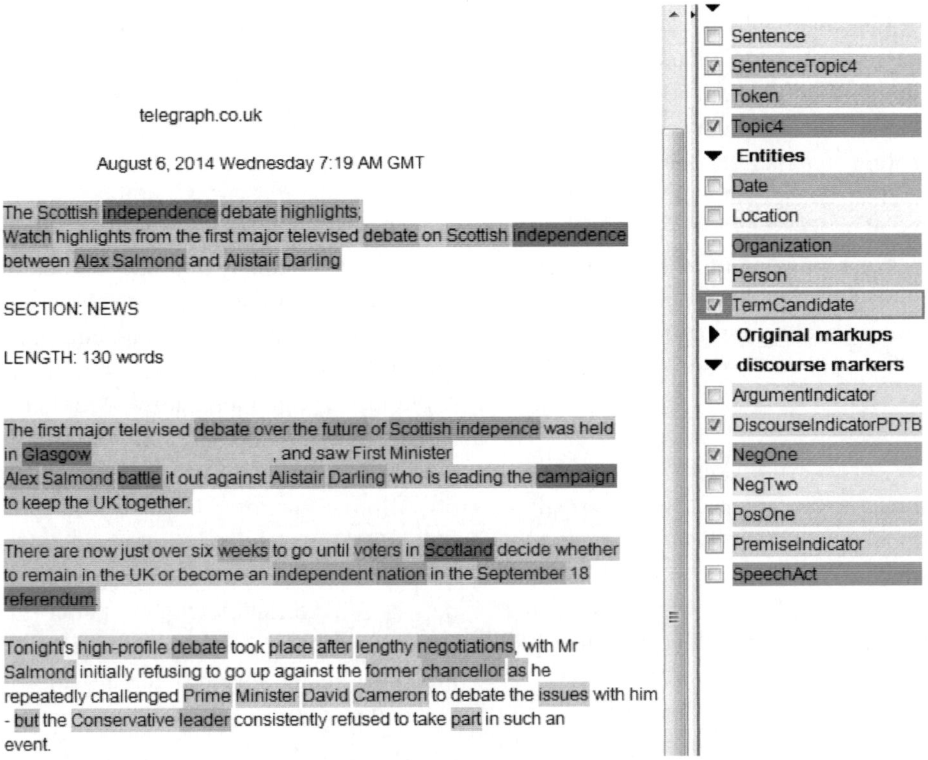

Figure 2: Highlighting Annotations in the Text

a selection of available annotation types (differentiated by colour in the original): Topic4 (labels indicative of Topic 4); SentenceTopic4 (Sentences in which Topic4 labels occur); various discourse level information types such as discourse/argument markers and speech acts. Other annotations are available, e.g. sentiment and epistemic. The argumentation engineer can now focus on the close reading of sentences that represent relevant topics, contain the required terminology and argumentational aspects.

For corpus-level exploration and selection, search patterns can be formulated and examined by means of the ANNIC (Annotation in Context) querying and visualization tool in GATE (Aswani et al.(2005)). This tool can index documents not only by content, but also by their annotations and features. It also enables users to formulate versatile queries mixing keywords and information available from any annotation types (e.g. linguistic, conceptual). The result consists of the matching texts in the corpus, displayed within the context of linguistic annotations (not just text, as is customary for KWIC systems). The data is displayed in a GUI, facilitating exploration and the discovery of new patterns.

Searching in the corpus for single annotations returns all those strings that are annotated with the search annotation along with their context and source document. Figure 3 illustrates a more complex query in the top pane by means of which an argumentation engineer wants to explore up to seven token corpus contexts that contain particular term candidates and argument indicators. The query finds all sequences of annotated text where the first string is annotated with *ArgumentationIndicator*, followed by zero to five other *Tokens*, followed by a string with a *TermCandidate* annotation. One of the search results is visualised in the bottom pane by means of query matches and left/right contexts. The coloured bars form an annotation stack that shows the occurrence of selected annotations in the contexts. In this case we see an emphasis argument indicator "obviously" co-occurring with the term candidates "Scotland", "independent Scotland" and "choice".

By inspecting the document more closely the argumentation engineer will be able to produce a structured representation of the identified argument. The ANNIC interface thus uses the annotations to reduce the search space for human engineers, and focuses their attention on passages that are relevant for sourcing arguments. The tool allows incremental refinement of searches, allowing for a interactive way to examine the semantic content of the texts. Also, the argumentation engineer can provide feedback in the form of changing/adding annotations, which will be used in GATE to improve the automated analysis.

5 Related Work

The paper presents developments of an implemented, semi-automatic, interactive text analytic tool that combines rule-based and statistically-oriented approaches. The tool supports analysts in identifying "hot zones" of relevant textual material as well as fine-grained, relevant textual passages; these passages can be used to compose argument graphs in a tool such as DebateGraph. As such, the tool evaluated with respect to user facilitation (i.e. analysts qualitative evaluation of using the tool or not) rather than with respect to *recall* and *precision* (Mitkof(2003)) in comparison to a gold standard. The tool is an advance over graphically-based argument extraction tools that rely on the analysts' unstructured, implicit, non-operationalised knowledge of discourse indicators and content (van Gelder(2007); Rowe and Reed(2008); Liddo and Shum(2010); Bex et al.(2014)). There are a variety of rule-based approaches to argument annotation: (Pallotta and Delmonte(2011)) classify statements according to rhetorical roles using full sentence parsing and semantic translation; (Saint-Dizier(2012)) provides a rule-oriented approach to process specific, highly structured argumentative texts; (Moens et al.(2007)) manually annotates legal texts then constructs a grammar that is tailored to automatically annotated the passages. Such rule-oriented approaches share some generic components with our approach, e.g. discourse indicators, negation indicators. However, they do not exploit a terminological analysis, do not straightforwardly provide for complex annotation querying, and are stand-alone tools that are not integrated with other NLP tools. Importantly, the rule-based approach outlined here could be used to support the creation of gold standard corpora on which statistical models can be trained. Finally, we are not aware of statistical models to extract the fine-grained information that is required for extracting argument elements.

The tool is used to construct or reconstruct arguments in *complex*, *high volume*, *fragmentary*, and *alinearly* presented comments or statements. This is in contrast to many approaches that, by and large, follow the structure of arguments within a particular (large and complex) document, e.g. the BBC's Moral Maze (Bex et al.(2014)), manuals (Saint-Dizier(2012)), and legal texts (Moens et al.(2007)).

The tool can be modularly developed, adding further argumentation elements, domain models, disambiguating discourse indicators (Webber et al.(2011)), auxilary linguistic indicators, and other parts of speech that distinguish sentence components. More elaborate query patterns could be executed to refine results. In general, the openness and flexibility of the tool provide a platform for future, detailed solutions to issues in argumentation.

6 Discussion

The tool offers a very flexible, useful and meaningful way to query a corpus of text for relevant argument passages, leaving the argument engineer to further analyse and use the results. Having developed in in conjunction with an industrial partner, the next task is to evaluate it with user studies, inquiring whether the tool facilitates or changes the capability to develop arguments for graphs. As a result of this feedback, the tool can be developed further, e.g. adding a summarisation component, automating extraction, augmenting the base terminology (speech acts, propositional attitudes, etc), and creating discourse indicator patterns. The tool can also be used to examine the role of the various components in the overall argument pattern search, investigating the use of, e.g. discourse indicators or speech acts in different discourse contexts.

Acknowledgments

The authors gratefully acknowledge funding from the Semantic Media Network project *Semantic Media: a new paradigm for navigable content for the 21st Century* (EPSRC grant EP/J010375/1). Thanks to Ebuka Ibeke and Georgios Klados for their contributions to the project.

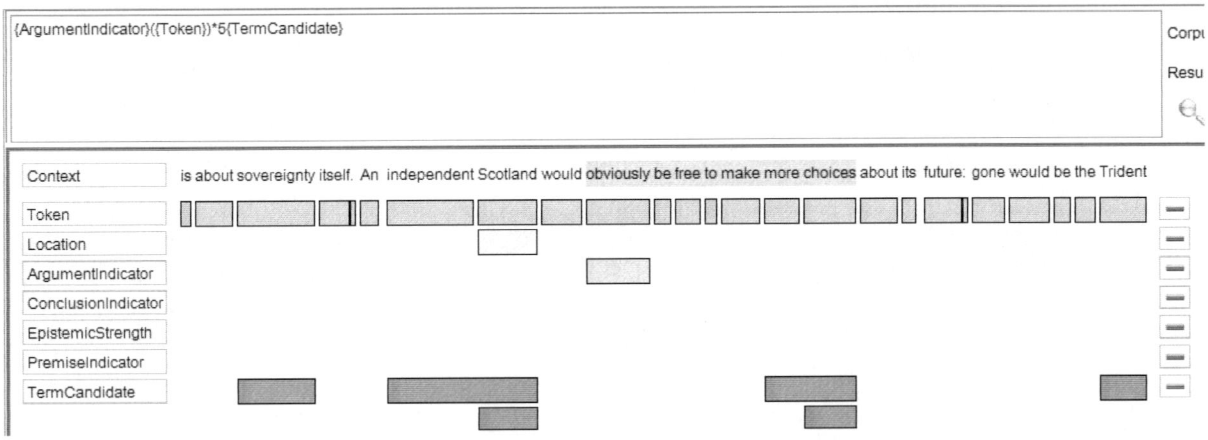

Figure 3: Searching for Patterns in the Corpus

References

Niraj Aswani, Valentin Tablan, Kalina Bontcheva, and Hamish Cunningham. Indexing and Querying Linguistic Metadata and Document Content. In *Proceedings RANLP 2005*, Borovets, Bulgaria, 2005.

Floris Bex, Mark Snaith, John Lawrence, and Chris Reed. Argublogging: An application for the argument web. *J. Web Sem.*, 25:9–15, 2014.

David Blei, Andrew Ng, and Michael Jordan. Latent dirichlet allocation. *Journal of Machine Learning Research*, 3(4-5):9931022, 2008.

Hamish Cunningham, Diana Maynard, Kalina Bontcheva, and Valentin Tablan. GATE: A framework and graphical development environment for robust NLP tools and applications. In *Proceedings of ACL 2002*, pages 168–175, 2002.

Anna De Liddo and Simon Buckingham Shum. Cohere: A prototype for contested collective intelligence. In *ACM CSCW 2010 - Collective Intelligence In Organizations*, Savannah, Georgia, USA, February 2010.

Diana Maynard, Yaoyong Li, and Wim Peters. NLP techniques for term extraction and ontology population. In *Proceedings of OLP 2008*, pages 107–127, Amsterdam, The Netherlands, The Netherlands, 2008. IOS Press.

Ruslan Mitkof, editor. *The Oxford Handbook of Computational Linguistics*. Oxford University Press, 2003.

Marie-Francine Moens, Erik Boiy, Raquel Mochales-Palau, and Chris Reed. Automatic detection of arguments in legal texts. In *Proceedings ICAIL '07*, pages 225–230, New York, NY, USA, 2007. ACM Press.

Vincenzo Pallotta and Rodolfo Delmonte. Automatic argumentative analysis for interaction mining. *Argument and Computation*, 2(2-3):77–106, 2011.

Glenn Rowe and Chris Reed. Argument diagramming: The Araucaria Project. In Alexandra Okada, Simon Buckingham Shum, and Tony Sherborne, editors, *Knowledge Cartography: Software Tools and Mapping Techniques*, pages 163–181. Springer, 2008.

Patrick Saint-Dizier. Processing natural language arguments with the <TextCoop> platform. *Argument & Computation*, 3(1):49–82, 2012.

Tim van Gelder. The rationale for Rationale. *Law, Probability and Risk*, 6(1-4):23–42, 2007.

Bonnie Webber, Markus Egg, and Valia Kordoni. Discourse structure and language technology. *Natural Language Engineering*, December 2011.

Adam Wyner. Mining fine-grained argument elements. In Elena Cabrio, Serena Villata, and Adam Wyner, editors, *Proceedings of ArgNLP2014*, volume 1341, Bertinoro, Italy, July 2015. CEUR Workshop Proceedings.

Adam Wyner and Wim Peters. On rule extraction from regulations. In Katie Atkinson, editor, *Proceedings of JURIX 2011*, pages 113–122. IOS Press, 2011.

Adam Wyner, Jodi Schneider, Katie Atkinson, and Trevor Bench-Capon. Semi-automated argumentative analysis of online product reviews. In *Proceedings of COMMA 2012)*, pages 43–50. IOS Press, 2012.

Automatic Claim Negation: Why, How and When

Yonatan Bilu
IBM Haifa Research Lab
Mount Carmel
Haifa, 31905, Israel
yonatanb@il.ibm.com

Daniel Hershcovich
IBM Haifa Research Lab
Mount Carmel
Haifa, 31905, Israel
danielh@il.ibm.com

Noam Slonim
IBM Haifa Research Lab
Mount Carmel
Haifa, 31905, Israel
noams@il.ibm.com

Abstract

The main goal of argumentation mining is to analyze argumentative structures within an argument-rich document, and reason about their composition. Recently, there is also interest in the task of simply detecting claims (sometimes called conclusion) in general documents. In this work we ask how this set of detected claims can be augmented further, by adding to it the negation of each detected claim. This presents two NLP problems: how to automatically negate a claim, and when such a negated claim can plausibly be used. We present first steps into solving both these problems, using a rule-based approach for the former and a statistical one towards the latter.

1 Introduction

In Monty Python's famous Argument Clinic Sketch (Chapman and Cleese, 1972), Michael Palin is seeking a good argument, and John Cleese, too lazy to provide a real argument, simply contradicts whatever Mr. Palin is saying.

> MP: An argument isn't just contradiction.
> JC: Well! it *can* be!
> MP: No it can't! An argument is a connected series of statements intended to establish a proposition.
> JC: No it isn't!
> MP: Yes it is! It isn't just contradiction!
> JC: Look, if I *argue* with you, I must take up a contrary position!
> MP: Yes, but it isn't just saying 'no it isn't'.

In this work we aim to explore this last statement from the perspective of an automatic system, aiming to refute an examined claim. Specifically, given a claim, *how* should we contradict it? Is it enough to say "No it isn't", or is a more complicated algorithm required? And *when* can we plausibly use an automatically generated contradiction? When would it be considered a valid counter claim, and when would it seem as an even less comprehensible version of John Cleese? The answers to these questions turn out to be less simple than one might expect at first glance.

The main goal of argumentation mining is to analyze argumentative structures within a document. Typically, documents in which such structures are abundant, such as from the legal domain (Mochales Palau and Moens, 2011; Bach et al., 2013; Ashley and Walker, 2013; Wyner et al., 2010), are analyzed, and compound argumentative structures, or argumentation schemes, are sought (Walton, 2012).

More recently, there is also interest in automatically detecting simple argumentative structures, or the building blocks of such structures, in documents which are not argumentative by nature. For example, in (Aharoni et al., 2014; Levy et al., 2014) it was shown that context-dependent Claims and Evidences (sometimes called Conclusion and Grounds, respectively) are fairly common in Wikipedia articles, and can be detected automatically. In this setting, detection is done within a given context of a pre-specified debatable topic. Then, the objective is to search a given set of documents, and mine Claims and Evidence pertaining to this topic.

Proceedings of the 2nd Workshop on Argumentation Mining, pages 84–93,
Denver, Colorado, June 4, 2015.

One motivation for such context-dependent argumentation mining is that it serves as the first component in a debate-support system. In a second stage, Claims and Evidence can be combined into full fledged Arguments, highlighting to the user the various opinions surrounding the debatable topic.

In order to provide a comprehensive view of these various opinions, it might not be sufficient to rely on the initial set of detected argumentative elements. For example, for practical reasons, an automatic Claim detection system as in (Levy et al., 2014) will present to the user only its top scoring predictions, which will probably represent only a subset of the relevant Claims. Furthermore, the examined corpus might be biased, hence enriched with claims supporting only one side of the debate. Thus, it is of interest to augment the initial set of predictions made by such systems through various means.

Here, motivated by the observation that negating previous arguments has an important function in argumentation (Apothéloz et al., 1993), we suggest a system to augment a given set of relevant Claims by automatically suggesting a meaningful negation per mentioned Claim. More specifically, we require that the automatically suggested negation will be not only grammatically correct, but also plausible to use in a discussion about the given topic. As we discuss and demonstrate, this latter requirement poses a nontrivial challenge. Accordingly, we propose a Machine Learning approach that exploits NLP-based features in order to determine if it is plausible to use the suggested negation. Our results demonstrate the feasibility and practical potential of the suggested approach.

2 Related work

Negation detection has received much attention in NLP. This includes the detection of negated clauses and subclauses, and of negation expressions and of their scope. Methods employed in this detection include conditional random fields (CRFs) (Councill et al., 2010), regular expressions (Chapman et al., 2013), and syntactic rules (Lotan et al., 2013; Mutalik et al., 2001). Negation detection is critical for medical applications, for example, in order to classify whether the text contains the existence or absence of a condition (Chapman et al., 2013). It was also shown to improve the results in sentiment analysis (Wiegand et al., 2010; Zhu et al., 2014), as negation alters the sentiment of the text in its scope. Despite these results, it is not trivial, in general, to infer the meaning of a negated utterance, or what is in fact negated—it depends on the focus of the original sentence (Blanco and Moldovan, 2011). By contrast, here we deal with negating typically short claims (12 words long on average), where focus and scope are usually relatively easy to infer.

Several works have tackled the task of surface realization—the transformation from a logical representation to human-readable text—providing systems such as SimpleNLG (Gatt and Reiter, 2009). However, these earlier works do not provide a principled method of negating existing sentences given as free text statements.

To our knowledge, there has been just one work on generating the negations of existing sentences (Ahmed and Lin, 2014). Ahmed and Lin use a set of syntactic rules to phrase all possible negations of a given sentence, according to the possible scopes of negation. Their focus is rather different from ours. First, they are interested in sentences in general, rather than Claims – which, in our corpus, tend to have a typically simple structure. Second, their interest is mainly in finding the scopes where negation can be applied, and applying it using simple rules. Here we consider only one scope, and explore the fluency and plausibility of the resulting statement and its argumentative value. Finally, Ahmed and Lin exemplify their technique on a small set of sentences, whereas here the statistical analysis and learning are done on much larger data.

3 Problem definition and associated challenges

Similarly to (Aharoni et al., 2014; Levy et al., 2014) we define the following two concepts:

- **Topic** – a short phrase that frames the discussion.
- **Context Dependent Claim (CDC)** – a general, concise statement that directly supports or contests the given Topic.

For brevity, henceforth we refer to a CDC as simply a Claim. Given such a Claim, our goal is to automatically generate its *Claim Negation*, defined here as *a statement that asserts the opposite of the original Claim, and can be plausibly used while discussing the Topic.*

For example, given the Claim *affirmative action is effective*, its Claim Negation could be stated as follows: *affirmative action is* **not** *effective*. However, for many Claims, the situation is somewhat more complex. Specifically, we identify four levels of complexity when trying to automatically generate Claim Negations.

- *Grammar*—as with any task in which text is automatically generated or modified, one has to make sure the new text is grammatically correct. For example, a naïve system which simply inserts the word "does not" before the verb "have", might transform the Claim:

  > *As a standard embryo does have a highly valuable future, killing it is seriously wrong.*

  into the grammatically incorrect statement:

  > *As a standard embryo does* ***does not*** *have a highly valuable future, killing it is seriously wrong.*

  As will be discussed in the sequal, such errors are rare, and, by and large, are a result of errors in the negation algorithm, which in retrospect could have been easily fixed.

- *Clarity*—an automatically generated negation might be grammatically correct, but unclear and incoherent. For example, an automatic system trying to negate the Claim:

  > *School should be made to fit the child, rather than the other way around.*

  may suggest the following statement, which is grammatically correct, yet unintelligible:

  > *School should* ***not*** *be made to fit the child, rather than the other way around.*

- *Opposition*—a naïve negation might be grammatically correct, and even clear, but still not expressing the opposite of the original Claim. For example, given the Claim:

  > *Children who fail to engage in regular physical activity are at greater risk of obesity.*

  the following suggested negation is not stating its opposite, hence is not a valid Claim Negation (the scope is wrong):

  > *Children who* ***do not*** *fail to engage in regular physical activity are at greater risk of obesity*

- *Usability*—finally, a suggested negation that satisfies the above three criteria, may still not be plausible to use while discussing the Topic. Consider the following two Claims:

  > *Affirmative action has* ***undesirable*** *side-effects in addition to failing to achieve its goals.*
  >
  > *The selection process* **should not** *be based on some arbitrary or irrelevant criterion.*

  and their corresponding candidate negations:

  > *Affirmative action has* **desirable** *side-effects in addition to failing to achieve its goals.*
  >
  > *The selection process* **should** *be based on some arbitrary or irrelevant criterion.*

  Both suggested negations pass the previous three criteria, but nonetheless it is hard to imagine someone stating them in earnest.

Finally, it is interesting to note that for some Claims, a corresponding Claim Negation does not necessarily exist. Consider the following two Claims:

> *People continue to die at a high rate due in large part to lack of sufficient aid.*
>
> *Rather than 'punish' the banks and others truly responsible for the crisis, the government is instead 'punishing' regular people for the 'crimes' of others.*

While one can think of many ways to try and refute these Claims, it is less clear how one states the exact opposite of either of them.

4 Automatic claim negation algorithm

In this section we describe our technical approach to automatically generating a Claim Negation. We start with a description of some preliminary analysis. Motivated by this analysis, we defined a two-stage approach. In the first stage, described in section 4.2, given a Claim, a simple rule–based algorithm is applied to generate its candidate negation. In the second stage, described in section 4.3, an automatic classification scheme is used to assess the plausibility of using the suggested negation (i.e. whether or not it passes the Usability criterion).

4.1 Preliminary analysis

The purpose of the preliminary analysis was to better understand where most of the challenge lies. Is it difficult to suggest a grammatically correct negation? Or perhaps the main difficulty is in automatically determining if the suggested negation is plausible to use? Furthermore, how often one should expect a Claim Negation to actually exist—clearly a prerequisite for the system to correctly produce one?

Towards that end we asked a team of five annotators to manually analyze the first 200 Claims in the dataset published in (Aharoni et al., 2014). Each annotator was asked to examine each Claim, and to determine the *difficulty* of generating a negation of that Claim. Specifically, the annotator was asked to label the negation difficulty as "Type 1" (namely, "simple"), if it can be derived from the original Claim by one of the following alterations:

1. Adding the word "no" or "not".

2. Removing the word "no" or "not".

3. Adding the phrase "does not" or "do not", and possibly changing the conjugation of an adjacent verb.

The annotator was asked to define the negation difficulty as "Type 2" (namely, "complex") if she could think of a negation, but not of one derived through the simple modifications mentioned above. If the annotator could not easily phrase a clear negation to the examined Claim, she was asked to define the negation difficulty as "Type 3" (namely, "none available").

Given the annotation results, the negation difficulty of an examined Claim was defined as the majority vote of the five annotators. By this scheme, 128 Claims were annotated as having a *simple* negation, 37 as having a *complex* negation, and 25 with *none available*. For an additional 10 Claims the vote was a 2-2-1 split. This was rather encouraging, suggesting that for about 75% of the Claims that can be negated, simple rules may suffice.

In addition, each annotator was asked to determine if it is plausible to use the envisioned negation in a debate. For only 47 out of the 200 Claims examined, the majority of the labelers determined that the negation would be usable. These results suggested that the main challenge for automatic Claim negation would lie in determining usability rather than in generating a grammatically correct negation, which led us to the approach described in the sequel.

4.2 Claim negation: How?

The first stage of our algorithm receives a Claim as input, and uses a simple rule–based machinery to generate its candidate negation, aiming for it to be a Negated Claim. Specifically, the algorithm runs as follows:

1. Tokenize the Claim and label the tokens for parts-of-speech using the Stanford Core NLP pipeline (Manning et al., 2014).

2. Find the first token labeled as one of the following: a modal verb, a verb in the present tense, or a verb ending in "n't". We denote this token as T_1.

3. If T_1 is followed or preceded by one of several negation strings (e.g., "no", "not""), remove this negation and finish.

4. If T_1 ends in "n't", remove this suffix and finish (so, e.g., "can't" would be transformed to "can").

5. If T_1 is a modal verb, is a form of the verb "to be" (e.g. "is" or "are"). or is followed by a gerund, then:

(a) If T_1 is followed by a word composed of a negation prefix (e.g. "un", "non") and a WordNet (Miller, 1995) adjective (e.g., "unworkable"), remove the negation prefix and finish.

(b) Otherwise, insert the word "not" after T_1, and finish.

6. Otherwise, insert the words "does not" or "do not" (according to plurality) before T_1, and replace T_1 with its lemmatized form.

Note that the algorithm may fail in step 2, if no appropriate token exists. This happened in five of the 200 Claims we initially considered, so for the remainder of this paper we ignore this problem.

4.3 Claim negation: When?

The second stage of our algorithm, receives as input the output of the first stage – namely, a candidate negation, and aims to determine its Usability, i.e., whether or not it is plausible to use the suggested negation in a debate about the Topic. To this end, we used a Logistic Regression classifier. Specifically, we developed a set of 19 features, and, accordingly, each candidate negation was transformed into an 19-dimensional feature vector. The classifier was trained and tested based on these representations. Importantly, to avoid overfitting, the features were designed and developed by examining only the initial results of the algorithm on the set of 200 Claims exploited in our preliminary analysis (section 4.1), and all of them were used in later experiments.

The features eventually included in our algorithm were as follows, and are discussed in greater detail below:

1. Counts: Number of words in the Claim.
2. Tokens: Whether or not the Claim contains the following tokens: "and", "or", "than", "," (one feature per token).
3. PoS Tags: Whether or not the Claim contains the following PoS Tags: "VBZ", "VBP", "MD" (one feature per PoS tag).
4. Sentiment: Number of words with positive sentiment and number of words with negative sentiment, taken from (Hu and Liu, 2004) (two features).
5. Algorithm step: Which step in the rule-based algorithm of section 4.2 yielded the negation (8 features; some steps are divided in 2).
6. Frequency in real world corpora – of the altered phrase in the suggested negation, compared to that of the original phrase, in the original Claim.

The motivation for selecting the first five types of features is that it is probably more challenging to automatically generate valid Claim Negations to complex and comparative Claims. In addition, removing an existing negation may behave differently from inserting a negation.

The relative frequency feature is motivated by examples like the non-usable negation mentioned in section 3:

> *Affirmative action has desirable side-effects.*

The relatively low frequency of the phrase "desirable side effects" compared to that of the original phrase "undesirable side effects" may be indicative to the implausibility of using the former. For example, in the Wikipedia dump we examined, the former appears just five times and the latter 120 times.

More specifically, the frequency feature, denoted f, was computed as follows. We tokenized both the original Claim and the suggested negation, yielding two sequences of tokens, denoted $\{c_1, c_2, \ldots, c_{k_1}\}$ and $\{n_1, n_2, \ldots, n_{k_2}\}$. We then found the last token up to which both sequences agree, and denoted its position i. Thus, in these notations, c_i and n_i are the same token (e.g., "has" in the aforementioned example), while c_{i+1} differs from n_{i+1} (e.g., "undesirable" versus "desirable" in the same example). We then considered the following sequences of 5 tokens - $\{c_i, \ldots, c_{i+4}\}$ and $\{n_i, \ldots, n_{i+4}\}$, and their respective frequency in Google n-grams (Michel et al., 2011) for $n = 5$, denoted f_c and f_n, respectively. If both sequences were not found (or if either sentence had less than $i + 4$ tokens), we repeated the process for sequences of 4 tokens, and if needed, for sequences of 3 tokens, until one of the sequences was present at least once in the corresponding Google n-grams corpus. Finally, we defined $f = (f_n + 1)/(f_c + 1)$. Thus, if the sequence obtained in the suggested negation ("has desirable side effects" in our example) was rare in Google n-grams compared to the corresponding sequence of tokens in the original Claim ("has undesirable side effects" in our example) then f was correspondingly receiving a relatively low value.

5 Experimental results

5.1 Experimental setup

We started with a data set of 1,240 Claims, collected in the context of various debatable topics, using the same protocol described in (Aharoni et al., 2014). Given this data, the algorithm described in section 4.2 was used to generate 1,240 pairs of the form (Claim, candidate negation). Each pair was annotated by 5 annotators, out of a set of 11 annotators. Specifically, each annotator was asked to assess the candidate negation according to the 4 criteria mentioned in section 3 – i.e., whether the candidate negation is grammatically correct; clear; states the opposite of the original Claim; and usable in a debate to rebut the Claim. Taking the majority over the 5 annotators determined the candidate negation's label. Thus, a candidate negation was considered "usable" if at least three annotators determined it was such. We note that each pair of annotators either considered no pairs of (Claim, candidate negation) in common, or at least 250. This was important when measuring agreement (section 5.2), ensuring a reasonable sample size.

Next, a logistic-regression classifier was trained and tested based on the features described in section 4.3, in a 10-fold cross validation framework, using the "usable" (yes/no) annotation as the class label. That is, the data set was divided into 10 chunks of consecutive Claims. At each of the 10 iterations, a logistic-regression classifier was trained on 9 of the chunks, and predicted whether or not each of the candidate negations in the remaining chunk should be considered "usable". There is a caveat here - on the one hand each fold should be of the same size, while on the other hand including claims from the same topic in both train and test set may conceivably create a bias (if deciding successful negation is somehow topic-dependant). As a compromise we ordered the claims according to topic. This way folds are of the same size, and at most two topics are split between the train and test sets.

	Grammar	Clarity	Opp.	Use
Frac. pass	0.96	0.85	0.79	0.50
Mean agree	0.90	0.84	0.84	0.72

Table 1: Fraction of negated claims which passed each criteria according to majority vote, and mean pairwise agreement among annotators. Pairwise agreement is defined as the fraction of candidate negations for which the two annotators give the same "yes/no" label.

The weights assigned to each train sample were the product of two numbers - a normalizing factor and a confidence score. The normalization factor is assigned so that the total weight for positive samples is the same as that of negative samples. Namely, if k out of n samples are positive, then the normalization factor for positive samples is $(n-k)/k$ (and 1 for negative samples). The confidence score was defined as the size of the majority which determined the label, divided by 5. So 0.6 in the case of a 3-2 split, 0.8 in the case of a 4-1 split and 1.0 in the case of a unanimous vote.

The complete data-set, including the Claims, candidate negations, and associated annotations, are available upon request for research purposes.

5.2 Results

The first stage – rule-based part – of the Claim negation algorithm performed quite well on the first three levels of this task, being labeled as correct on 96% of the Claims for Grammar, and on about 80% of them for Clarity and Opposition. On the other hand, the generated negations were deemed usable for only 50% of the instances (Table 1).

It is interesting to note that this number is still twice as much as would be expected from our initial study, where only 23.5% of the Claims were annotated as having a usable negation. This may be due to the sample size, or differences in the phrasing of the guidelines—one difference is that in the initial task we asked whether a given Claim has a usable negation, whereas in this task we explicitly stated a candidate negation. The second difference is that in the initial guidelines we asked whether the negation was useful in a debate, and here we asked whether it is useful for refuting the original Claim. We made this second change because we felt that the failing to

Frac. in	Grammar	Clarity	Opp.	Use
Grammar	1.00	0.88	0.82	0.52
Clarity	0.99	1.00	0.91	0.59
Opp.	0.99	0.98	1.00	0.63
Use	1.00	1.00	1.00	1.00

Table 2: Fraction of claims which pass both criteria from those which pass the one listed on the left column. If n_1 claims pass criterion i, and n_2 pass both i and j, the (i, j) entry in the table is $n2/n1$.

Kappa	Mean	Std	Min.	Max.
Annot.	0.43	0.09	0.23	0.63
Class.	0.29	0.10	0.21	0.36

Table 3: Pairwise Cohen's kappa statistics among annotators (first line), and comparing annotators to classifier (second line).

explicitly mention the context of rebuttal in the initial phrasing may indeed have led the annotators to be too strict in their evaluation.

Next, we observe that the suggested negations that pass each criterion form almost a perfect hierarchy with respect to containment (Table 2). All suggested negations that pass the Usability criterion also pass the Clarity criterion and the Opposition criterion. Suggested negations that pass the Clarity criterion and those that pass the Opposition criterion are almost the same ones (intersection covers 91.6% and 97.6% of the original sets, respectively), and both sets almost always pass the Grammar criterion (98.9% and 99.1%, respectively).

Determining whether or not a suggested negation is usable is inherently subjective, and as seen in Table 3, agreement between annotators achieved mean pairwise Cohen's kappa coefficients of 0.43 (this is considered fair to good agreement (Landis and Kock, 1977; Fleiss, 1981)). This is similar to what was obtained in (Aharoni et al., 2014) for a similar task: Claim and Evidence confirmation—the task in which one is presented with a Claim or Evidence candidate and needs to determine whether or not it is indeed one. There the reported mean kappas are 0.39 for Claims and 0.4 for Evidence.

Nonetheless, taking majority vote as labels and training a logistic-regression classifier, prediction accuracy was 0.66%, notably higher than expected at random. Similarly, among the top scoring predictions of each fold, some 80% were indeed annotated as usable (Figure 1). That is, for each fold the 124 suggested negations on which the classifier was tested were sorted according to the classifier's score. Then, for each $k = 1, \ldots, 124$, the fraction of Usable negations among the top k was computed, and averaged across folds. Specifically, on average 86% of the suggested negations for $k = 5$ passed the Usability criterion, 83% for $k = 10$, and 78% for $k = 20$.

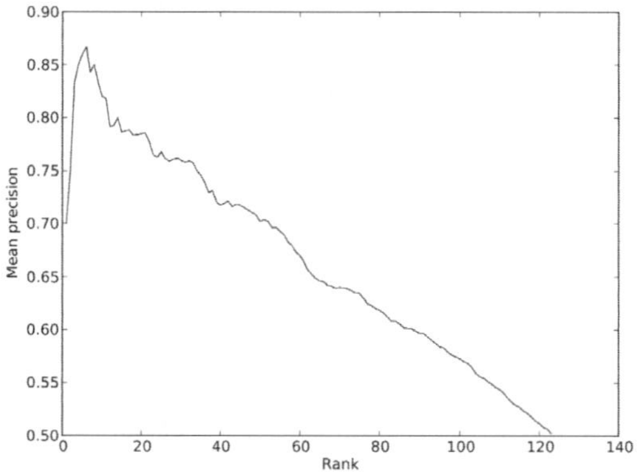

Figure 1: Mean precision (over 10 folds) of the top-ranked candidates, according to classifier score.

Another way to appreciate the classifier's predictions on this subjective task is comparing the annotators' agreement with these predictions to the agreement among the annotators themselves. As seen in (Table 3), while agreement with the former is lower than the latter, the difference in kappa coefficients is less than two standard deviations, and mean agreement with the classifier's predictions is within the range of pairwise agreements displayed among annotators.

It is interesting to understand the relative importance of each of the 19 features, as expressed by the coefficient in the logistic-regression model (when trained on the entire set). The Counts and Sentiment features are normalized, so all values are roughly of the same scale. For the indicators of tokens and for the PoS tag "VBZ", coefficients are less than 10^{-4}. Indeed, the same results are obtained with and without them (not shown). Other features have roughly the same magnitude of coefficients, with the highest obtained for the Counts feature (1.9), and lowest for the negative Sentiment feature (0.12).

A different way to examine this is via the correlation between feature values and labels. Towards this end we computed the Spearman Correlation between the vector l of $0-1$ labels, and the vector f_i of feature values for each feature i. Namely, l_c is 1 if the negation suggested for Claim c was determined "usable" by the majority of the annotators, and 0 otherwise; f_{ic} is the value of feature i computed for Claim c. The highest Spearman Correlation so attained (in absolute value) is with the Counts feature (-0.35) and the PoS "MD" Indicator (-0.21). The n-gram frequency feature comes in third, with correlation coefficient of 0.07.

Note that since the suggested criteria form a hierarchy, getting good predictions for lower levels of the hierarchy may already yield non-trivial results for higher levels. For example, suppose we had a perfect classifier for Clarity, and we would use it to predict Usability. Predicting that a negation that fails the Clarity criterion is also not usable would always be correct – since all negations which fail Clarity also fail Usability. Conversely, predicting that a negation that passes the Clarity criterion is also usable would be correct 59% of the time (as per Table 2). Since 85% of the automatically suggested negations pass the Clarity criterion, overall accuracy for such a hypothetical classifier would be $0.85 \cdot 0.59 + 0.15 \cdot 1.0 = 0.65$, similar to what is obtained here. Indeed, since many of the features we develop aim to capture the complexity of the Claim, they are probably relevant for classifying success at lower levels of the hierarchy as well. In other words, much of the classifier's success may be attributed to capturing Clarity, rather than Usability. We defer further investigation of these ideas to future work.

6 Conclusions and future work

We presented an algorithm that, given a Claim, automatically generates a possible negation, and further determines the plausibility of using this negation to refute the original Claim. Our results highlight the main challenges in generating a meaningful Claim Negation, and demonstrate the feasibility of the proposed approach.

Automatic Claim Negation can augment the results of automatic Claim Detection systems (Levy et al., 2014) and thus enhance the performance of debate support systems. In particular, this could be useful in a setting where the context includes, in addition to a debatable topic, some initial Claims regarding it. For example, in the legal domain, where some Claims have already been made, and one is interested in substantiating them further, or in refuting them. The most basic refutation of a Claim is simply claiming its negation. Of course, for this to be useful, the system would also need to detect Evidence supporting the automatically generated Claim Negation.

The algorithm we presented here for automatic Claim negation is rather naïve. While the results may suggest that the main challenge is in the "when" rather than the "how", improving the first stage – rule based part – of the algorithm is certainly an important step in achieving better automatic negation system. For example, the algorithm negates modal verbs by adding "not" after them (see section 4.2). However, after "must" or "may", this is often erroneous, as in:

> *Countries must be prepared to allow Open borders for people fleeing conflict.*

or

> *National security may simply serve as a pretext for suppressing unfavorable political and social views.*

This may be the reason why the indicator of modal verbs was found to be negatively correlated with the "usable" label, and suggests that more subtle rules, which take negation scope into account, may carry important potential. A database of modal verbs, such as the one in (Pakray et al., 2012), may be helpful for this purpose.

When the algorithm introduces negation, rather than removes it, it always negates the verb. As pointed out in (Ahmed and Lin, 2014), this is the easy case. While this also turns out to be the most common negation scope when it comes to Claims, one could probably improve the negation algorithm by considering other scopes, as done in (Ahmed and Lin, 2014). Determining which of these scopes is the one which actually states the intuitive contradiction of the original claim may be an interesting task in itself, and may make use of corpus-frequency features like the n-gram one described here

As for improving the decision for when a suggested negation is usable, one should keep in mind that while Claims are at the heart of an argument, they usually require supporting Evidence for the argument to be whole. Hence, the existence or absence of supporting Evidence for the suggested negation (or opposing Evidence to the original Claim) may be a strong indicator regarding the suggested negation usability.

Finally, automatic Claim negation may be seen as a special (and relatively simple) case of augmenting a set of Claims via *automatic Claim generation*. That is, rather than building the text from atomic elements, as is usually done in Natural Language Generation, this paradigm suggests to generate new Claims by modifying existing ones. Examples of this are Claim rephrasing towards a specific goal (e.g., making them more assertive or more persuasive), and combining existing Claims into novel ones (e.g., combine the Claim *X causes Y* and *Y causes Z* into *X causes Z*). We believe that any Claim generation task would benefit from the four-tier analysis we suggested here, namely - Grammar, Clarity, Goal attainment (Opposition in the case of Claim Negation), and Usability. In this sense, the present work can be seen as a first step towards constructing more general automatic Claim generation systems.

Acknowledgements

We thank Ido Dagan and Ruty Rinot for helpful comments and suggestions.

References

Ehud Aharoni, Anatoly Polnarov, Tamar Lavee, Daniel Hershcovich, Ran Levy, Ruty Rinott, Dan Gutfreund, Noam Slonim. A Benchmark Dataset for Automatic Detection of Claims and Evidence in the Context of Controversial Topics 2014. *Workshop on Argumentation Mining, ACL*

Afroza Ahmed and King Ip Lin. Negative Sentence Generation by Using Semantic Heuristics. 2014. *The 52nd Annual ACM Southeast Conference (ACMSE 2014), Kennesaw, GA, USA.*

Denis Apothéloz, Pierre-Yves Brandt and Gustav Quiroz. The function of negation in argumentation. 1993. *Journal of Pragmatics*, 19 23-38. North-Holland.

Kevin D. Ashley and Vern R. Walker. From Information Retrieval (IR) to Argument Retrieval (AR) for Legal Cases: Report on a Baseline Study. 2013.

Ngo Xuan Bach, Nguyen Le Minh, Tran Thi Oanh, and Akira Shimazu. A Two-Phase Framework for Learning Logical Structures of Paragraphs in Legal Articles. 2013. *In ACM Transactions on Asian Language Information Processing (TALIP)*. 12(1):3

Eduardo Blanco, and Dan I. Moldovan. Some Issues on Detecting Negation from Text. 2011. *FLAIRS Conference.*

W.W. Chapman, D. Hilert, S. Velupillai, et al. Extending the NegEx Lexicon for Multiple Languages. 2013. *Studies in health technology and informatics*, 192:677-6813.

Graham Chapman and John Cleese. The Argument Clinic. 1972. *Monty Python's Flying Circus*, 29:12.

I. Councill, R. McDonald and L. Velikovich. What's great and what's not: learning to classify the scope of negation for improved sentiment analysis. 2010. *Proceedings of the Workshop on Negation and Speculation in Natural Language Processing.*

J.L. Fleiss. Statistical methods for rates and proportions (2nd ed.) 1981.

A Gatt and E Reiter (2009). SimpleNLG: A realisation engine for practical applications. 2009. *Proceedings of ENLG-2009.*

Minqing Hu and Bing Liu. 2004. Mining and summarizing customer reviews. 2004. *In Knowledge Discovery and Data Mining*: 168-177.

J.R. Landis and G.G. Kock. The measurement of observer agreement for categorical data". 1977. *Biometrics* 33 (1): 159174.

Landis, J.R.; Koch, G.G. (1977). "The measurement of observer agreement for categorical data". Biometrics 33 (1): 159174.

Ran Levy, Yonatan Bilu, Daniel Hershcovich, Ehud Aharoni and Noam Slonim. Context Dependent Claim Detection 2014. *In The 25th International Conference on Computational Linguistics*

Amnon Lotan, Asher Stern, and Ido Dagan. 2013. TruthTeller: Annotating predicate truth. 2013. *In Proceedings of the Annual Meeting of the North American Chapter of the ACL, pages 752757, Atlanta, Georgia.*

Christopher D. Manning, Mihai Surdeanu, John Bauer, Jenny Finkel, Steven J. Bethard, and David McClosky. 2014. The Stanford CoreNLP Natural Language Processing Toolkit. 2014. *In Proceedings of 52nd Annual Meeting of the Association for Computational Linguistics: System Demonstrations* 55-60.

Jean-Baptiste Michel, Yuan Kui Shen, Aviva Presser Aiden, Adrian Veres, Matthew K. Gray, William Brockman, The Google Books Team, Joseph P. Pickett, Dale Hoiberg, Dan Clancy, Peter Norvig, Jon

Orwant, Steven Pinker, Martin A. Nowak, and Erez Lieberman Aiden. Quantitative Analysis of Culture Using Millions of Digitized Books. 2011. *Science* 331(6014):176-182

George A. Miller. WordNet: A Lexical Database for English. *COMMUNICATIONS OF THE ACM*, 38:39-41.

Mochales Palau, Raquel and Moens, Marie-Francine. Argumentation mining. 2011. *In Artificial Intelligence and Law*, 19(1): 1-22.

Douglas Walton, Argument Mining by Applying Argumentation Schemes 2012. *In Studies in Logic* 4(1):38-64

Michael Wiegand, Alexandra Balahur, Benjamin Roth, Dietrich Klakow, and Andrs Montoyo. A survey on the role of negation in sentiment analysis. 2010. *In Proceedings of the Workshop on Negation and Speculation in Natural Language Processing, pages 6068, Uppsala.*

Adam Wyner, Raquel Mochales-Palau, Marie-Francine Moens, and David Milward. Approaches to text mining arguments from legal cases. 2010. *In Semantic processing of legal texts* 60-79.

Xiaodan Zhu, Hongyu Guo, Svetlana Kiritchenko, Saif Mohammad. An Empirical Study on the Effect of Negation Words on Sentiment. 2014. *The 52th Annual Meeting of the Association for Computational Linguistics (ACL-2014). Baltimore, USA.*

Partha Pakray, Pinaki Bhaskar, Somnath Banerjee, Sivaji Bandyopadhyay, Alexander F. Gelbukh. An Automatic System for Modality and Negation Detection. 2012. *In proceedings of CLEF (Online Working Notes/Labs/Workshop).*

Mutalik PG, Deshpande A, Nadkarni PM. Use of general-purpose negation detection to augment concept indexing of medical documents: a quantitative study using the UMLS. 2001. *J Am Med Inform Assoc. 2001 Nov-Dec;8(6):598-609.*

Learning Sentence Ordering for Opinion Generation of Debate

Toshihiko Yanase **Toshinori Miyoshi** **Kohsuke Yanai** **Misa Sato**
Research & Development Group, Hitachi, Ltd.
{toshihiko.yanase.gm, toshinori.miyoshi.pd, kohsuke.yanai.cs, misa.sato.mw}
@hitachi.com

Makoto Iwayama **Yoshiki Niwa**
Research & Development Group, Hitachi, Ltd.
{makoto.iwayama.nw, yoshiki.niwa.tx}
@hitachi.com

Paul Reisert **Kentaro Inui**
Tohoku University
{preisert, inui}@ecei.tohoku.ac.jp

Abstract

We propose a sentence ordering method to help compose persuasive opinions for debating. In debate texts, support of an opinion such as evidence and reason typically follows the main claim. We focused on this claim-support structure to order sentences, and developed a two-step method. First, we select from among candidate sentences a first sentence that is likely to be a claim. Second, we order the remaining sentences by using a ranking-based method. We tested the effectiveness of the proposed method by comparing it with a general-purpose method of sentence ordering and found through experiment that it improves the accuracy of first sentence selection by about 19 percentage points and had a superior performance over all metrics. We also applied the proposed method to a constructive speech generation task.

1 Introduction

There are increasing demands for information structuring technologies to support decision making using a large amount of data. Argumentation in debating which composes texts in a persuasive manner is a research target suitable for such information structuring. In this paper, we discuss sentence ordering for constructive speech generation of debate.

The following is an example of constructive speech excerpts that provide affirmative opinions on the banning of gambling[1].

> Motion: This House should ban gambling.
> (1) Poor people are more likely to gamble, in the hope of getting rich.
> (2) In 1999, the National Gambling Impact Commission in the United States found that 80 percent of gambling revenue came from lower-income households.

We can observe a typical structure of constructive speech in this example. The first sentence describes a claim that is the main statement of the opinion and the second sentence supports the main statement. In this paper, we focus on this claim-support structure to order sentences.

Regarding the structures of arguments, we can find research on the modeling of arguments (Freeley and Steinberg, 2008) and on recognition such as claim detection (Aharoni et al., 2014). To the best of our knowledge, there is no research that examines the claim-support structure of debate texts for the sentence ordering problem. Most of the previous works on sentence ordering (Barzilay et al., 2002; Lapata, 2003; Bollegala et al., 2006; Tan et al., 2013) focus on the sentence order of news articles and do not consider the structures of arguments. These methods mingle claim and supportive sentences together, which decreases the persuasiveness of generated opinions.

In this paper, we propose a sentence ordering method in which a motion and a set of sentences are given as input. Ordering all paragraphs of debate texts at once is a quite difficult task, so we have

[1]This example is excerpted from Debatabase (http://idebate.org/debatabase). Copyright 2005 International Debate Education Association. All Rights Reserved.

Proceedings of the 2nd Workshop on Argumentation Mining, pages 94–103,
Denver, Colorado, June 4, 2015. ©2015 Association for Computational Linguistics

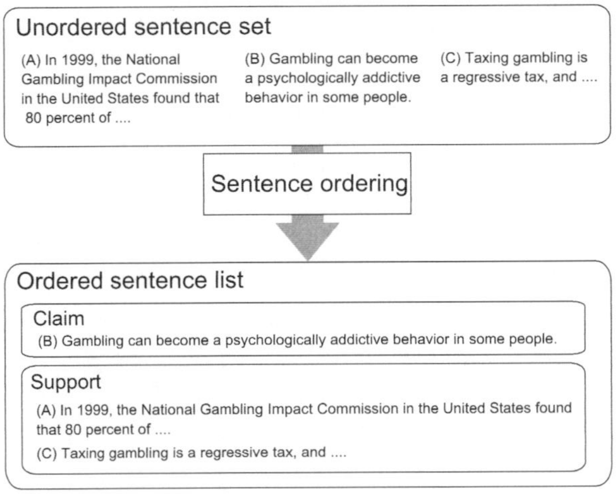

Figure 1: Target sentence ordering problem.

simplified by assuming that all input sentences stand for a single viewpoint regarding the motion.

We use this claim-support structure as a cue of sentence ordering. We employ two-step ordering based on machine learning, as shown in Fig. 1. First, we select a first sentence that corresponds to a claim, and second, we order the supportive sentences of the claims in terms of consistency. For each step, we design machine learning features to capture the characteristics of sentences in terms of the claim-support structure. The dataset for training and testing is made up of content from an online debate site.

The remainder of this paper is structured as follows. The next section describes related works dealing with sentence ordering. In the third section, we examine the characteristics of debate texts. Next, we describe our proposed method, explain the experiments we performed to evaluate the performance, and discuss the results. After that, we describe our application of the proposed sentence ordering to automated constructive speech generation. We conclude the paper with a summary and a brief mention of future work.

2 Related Works

Previous research on sentence ordering has been conducted as a part of multi-document summarization. There are four major feature types to order sentences: publication dates of source documents, topical similarity, transitional association cues, and rhetorical cues.

Arranging sentences by order of publication dates of source documents is known as the chronological ordering (Barzilay et al., 2002). It is effective for news article summarization because descriptions of a certain event tend to follow the order of publication. It is, however, not suitable for opinion generation because such generation requires statements and evidence rather than the simple summarization of an event.

Topical similarity is based on an assumption that neighboring sentences have a higher similarity than non-neighboring ones. For example, bag-of-words-based cosine similarities of sentence pairs are used in (Bollegala et al., 2006; Tan et al., 2013). Another method, the Lexical Chain, models the semantic distances of word pairs on the basis of synonym dictionaries such as WordNet (Barzilay and Elhadad, 1997; Chen et al., 2005). The effectiveness of this feature depends highly on the method used to calculate similarity.

Transitional association is used to measure the likelihood of two consecutive sentences. Lapata proposed a sentence ordering method based on a probabilistic model (Lapata, 2003). This method uses conditional probability to represent transitional probability from the previous sentence to the target sentence.

Dias et al. used rhetorical structures to order sentences (de S. Dias et al., 2014). The rhetorical structure theory (RST) (Mann and Thompson, 1988) explains the textual organization such as background and causal effect that can be useful to determine the sentence order. For example, causes are likely to precede results. However, it is important to restrict the types of rhetorical relation because original RST defines many relations and a large amount of data is required for accurate estimation.

There has been research on integrating different types of features. Bollegara et al. proposed machine learning-based integration of different kinds of features (Bollegala et al., 2006) by using a binary classifier to determine if the order of a given sentence pair is acceptable or not. Tan et al. formulated sentence ordering as a ranking problem of sentences (Tan et al., 2013). Their experimental results showed that the ranking-based method outperformed classification-based methods.

Viewpoint	Debate	News
Word overlap in neighbors	3.14	4.30
Word overlap in non-neighbors	3.09	4.22
Occurrence of named entity	0.372	0.832

Table 1: Characteristics of debate texts and news articles.

3 Characteristics of Debate Texts

Topical similarity can be measured by the word overlap between two sentences. This metric assumes that the closer a sentence pair is, the more word overlap exists. In order to examine this assumption, we compared characteristics between debate texts and news articles, as shown in Table 1. In the Debate column, we show the statistics of constructive speech of Debatabase, an online debate site. Each constructive speech item in the debate dataset has 7.2 sentences on average. Details of the debate dataset are described in the experiment section. In the News column, we show the statistics of a subset of Annotated English Gigaword (Napoles et al., 2012). We randomly selected 80,000 articles and extracted seven leading sentences per article.

Overall, we found less word overlap in debate texts than in news articles in both neighbor pairs and non-neighbor pairs. This is mainly because debaters usually try to add as much information as possible. We assume from this result that conventional topical similarity is less effective for debate texts and have therefore focused on the claim-support structure of debate texts.

We also examined the occurrence of named entity (NE) in each sentence. We can observe that most of the sentences in news articles contain NEs while much fewer sentences in debate texts have NEs. This suggests that debate texts deal more with general opinions and related examples while news articles describe specific events.

4 Proposed Method

4.1 Two-Step Ordering

In this study, we focused on a simple but common style of constructive speech. We assumed that a constructive speech item has a claim and one or more supporting sentences. The flow of the proposed ordering method is shown in Fig. 2. The system re-

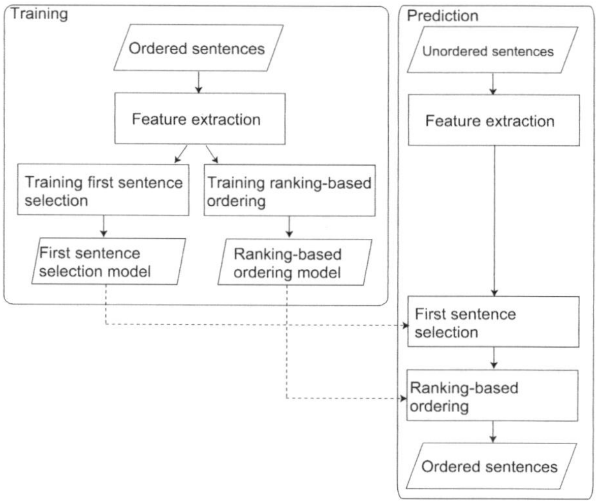

Figure 2: Flowchart of two-step ordering.

ceives a motion and a set of sentences as input and then it outputs ordered sentences. First, syntactic parsing is applied to the input texts, and then features for the machine learning models are then extracted from the results. Second, we select the first sentence, which is likely to be the claim sentence, from the candidate sentences. This problem is formulated as a binary-classification problem, where first sentences of constructive speech items are positive and all others are negative. Third, we order the remaining sentences on the basis of connectivity of pairs of sentences. This problem is formulated as a ranking problem, similarly to (Tan et al., 2013).

4.2 Feature Extraction

We obtained the part of speech, lemma, syntactic parse tree, and NEs of each input sentence by using the Stanford Core NLP (Manning et al., 2014).

The following features, which are commonly used in sentence ordering methods to measure local coherence (Bollegala et al., 2006; Tan et al., 2013; Lapata, 2003), are then extracted.

Sentence similarity: Cosine similarity between sentence u and v. We simply counted the frequency of each word to measure cosine similarity. In addition to that, we also measured the cosine similarity between latter half of u (denoted as $\mathrm{latter}(u)$) and former half of v (denoted as $\mathrm{former}(v)$). The sentences are separated by the most centered comma (if exists) or word (if no comma exists).

Overlap: Commonly shared words of u and v. Let $\text{overlap}_j(u,v)$ be the number of commonly shared words of u and v, for $j = 1,2,3$ representing lemmatized noun, verb and adjective or adverb, respectively. We calculated $\text{overlap}_j(u,v)/\min(|u|,|v|)$ and $\text{overlap}_j(\text{latter}(u),\text{former}(v))/\text{overlap}_j(u,v)$, where $|u|$ is the number of words of sentence u. The value will be set to 0 if the denominator is 0.

Expanded sentence similarity: Cosine similarity between candidate sentences expanded with synonyms. We used WordNet (Miller, 1995) to expand the nouns and verbs into synonyms.

Word transitional probability: Calculate conditional probability $P(w_v|w_u)$, where w_u, w_v denote the words in sentences u, v, respectively. In the case of the first sentence, we used $P(w_u)$. A probabilistic model based on Lapata's method (Lapata, 2003) was created.

The following features are used to capture the characteristics of claim sentences.

Motion similarity: Cosine similarity between the motion and the target sentence. This feature examines the existence of the motion keywords.

Expanded motion similarity: Cosine similarity of the target sentence to the motion expanded with synonyms.

Value relevance: Ratio of value expressions. In this study, we defined human values as the topics obviously considered to be positive or negative and highly relevant to people's values and then created a dictionary of value expressions. For example, health, education, and the environment are considered positive for people's values while crime, pollution, and high costs are considered negative.

Sentiment: Ratio of positive or negative words. The dictionary of sentimental words is from (Hu and Liu, 2004). This feature is used to examine whether the stance of the target sentence is positive, negative, or neutral.

Type	1st step	2nd step
Sentence similarity		✓
Expanded sentence similarity		✓
Overlap		✓
Word transitional probability	✓	✓
Motion similarity	✓	✓
Expanded motion similarity	✓	✓
Value relevance	✓	✓
Sentiment	✓	✓
Concreteness	✓	✓
Estimated first sentence similarity		✓

Table 2: Features used in each step.

Concreteness features are used to measure the relevance of support.

Concreteness features: The ratio of tokens that are a part of capital words, numerical expression, NE, organization, person, location, or temporal expression. These features are used to capture characteristics of the supporting sentences.

We use the estimated results of the first step as a feature of the second step.

Estimated first sentence similarity: Cosine similarity between the target sentence and the estimated first sentence.

4.3 First Step: First Sentence Selection

In the first step, we choose a first sentence from input sentences. This task can be formulated as a binary classification problem. We employ a machine learning approach to solve this problem.

In the training phase, we extract N feature vectors from N sentences in a document, and train a binary classification function f_{first} defined by

$$f_{\text{first}}(s_i) = \begin{cases} +1 & (i = 0) \\ -1 & (i \neq 0) \end{cases}, \quad (1)$$

where s_i denotes the feature vector corresponding to the i-th sentence. The function f_{first} returns $+1$ if s_i is the first sentence.

In the prediction phase, we applied f_{first} to all sentences and determined the first sentence that has the maximum posterior probability of $f_{\text{first}}(s_i) = +1$.

We used Classias[2] (Okazaki, 2009), an implementation of logistic regression, as a binary classifier.

4.4 Second Step: Ranking-Based Ordering

In the second step, we assume that the first sentence has already been determined. The number of sentences in this step is $N_{\text{second}} = N - 1$. We use a ranking-based framework proposed by Tan et al. (2013) to order sentences.

In the training phase, we generate $N_{\text{second}}(N_{\text{second}} - 1)$ pairs of sentences from N_{second} sentences in a document and train an association strength function f_{pair} defined by

$$f_{\text{pair}}(s_i, s_j) = \begin{cases} N_{\text{second}} - (j - i) & (j > i) \\ 0 & (j \leq i) \end{cases}. \quad (2)$$

For forward direction pairs, the rank values are set to $N - (j - i)$. This means that the shorter the distance between the pair is, the larger the rank value is. For the backward direction pairs, the rank values are set to 0.

In the prediction phase, the total ranking value of a sentence permutation ρ is defined by

$$f_{\text{rank}}(\rho) = \sum_{u,v;\rho(u)>\rho(v)} f_{\text{pair}}(u, v), \quad (3)$$

where $\rho(u) > \rho(v)$ denotes that sentence u precedes sentence v in ρ. A learning to rank algorithm based on Support Vector Machine (Joachims, 2002) is used as a machine learning model. We used svm^{rank} [3] to implement the training and the prediction of f_{pair}.

We used the sentence similarity, the expanded sentence similarity, the overlap, and the transitional probability in addition to the same features as the first step classification. These additional features are defined by a sentence pair (u, v). We applied the feature normalization proposed by Tan et al. (2013) to each additional feature. The normalization functions are defined as

$$V_{i,1} = f_i(u, v), \quad (4)$$

$$V_{i,2} = \begin{cases} 1/2, & \text{if } f_i(u,v) + f_i(v,u) = 0 \\ \frac{f_i(u,v)}{f_i(u,v)+f_i(v,u)}, & \text{otherwise} \end{cases} \quad (5)$$

$$V_{i,3} = \begin{cases} 1/|S|, & \text{if } \sum_{y \in S \setminus \{u\}} f_i(u,y) = 0 \\ \frac{f_i(u,v)}{\sum_{y \in S \setminus \{u\}} f_i(u,y)}, & \text{otherwise} \end{cases} \quad (6)$$

$$V_{i,4} = \begin{cases} 1/|S|, & \text{if } \sum_{x \in S \setminus \{v\}} f_i(x,v) = 0 \\ \frac{f_i(u,v)}{\sum_{x \in S \setminus \{v\}} f_i(x,v)}, & \text{otherwise} \end{cases} \quad (7)$$

where f_i is the i-th feature function, S is a set of candidate sentences, and $|S|$ is the number of sentences in S. Equation (4) is an original value of the i-th feature function. Equation (5) examines the priority of (u, v) to its inversion (v, u). Equation (6) measures the priority of (u, v) to the sentence pairs that have u as a first element. Equation (7) the priority of (u, v) to the sentence pairs that have v as a second element, similarly to Equation (6).

5 Experiments

5.1 Reconstructing Shuffled Sentences

We evaluated the proposed method by reconstructing the original order from randomly shuffled texts. We compared the proposed method with the Random method, which is a base line method that randomly selects a sentence, and the Ranking method, which is a form of Tan et al.'s method (Tan et al., 2013) that arranges sentences using the same procedure as the second step of the proposed method excluding estimated first sentence similarity feature.

Dataset

We created a dataset of constructive speech items from Debatabase to train and evaluate the proposed method. The speech item of this dataset is a whole turn of affirmative/negative constructive speech which consists of several ordered sentences. Details of the dataset were shown in Table 3. The dataset has 501 motions related to 14 themes (e.g., politics, education) and contains a total of 3,754 constructive speech items. The average sentence length per item is 7.2. Each constructive speech item has a short title sentence from which we extract the value (e.g., "health", "crime") of the item.

[2]http://www.chokkan.org/software/classias/

[3]http://www.cs.cornell.edu/people/tj/svm_light/svm_rank.html

Affirmative	no. of constructive speech items	1,939
	no. of sentences	14,021
Negative	no. of constructive speech items	1,815
	no. of sentences	13,041

Table 3: Details of constructive speech dataset created from Debatabase.

Method	Mean accuracy [%]	Std.
Random	17.9	0.81
Ranking	23.3	0.61
Proposed	42.6	1.58

Table 4: Results of the first sentence estimation.

Metrics

The overall performance of ordering sentences is evaluated by Kendall's τ, Spearman Rank Correlation, and Average Continuity.

Kendall's τ is defined by

$$\tau_k = 1 - \frac{2n_{\text{inv}}}{N(N-1)/2}, \quad (8)$$

where N is the number of sentences and n_{inv} is the number of inversions of sentence pairs. The metric ranges from -1 (inversed order) to 1 (identical order). Kendall's τ measures the efforts of human readers to correct wrong sentence orders.

Spearman Rank Correlation is defined by

$$\tau_s = 1 - \frac{6}{N(N+1)(N-1)} \sum_{i=1}^{N} d(i)^2, \quad (9)$$

where $d(i)$ is the difference between the correct rank and the answered rank at the i-th sentence. Spearman Rank Correlation takes the distance of wrong answers directly into account.

Average Continuity is based on the number of matched n-grams, and is defined using P_n. P_n is defined by

$$P_n = \frac{m}{N-n+1}, \quad (10)$$

where m is the number of matched n-grams. P_n measures the ratio of correct n-grams in a sequence. Average Continuity is then defined by

$$\tau_a = \exp\left(\sum_{n=2}^{k} \log(P_n + \alpha)\right), \quad (11)$$

where k is the maximum n of n-grams, and α is a small positive value to prevent divergence of score. In this experiment, we used $k = 4, \alpha = 0.01$ in accordance with (Bollegala et al., 2006).

Results

We applied 5-fold cross validation to each ordering method. The machine learning models were trained by 3,003 constructive speech items and then evaluated using 751 items.

The results of first sentence estimation are shown in Table 4. The accuracy of the proposed method is higher than that of Ranking, which represents the sentence ranking technique without the first sentence selection, by 19.3 percentage points. Although the proposed method showed the best accuracy, we observed that $f_{\text{first}}(s_0)$ tended to be -1 rather than 1. This is mainly because the two classes were unbalanced. The number of negative examples in the training data was 6.2 times larger than that of positive ones. We need to address the unbalanced data problem for further improvement (Chawla et al., 2004).

The results of overall sentence ordering are shown in Table 5. We carried out a one-way analysis of variance (ANOVA) to examine the effects of different algorithms for sentence ordering. The ANOVA revealed reliable effects with all metrics ($p < 0.01$). We performed a Tukey Honest Significant Differences (HSD) test to compare differences among these algorithms. In terms of Kendall's τ and Spearman Rank Correlation, the Tukey HSD test revealed that the proposed method was significantly better than the rests ($p < 0.01$). In terms of Average Continuity, it was also significantly better than the Random method, whereas it is not significantly different from the Ranking method. These results show that the proposed two-step ordering is also effective for overall sentence ordering. However, the small difference of Average Continuity indicates that the ordering improvement is only regional.

5.2 Subjective Evaluation

In addition to our evaluation of the reconstruction metrics, we also conducted a subjective evaluation

Method	Kendall's τ	Spearman	Average Continuity
Random	-6.92×10^{-4}	-1.91×10^{-3}	5.92×10^{-2}
Ranking	6.22×10^{-2}	7.89×10^{-2}	7.13×10^{-2}
Proposed	1.17×10^{-1}	1.44×10^{-1}	8.36×10^{-2}

Table 5: Results of overall sentence ordering.

with a human judge. In this evaluation, we selected target documents that were ordered uniquely by people as follows. First, the judge ordered shuffled sentences and then, we selected the correctly ordered documents as targets. The number of target documents is 24.

Each ordering was awarded one of four grades: Perfect, Acceptable, Poor or Unacceptable. The criteria of these grades are the same as those of (Bollegala et al., 2006). A perfect text cannot be improved by re-ordering. An acceptable text makes sense and does not require revision although there is some room for improvement in terms of readability. A poor text loses the thread of the story in some places and requires amendment to bring it up to an acceptable level. An unacceptable text leaves much to be improved and requires overall restructuring rather than partial revision.

The results of our subjective evaluation are shown in Figure 3. We have observed that about 70 % of randomly ordered sentences are perfect or acceptable. This is mainly because the target documents contain only 3.87 sentences on average, and those short documents are comprehensive even if they are randomly shuffled.

There are four documents containing more than six sentences in the targets. The number of unacceptably ordered documents of the Random method, the Ranking method, and the proposed method are 4, 3, and 1, respectively. We observed that the proposed method selected the claim sentences successfully and then arranged sentences related to the claim sentences. These are the expected results of the first sentence classification and the estimated first sentence similarity in the second step. These results show that the selection of the first sentence plays an important role to make opinions comprehensive.

On the other hand, we did not observe the improvement of the number of the perfectly selected

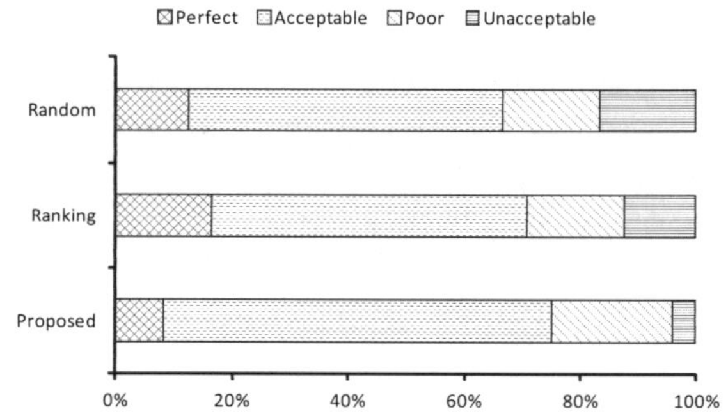

Figure 3: Results of subjective evaluation.

Position	Claim [%]	Support [%]
1	*62.5*	3.93
2	8.93	19.7
3	7.14	20.2
4	5.36	17.4
5+	16.1	*38.7*

Table 6: Sentence type annotation in constructive speech.

documents. We found misclassification of final sentences as first sentences in the results of the proposed method. Such final sentences described conclusions similar to the claim sentences. We need to extend the structure of constructive speech to handle conclusions correctly.

6 Discussion

6.1 Structures of Constructive Speech

We confirmed our assumption that claims are more likely to be described in the first sentence than others by manually examining constructive speech items. We selected seven motions from the top 100 debates in the Debatabase. These selected motions contain a total of 56 constructive speech items. A human annotator assigned claim tags and support tags for the sentences. The results are shown in Table 6.

Here, we can see that about two-thirds of claim

#	Text
1	The contributions of government funding have been shown to be capable of sustaining the costs of a museum, preventing those costs being passed on to the public in the form of admissions charges.
2	The examples of the British Labour government funding national museums has been noted above.
3	The National Museum of the American Indian in Washington was set up partially with government funding and partially with private funds, ensuring it has remained free since its opening in 2004 (Democracy Now , 2004).
4	In 2011 , China also announced that from 2012 all of its national museums would become publicly-funded and cease charging admissions fees (Zhu & Guo , 2011).

Table 7: A typical example ordered correctly by the proposed method. The motion is "This House would make all museums free of charge." The motion and sentences are from Debatabase.

sentences appeared at the beginning of constructive speech items, and that more than 90 % of supportive sentences appeared from the second sentences or later. This means that claims are followed by evidence in more than half of all constructive speech items.

6.2 Case Analysis

A typical example ordered correctly by the proposed method is shown in Table 7. This constructive speech item agrees with free admissions at museums. It has a clear claim-support structure. It first, makes a claim related to the contributions of government funding and then gives three examples. The first sentence has no NEs while the second and later sentences have NEs to give details about the actual museums and countries. Neighbor sentences were connected with common words such as "museum," "charge," and "government funding."

7 Application to Automated Constructive Speech Generation

We applied the proposed sentence ordering to the automated constructive speech generation.

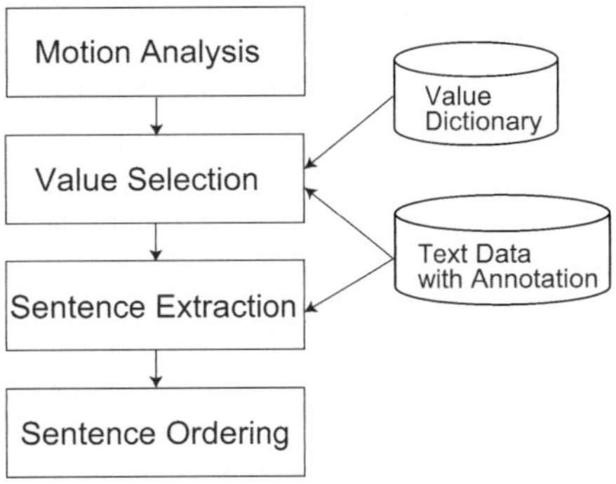

Figure 4: Flow of automated constructive speech generation.

System Description

The flowchart of constructive speech generation is shown in Fig. 4. Here, we give a brief overview of the system. The system is based on sentence extraction and sentence ordering, which we explain with the example motion "This House should ban smoking in public spaces." First, a motion analysis component extracts keywords such as "smoking" and "public spaces" from the motion. Second, a value selection component searches for related sentences with the motion keywords and human value information. More specifically, it generates pairs of motion keywords and values (such as (smoking, health), (smoking, education), and (smoking, crime)) and uses them as search queries. Then, it selects the values of constructive speech in accordance with the number of related sentences to values. In the third step, a sentence extraction component examines the relevancy of each sentence with textual annotation such as promote/suppress relationship and positive/negative relationship. Finally, a sentence ordering component arranges the extracted sentences for each value.

Ordering Results

The system outputs three paragraphs per motion. Each paragraph is composed of seven sentences. Currently, its performance is limited, as 49 out of the 150 generated paragraphs are understandable. To focus on the effect of sentence ordering, we manually extracted relevant sentences from generated constructive speech and then applied the proposed ordering method to them.

#	Text
1	Smoking is a serious public health problem that causes many diseases such as heart diseases, lung diseases, eye problems, as well as risks for women and babies.
2	Brendan McCormick, a spokesman for cigarette-maker Philip Morris USA, said, "We agree with the medical and scientific conclusions that cigarette smoking causes serious diseases in smokers, and that there is no such thing as a safe cigarette."
3	The study, released by the Rio de Janeiro State University and the Cancer Institute, showed that passive smoking could cause serious diseases, such as lung cancer, cerebral hemorrhage, angina pectoris, myocardial infection and coronary thrombosis.

Table 8: A result of sentence ordering in automated constructive speech generation. The motion is "This House would further restrict smoking." The motion is from Debatabase, and sentences are from Annotated English Gigaword.

The results are shown in Table 8[4]. We can observe that the first sentence mentions the health problem of smoking while the second and third sentences show support for the problem, i.e., the names of authorities such as spokesmen and institutes. The proposed ordering method successfully ordered the types of opinions that have a clear claim-support structure.

8 Conclusion

In this paper, we discussed sentence ordering for debate texts. We proposed a sentence ordering method that employs a two-step approach based on the claim-support structure. We then constructed a dataset from an on-line debate site to train and evaluate the ordering method. The evaluation results of reconstruction from shuffled constructive speech showed that our proposed method outperformed a general-purpose ordering method. The subjective evaluation showed that our proposed method is suitable for constructive speech containing explicit claim sentences and supporting examples.

In this study, we focused on a very simple structure, i.e., claims and support. We will extend this structure to handle different types of arguments in the future. More specifically, we plan to take conclusion sentences into account as a component of the structure.

[4]These sentences are extracted from Annotated English Gigaword. Portions ©1994-2010 Agence France Presse, ©1994-2010 The Associated Press, ©1997-2010 Central News Agency (Taiwan), ©1994-1998, 2003-2009 Los Angeles Times-Washington Post News Service, Inc., ©1994-2010 New York Times, ©2010 The Washington Post News Service with Bloomberg News, ©1995-2010 Xinhua News Agency, ©2012 Matthew R. Gormley, ©2003, 2005, 2007, 2009, 2011, 2012 Trustees of the University of Pennsylvania

References

Ehud Aharoni, Anatoly Polnarov, Tamar Lavee, Daniel Hershcovich, Ran Levy, Ruty Rinott, Dan Gutfreund, and Noam Slonim. 2014. A benchmark dataset for automatic detection of claims and evidence in the context of controversial topics. In *Proceedings of the First Workshop on Argumentation Mining*, pages 64–68. Association for Computational Linguistics.

Regina Barzilay and Michael Elhadad. 1997. Using lexical chains for text summarization. In *Proceedings of the ACL Workshop on Intelligent Scalable Text Summarization*, pages 10–17.

Regina Barzilay, Noemie Elhadad, and Kathleen R. McKeown. 2002. Inferring strategies for sentence ordering in multidocument news summarization. *J. Artif. Int. Res.*, 17(1):35–55, August.

Danushka Bollegala, Naoaki Okazaki, and Mitsuru Ishizuka. 2006. A bottom-up approach to sentence ordering for multi-document summarization. In *Proceedings of the 21st International Conference on Computational Linguistics and the 44th Annual Meeting of the Association for Computational Linguistics*, ACL-44, pages 385–392, Stroudsburg, PA, USA. Association for Computational Linguistics.

Nitesh V. Chawla, Nathalie Japkowicz, and Aleksander Kotcz. 2004. Editorial: Special issue on learning from imbalanced data sets. *SIGKDD Explor. Newsl.*, 6(1):1–6, June.

Yan-Min Chen, Xiao-Long Wang, and Bing-Quan Liu. 2005. Multi-document summarization based on lexical chains. In *Proceedings of 2005 International Conference on Machine Learning and Cybernetics 2005*, volume 3, pages 1937–1942 Vol. 3, Aug.

Márcio de S. Dias, Valéria D. Feltrim, and Thiago Alexandre Salgueiro Pardo. 2014. Using rhetorical structure theory and entity grids to automatically evaluate local coherence in texts. *Proceedings of the 11th International Conference, PROPOR 2014*, pages 232–243.

Austin J. Freeley and David L. Steinberg. 2008. *Argumentation and Debate*. WADSWORTH CENGAGE Learning.

Minqing Hu and Bing Liu. 2004. Mining and summarizing customer reviews. *Proceedings of the tenth ACM SIGKDD international conference on Knowledge discovery and data mining*, pages 168–177.

Thorsten Joachims. 2002. Optimizing search engines using clickthrough data. In *Proceedings of the Eighth ACM SIGKDD International Conference on Knowledge Discovery and Data Mining*, KDD '02, pages 133–142, New York, NY, USA. ACM.

Mirella Lapata. 2003. Probabilistic text structuring: Experiments with sentence ordering. In *Proceedings of the 41st Annual Meeting on Association for Computational Linguistics - Volume 1*, ACL '03, pages 545–552, Stroudsburg, PA, USA. Association for Computational Linguistics.

William C. Mann and Sandra A. Thompson. 1988. Rhetorical structure theory: Toward a functional theory of text organization. *Text*, 8(3):243–281.

Christopher D. Manning, Mihai Surdeanu, John Bauer, Jenny Finkel, Steven J. Bethard, and David McClosky. 2014. The Stanford CoreNLP natural language processing toolkit. In *Proceedings of 52nd Annual Meeting of the Association for Computational Linguistics: System Demonstrations*, pages 55–60.

George A. Miller. 1995. Wordnet: A lexical database for English. *Communications of the ACM*, 38(11):39–41.

Courtney Napoles, Matthew Gormley, and Benjamin Van Durme. 2012. Annotated English Gigaword ldc2012t21. AKBC-WEKEX '12, pages 95–100. Association for Computational Linguistics.

Naoaki Okazaki. 2009. Classias: a collection of machine-learning algorithms for classification.

Jiwei Tan, Xiaojun Wan, and Jianguo Xiao. 2013. Learning to order natural language texts. *Proceedings of the 51st Annual Meeting of the Association for Computational Linguistics*, pages 87–91.

Towards Detecting Counter-considerations in Text

Andreas Peldszus
Applied Computational Linguistics
FSP Cognitive Science
University of Potsdam
peldszus@uni-potsdam.de

Manfred Stede
Applied Computational Linguistics
FSP Cognitive Science
University of Potsdam
stede@uni-potsdam.de

Abstract

Argumentation mining obviously involves finding support relations between statements, but many interesting instances of argumentation also contain counter-considerations, which the author mentions in order to preempt possible objections by the readers. A counter-consideration in monologue text thus involves a switch of perspective toward an imaginary opponent. We present a classification approach to classifying counter-considerations and apply it to two different corpora: a selection of very short argumentative texts produced in a text generation experiment, and a set of newspaper commentaries. As expected, the latter pose more difficulties, which we investigate in a brief error anaylsis.

1 Introduction

The exchange of argument and objection is obviously most typical for dialogue, but to a good extent it is also present in monologue text: Authors do not only provide justifications for their own position – they can also mention potential objections and then refute or outweigh them. In this way they demonstrate to have considered the position of "the other side", which altogether is designed to reinforce their own position. We use the term 'counter-consideration' in a general sense to cover all such moves of an author, no matter whether they are directed at the conclusion of the text or at an intermediate argument, or at some support relation, and irrespective of whether they are explicitly refuted by the author or merely mentioned and left outweighed by the mass of arguments in favour of the main claim.[1]

For an author, presenting a counter-consideration involves a switch of perspective by temporarily adopting the opposing viewpoint and then moving back to one's own. This is a move that generally requires some form of explicit linguistic marking so that the reader can follow the line of argumentation. The kinds of marking include explicit belief attribution followed by a contrastive connective signaling the return ("Some people think that X. However, this ..."), and there can also be quite compact mentions of objections, as in "Even though the project is expensive, we need to pursue it, because..."

Detecting counter-considerations is thus a subtask of argumentation mining. It involves identifying the two points of perspective switching, which we henceforth call a move from the *proponent role* to the *opponent role* and back. Thus the task can be operationalized as labelling segments of argumentative text in terms of these two roles. Then, counter-considerations are segments labeled as "opponent".

We study this classification problem using two different corpora: a colletion of user-generated short "microtexts", where we expect the task to be relatively easy, and a set of argumentative newspaper pieces that explicitly argue in favour of or against a particular position ('ProCon'). These texts are longer and more complex, and the opponent role can be encoded in quite subtle ways, so that we expect

[1]Govier (2011) discusses the role of such counter-considerations in 'pro and con' argumentation in more depth. Also, for a comprehensive overview of different notions of objections in argument analysis, see Walton (2009).

Proceedings of the 2nd Workshop on Argumentation Mining, pages 104–109,
Denver, Colorado, June 4, 2015.

the classification to be more difficult.

After looking at related work, Section 3 describes our corpora and the machine learning experiments. In Section 4, we evaluate the results and discuss the most common problems with the ProCon texts, and Section 5 concludes.

2 Related work

The majority of work on text-oriented argumentation mining concentrates on identifying just the "gist" of arguments, i.e., premises and conclusions. This holds, for example, for the well-known early approach of Mochales Palau and Moens (2009), and for the follow-up step on scheme classification (on top of detected premises/conclusions) by Feng and Hirst (2011).

Among the few approaches that do consider counter-considerations, Kang and Saint-Dizier (2014) analyze technical douments (largely instructional text), where the notion of exception to an argument plays a role, but its function is quite different from the perspective-switching that we discuss here.

Ong et al. (2014) work on student essays, which are somewhat more similar to "our" genres. Their task includes the recognition of sentence types (CurrentStudy, Hypothesis, Claim, Citation) and of *support* and *oppose* relations between sentences. For the complete task, the authors use eight hand-coded rules performing string matching using word lists and numbers (for identifying the year of a citation); thus the approach is geared toward finding relationships specifically between citations and will not generalize well to the broad class of counter-considerations.

A support/oppose distinction is also made by Stab and Gurevych (2014), who annotated a corpus of 90 essays (1673 sentences) with the central claim of the text (90 instances), claims of paragraph-size units (429), and premises (1033). Claims are marked with an attribute 'for' (365) or 'against' (64), but the authors do not report numbers on the stance of premises. Note however, that the stance of premises could be inferred by the relation structure, i.e. the sequence of supposing and opposing relations. Of the 1473 relations in the corpus, 161 are opposing. As the proportion of 'against' claims is also relatively low, the authors restrict their classification task, again, to the 'for' claims and the support relations.

Looking beyond the argumentation mining literature, elaborate approaches to subjectivity analysis are also relevant to us, as found in the *appraisal theory* of Martin and White (2005), whose multidimensional analysis also covers a speaker's consideration of conflicting standpoints. Appraisal is a very comprehensive scheme that is difficult to annotate (Read and Carroll, 2012a); thus its automatic classification is hard, as experiments by Read and Carroll (2012b) show. Our smaller task of role identification addressed here can be considered a subproblem of appraisal analysis.

3 Classification study

3.1 Corpora

As stated earlier, we worked with two different corpora in order to study the difference in task difficulty for short and simple "user-generated" texts versus newspaper articles.

The "argumentative microtext" corpus (Peldszus and Stede, 2015) is a new, freely available collection of 112 very short texts that were collected from human subjects, originally in German. Subjects received a prompt on an issue of public debate, usually in the form of a yes/no question (e.g., "Should shopping malls be open on Sundays?"), and they were asked to provide their answer to the question along with arguments in support. They were encouraged to also mention potential counter-considerations. The target length suggested to the subjects was five sentences. After the texts were collected, they were professionally translated to English, so that the corpus is now available in two languages. An example of an English text is:

> Health insurance companies should naturally cover alternative medical treatments. Not all practices and approaches that are lumped together under this term may have been proven in clinical trials, yet it's precisely their positive effect when accompanying conventional 'western' medical therapies that's been demonstrated as beneficial. Besides, many general practitioners offer such counselling and treatments in parallel anyway - and who would want to question their broad expertise?

The annotation of argumentation structure (common to both language versions) follows the scheme outlined in Peldszus and Stede (2013), which in turn is based on the work of Freeman (1991), and it includes different types of support and attack relations. The argumentative role per segment can be inferred from the relational structure. 21.7% of the 576 individual discourse segments bear the opponent role. As reported in Peldszus (2014), naive and untrained annotators reached an agreement of κ=.52 in distinguishing proponent and opponent on a subset of the corpus, while expert annotators achieved perfect agreement.

The ProCon corpus consists of 124 texts taken from a "pro and contra" column of the German newspaper *Der Tagesspiegel*. The setting for the content is essentially the same: A "should we do X or not / Is X good or bad / ..." question on an issue of public interest. The texts, however, are written by journalists, and a pro and a contra article appear next to each other in the paper (but they don't refer to each other). Typically they are 10-12 sentences long. While the microtexts are manually segmented, we use an automatic segmentation module for German to split the ProCon texts. This is a statistical system trained on a similar corpus, which aims at identifying clause-size segments on the output of a dependency parser (Bohnet, 2010). Segmentation leads to 2074 segments, which have then been annotated with the proponent/opponent label by two expert annotators. 8.3% of the individual 2074 segments bear the opponent role. Agreement between these experts had been tested on 24 manually segmented ProCon texts and resulted in κ=.74. Table 1a summarizes the corpus statistics.

To get a clearer picture of the distribution of opponent segments, we study their frequency and position in the individual texts: Table 1b shows the number of texts by the number (n) of included opponent segments, and Table 1c gives the percentage of opponent segments occurring in the first to fifth chunk of the text. While there is clear tendency for opponent segments to appear in the opening of a ProCon text, they are more equally spread in the microtexts.

3.2 Experiments

Feature sets We compare three different feature sets: two simple bag-of-word models as baselines and one model with additional features from automatic linguistic analysis. The first model (B) only extracts binary features for each lemma occurring in the target segment. The second model (B+C) additionally extracts these features from the preceding and the subsequent segment, thus providing a small context window. The full model (B+C+L) adds parsing-based features for the whole context window, such as pos-tags, lemma- and pos-tag-based dependency-parse triples, the morphology of the main verb (Bohnet, 2010), as well as lemma-bigrams. Discourse connectives are taken from a list by Stede (2002) and used both as individual items and as indicating a coherence relation (Cause, Contrast, etc.). Furthermore, we use some positional statistics such as relative segment position, segment length, and punctuation count.

Approach The goal is to assign the labels 'proponent' and 'opponent' to the individual segments. We trained a linear log-loss model using stochastic gradient descent learning as implemented in the Scikit learn library (Pedregosa et al., 2011). The learning rate is set to optimal decrease, and the class weights are adjusted according to class distribution. We used a nested 5x3 cross validation (CV), with the inner CV for tuning the hyper parameters (the regularization parameter alpha and the number of best features to select) and the outer CV for evaluation. We optimize macro averaged F1-score. The folding is stratified, randomly distributing the texts of the corpus while aiming to reproduce the overall label distribution in both training and test set.

All results are reported as average and standard deviation over the 50 folds resulting from 10 iterations of 5-fold cross validation. We use the following metrics: Cohen's Kappa κ, Macro average F1, Precision, Recall and F1 for the opponent class.

Results The performance of the classifiers is shown in Table 2.[2] Comparing the results for the two datasets confirms our assumption that the task is much harder on the ProCon texts. When comparing the different models, we observe that the simple baseline model without context performs poorly; adding context improves the results significantly.

[2]Similar results for an earlier version of the microtext corpus for this and other argumentation mining tasks have been presented in Peldszus (2014).

	microtexts	ProCon
texts	112	124
segments	576	2074
segments (proponent)	451	1902
segments (opponent)	125	172
segments per text	5.1±0.8	16.9±3.1
opp. seg. per text	1.1±0.7	1.4±1.5

(a) general statistics (averages with std. dev.)

n	microtexts	ProCon
0	15	46
1	74	32
2	18	16
3	5	17
4		6
5		3
6		3

(b) opponent frequency

p	microtexts	ProCon
1/5	16.0%	35.5%
2/5	23.2%	18.6%
3/5	17.6%	19.1%
4/5	28.8%	12.8%
5/5	14.4%	11.6%

(c) opponent position

Table 1: Corpus statistics: For details see Section 3.1.

The full featureset (B+C+L) always yields best results, except for a small drop of precision on the ProCon texts. The improvement of the full model over B+C is significant for the microtexts ($p < 0.003$ for κ, F1 macro and opponent F1, using Wilcoxon signed-rank test over the 50 folds), but not significant for the ProCon texts.

Feature selection mostly supports the classification of the ProCon texts, where the mass of extracted features impairs the generalization. Typically only 25 features were chosen. For the microtexts, reducing the features to the 50 best-performing ones still yields good but not the best results. One reason for the difference in feature selection behaviour between the datasets might be that the proportion of proponent and opponent labels is more skewed for the ProCons than for the microtexts. Another reason might be the richer set of expressions marking the role switch in the ProCon texts.

A common observation for both corpora is that the connective *aber* ('but') in the subsequent segment is the best predictor for an opponent role. Other important lexical items (also as part of dependency triples) are the modal particles *natürlich* ('of course', 'naturally') and *ja* (here in the reading: 'as is well-known'), and the auxiliary verb *mögen* (here: 'may'). All of these occur in the opponent role segment itself, and they have in common that they "color" a statement as something that the author concedes (but will overturn in the next step), which corresponds to the temporary change of perspective. As for differences between the corpora, we find that the connective *zwar*, which introduces a concessive minor clause, is very important in the microtexts but less prominent in ProCon. We attribute this to the microtext instruction of writing rather short texts, which supposedly leads the students to often formulating their counter-considerations as compact minor clauses, for which *zwar* ('granted that') is the perfect marker. Presumably for the same reason, we observe that the concessive subordinator *obwohl* ('although') is among the top-10 features for microtexts but not even among the top-50 for ProCon. In ProCon, the group of connectives indicating the Contrast coherence relation is a very good feature, and it is absent from the microtext top-50; recall, though, that the single connective *aber* ('but') is their strongest predictor, and the very similar *doch* is also highly predictive.

4 Discussion and error analysis

Proponent/Opponent role identification is not an easy classification task. For the microtexts, we regard the results as fairly satisfactory. For ProCon, there is a significant drop in F1 macro, and even more so for the opponent prec/rec/F1. This was in principle to be expected, but we wanted to know reasons and thus performed a qualitative error analysis.

Segmentation. As pointed out, ProCon texts have been automatically segmented, which leads to a number of errors that generate some of the classification problems; we found, however, that this is only a small factor.

There are other points to remark on segmentation, though. First, we find 37 cases where more than one opponent role segment appear in a sequence (mostly two of them, but ranging up to six), as compared to 68 cases of individual segments. The sequences pose problems for segment-wise classification focusing on perspective *change* signals, especially when the context window is small. Many of

	microtexts			ProCon		
	B	B+C	B+C+R	B	B+C	B+C+R
κ	.375±.109	.503±.080	.545±.098	.187±.064	.320±.078	.323±.091
F1 macro	.685±.056	.751±.040	.772±.049	.588±.033	.659±.040	.660±.047
opponent P.	.548±.097	.647±.081	.668±.096	.428±.165	.370±.063	.361±.074
opponent R.	.474±.146	.575±.084	.626±.108	.163±.054	.400±.109	.422±.117
opponent F1	.497±.101	.604±.065	.640±.081	.225±.064	.378±.073	.382±.083

Table 2: Results for role-identification, reported as average and standard deviation

the sequences occur right at the beginning of the text, where the author provides an extended description from the opponent's view, and then switches to his own perspective. Correctly identifying complete sequences would require a deeper analysis of cohesive devices for finding continuation or break of topic/perspective/argumentative orientation.

Also, notice that many of the sequences actually contain argumentative sub-structure, where, for example, the possible objection is first backed up with purported evidence and then refuted.

Here, the question of segmentation grain-size arises. In the present annotation, we do not label segments as 'opponent role' when they include not only the opponent's objection but also the author's refutation or dismissal. This is because on the whole, the segment conveys the author's (proponent's) position. A translated example from the corpus is: "Not convincing at all is the argument that to the government, teachers should be worth more than a one-Euro-job." Besides such cases of explicit dismissal, we find, for instance, concessive PPs that include an opposing argument: "Despite the high cost, the building must be constructed now." We leave it to future work to dissect such complex segments and split them into an opponent and a proponent part.

Connectives. Contrastive connectives are very good indicators for changing back from the opponent role to the proponent role, but unfortunately they occur quite frequently also with other functions. There are 105 opponent segments or sequences thereof in the corpus, but 195 instances of the words *aber* and *doch*, which are the most frequent contrastive connectives. Therefore, their presence needs to be correlated with other features in order to serve as reliable indicators.

Language. While our focus in this paper was on the performance difference between the German microtexts and the ProCon texts, we want to mention that the overall classification results for microtexts do hardly differ between the German and the English version. This leads us to expect that for English pro/contra commentaries, we would also obtain results similar to those for German.

5 Conclusion

Counter-considerations may be regarded as not the most important aspects of an argumentation, but in many essayistic text genres, they constitute rhetorical moves that authors quite frequently advance to strengthen their points. After all, refuting a potential objection is in itself an argument in support of the conclusion. Almost two thirds of the newspaper pro/contra texts in our corpus have counter-considerations, and so we think these devices are definitely worth studying in order to arrive at complete argumentation analyses.

Casting the problem as a segment classification task, we obtained good results on our corpus of microtexts, whereas we see room for improvement for the longer and more complex pro/contra newspaper texts. Our error analysis identified several directions for future work, which will also include testing a sequence labelling approach to see whether the regularities in signalling perspective changes can be captured more easily, especially for the many cases of contiguous sequences of opponent role segments.

Acknowledgments

We are grateful to the anonymous reviewers for their thoughtful comments and suggestions on improving the paper. The first author was supported by a grant from Cusanuswerk.

References

Bernd Bohnet. 2010. Very high accuracy and fast dependency parsing is not a contradiction. In *Proceedings of the 23rd International Conference on Computational Linguistics*, COLING '10, pages 89–97, Stroudsburg, PA, USA. Association for Computational Linguistics.

Vanessa Wei Feng and Graeme Hirst. 2011. Classifying arguments by scheme. In *Proceedings of the 49th Annual Meeting of the Association for Computational Linguistics: Human Language Technologies - Volume 1*, pages 987–996, Stroudsburg, PA, USA. Association for Computational Linguistics.

James B. Freeman. 1991. *Dialectics and the Macrostructure of Argument*. Foris, Berlin.

Trudy Govier. 2011. More on counter-considerations. In *Proceedings of International Conference of the Ontario Society for the Study of Argumentation (OSSA)*, pages 1–10, Windsor/Ontario.

Juyeon Kang and Patrick Saint-Dizier. 2014. A discourse grammar for processing arguments in context. In *Computational Models of Argument - Proceedings of COMMA 2014, Atholl Palace Hotel, Scottish Highlands, UK, September 9-12, 2014*, volume 266 of *Frontiers in Artificial Intelligence and Applications*, pages 43–50. IOS Press.

James R. Martin and Peter R. R. White. 2005. *The Language of Evaluation: Appraisal in English*. Palgrave Macmillan, Houndsmills/New York.

Raquel Mochales Palau and Marie-Francine Moens. 2009. Argumentation mining: the detection, classification and structure of arguments in text. In *Proceedings of the Twelfth International Conference on Artificial Intelligence and Law (ICAIL 2009), Barcelona, Spain*, pages 98–109. ACM.

Nathan Ong, Diane Litman, and Alexandra Brusilovsky. 2014. Ontology-based argument mining and automatic essay scoring. In *Proceedings of the First Workshop on Argumentation Mining*, pages 24–28, Baltimore, Maryland, June. Association for Computational Linguistics.

F. Pedregosa, G. Varoquaux, A. Gramfort, V. Michel, B. Thirion, O. Grisel, M. Blondel, P. Prettenhofer, R. Weiss, V. Dubourg, J. Vanderplas, A. Passos, D. Cournapeau, M. Brucher, M. Perrot, and E. Duchesnay. 2011. Scikit-learn: Machine learning in Python. *Journal of Machine Learning Research*, 12:2825–2830.

Andreas Peldszus and Manfred Stede. 2013. From argument diagrams to automatic argument mining: A survey. *International Journal of Cognitive Informatics and Natural Intelligence (IJCINI)*, 7(1):1–31.

Andreas Peldszus and Manfred Stede. 2015. An annotated corpus of argumentative microtexts. In *Proceedings of the First Conference on Argumentation*, Lisbon, Portugal, June. to appear.

Andreas Peldszus. 2014. Towards segment-based recognition of argumentation structure in short texts. In *Proceedings of the First Workshop on Argumentation Mining*, Baltimore, U.S., June. Association for Computational Linguistics.

Jonathon Read and John Carroll. 2012a. Annotating expressions of appraisal in english. *Language Resources and Evaluation*, 421–447(3).

Jonathon Read and John Carroll. 2012b. Weakly-supervised appraisal analysis. *Linguistic Issues in Language Technology*, 8(2).

Christian Stab and Iryna Gurevych. 2014. Annotating argument components and relations in persuasive essays. In *Proceedings of COLING 2014, the 25th International Conference on Computational Linguistics: Technical Papers*, pages 1501–1510. Dublin City University and Association for Computational Linguistics.

Manfred Stede. 2002. DiMLex: A Lexical Approach to Discourse Markers. In Vittorio Di Tomaso Alessandro Lenci, editor, *Exploring the Lexicon - Theory and Computation*. Edizioni dell'Orso, Alessandria, Italy.

Douglas Walton. 2009. Objections, rebuttals and refutations. In *Proceedings of International Conference of the Ontario Society for the Study of Argumentation (OSSA)*, pages 1–10, Windsor/Ontario.

Identifying Prominent Arguments in Online Debates Using Semantic Textual Similarity

Filip Boltužić and **Jan Šnajder**
University of Zagreb, Faculty of Electrical Engineering and Computing
Text Analysis and Knowledge Engineering Lab
Unska 3, 10000 Zagreb, Croatia
{filip.boltuzic,jan.snajder}@fer.hr

Abstract

Online debates sparkle argumentative discussions from which generally accepted arguments often emerge. We consider the task of unsupervised identification of prominent argument in online debates. As a first step, in this paper we perform a cluster analysis using semantic textual similarity to detect similar arguments. We perform a preliminary cluster evaluation and error analysis based on cluster-class matching against a manually labeled dataset.

1 Introduction

Argumentation mining aims to detect the argumentative discourse structure in text. It is an emerging field in the intersection of natural language processing, logic-based reasoning, and argumentation theory; see (Moens, 2014) for a recent overview.

While most work on argumentation mining has focused on well-structured (e.g., legal) text, recently attention has also turned to user-generated content such as online debates and product reviews. The main motivation is to move beyond simple opinion mining and discover the reasons underlying opinions. As users' comments are generally less well-structured and noisy, argumentation mining proper (extraction of argumentative structures) is rather difficult. However, what seems to be a sensible first step is to identify the *arguments* (also referred to as *reasons* and *claims*) expressed by users to back up their opinions.

In this work we focus on online debates. Given a certain topic, a number of prominent arguments often emerge in the debate, and the majority of users will back up their stance by one or more of these arguments. The problem, however, is that linking users' statements to arguments is far from trivial. Besides language variability, due to which the same argument can be expressed in infinitely many ways, many other factors add to the variability, such as entailment, implicit premises, value judgments, etc. This is aggravated by the fact that most users express their arguments in rather confusing and poorly worded manner. Another principal problem is that, in general, the prominent arguments for a given topic are not known in advance. Thus, to identify the arguments expressed by the users, one first needs to come up with a set of prominent arguments. Manual analysis of the possible arguments does not generalize to unseen topic nor does it scale to large datasets.

In this paper, we are concerned with automatically identifying prominent arguments in online debates. This is a formidable task, but as a first step towards this goal, we present a cluster analysis of users' argumentative statements from online debates. The underlying assumption is that statements that express the same argument will be semantically more similar than statements that express different arguments, so that we can group together similar statements into clusters that correspond to arguments. We operationalize this by using hierarchical clustering based on semantic textual similarity (STS), defined as the degree of semantic equivalence between two texts (Agirre et al., 2012).

The purpose of our study is twofold. First, we wish to investigate the notion of prominent arguments, considering in particular the variability in expressing arguments, and how well it can be captured by semantic similarity. Secondly, from a more practical perspective, we investigate the possibility of automatically identifying prominent arguments, setting a baseline for the task of unsupervised argument identification.

2 Related Work

The pioneering work in argumentation mining is that of Moens et al. (2007), who addressed mining of argumentation from legal documents. Recently, the

Proceedings of the 2nd Workshop on Argumentation Mining, pages 110–115,
Denver, Colorado, June 4, 2015.

focus has also moved to mining from user-generated content, such as online debates (Cabrio and Villata, 2012), discussions on regulations (Park and Cardie, 2014), and product reviews (Ghosh et al., 2014).

Boltužić and Šnajder (2014) introduced *argument recognition* as the task of identifying what arguments, from a predefined set of arguments, have been used in users comments, and how. They frame the problem as multiclass classification and describe a model with similarity- and entailment-based features.

Essentially the same task of argument recognition, but at the level of sentences, is addressed by Hasan and Ng (2014). They use a probabilistic framework for argument recognition (reason classification) jointly with the related task of *stance classification*. Similarly, Conrad et al. (2012) detect spans of text containing *arguing subjectivity* and label them with *argument tags* using a model that relies on sentiment, discourse, and similarity features.

The above approaches are supervised and rely on datasets manually annotated with arguments from a predefined set of arguments. In contrast, in this work we explore unsupervised argument identification. A similar task is described by Trabelsi and Zaïane (2014), who use topic modeling to extract words and phrases describing *arguing expressions*, and also discuss how the arguing expressions could be clustered according to the arguments they express.

3 Data and Model

Dataset. We conduct our study on the dataset of users' posts compiled by Hasan and Ng (2014). The dataset is acquired from two-side online debate forums on four topics: "Obama", "Marijuana", "Gay rights", and "Abortion". Each post is assigned a stance label (*pro* or *con*), provided by the author of the post. Furthermore, each post is split up into sentences and each sentence is manually labeled with one argument from a predefined set of arguments (different for each topic). Note that all sentences in the dataset are argumentative; non-argumentative sentences were removed from the dataset (the ratio of argumentative sentences varies from 20.4% to 43.7%, depending on the topic). Hasan and Ng (2014) report high levels of inter-annotator agreement (between 0.61 and 0.67, depending on the topic).

For our analysis, we removed sentences labeled with rarely occurring arguments (<2%), allowing us to focus on prominent arguments. The dataset we work with contains 3104 sentences ("Abortion" 814, "Gay rights" 824, "Marijuana" 836, and "Obama" 630) and 47 different arguments (25 pro and 22 con, on average 12 arguments per topic). The majority of sentences (2028 sentences) is labeled with pro arguments. The average sentence length is 14 words.

Argument similarity. We experiment with two approaches for measuring the similarity of arguments.

Vector-space similarity: We represent statements as vectors in a semantic space. We use two representations: (1) a bag-of-word (BoW) vector, weighted by inverse sentence frequency, and (2) a distributed representation based on the recently proposed neural network skip-gram model of Mikolov et al. (2013a).

As noted by Ramage et al. (2009), BoW has shown to be a powerful baseline for semantic similarity. The rationale for weighting by inverse sentence frequency (akin to inverse document frequency) is that more frequently used words are less argument-specific and hence should contribute less to the similarity.

On the other hand, distributed representations have been shown to work exceptionally well (outperforming BoW) for representing the meaning of individual words. Furthermore, they have been shown to model quite well the semantic composition of short phrases via simple vector addition (Mikolov et al., 2013b). To build a vector for a sentence, we simply sum the distributed vectors of the individual words.[1]

For both representations, we remove the stopwords before building the vectors. To compute the similarity between two sentences, we compute the cosine similarity between their corresponding vectors.

Semantic textual similarity (STS): Following on the work of Boltužić and Šnajder (2014), we use an off-the-shelf STS system developed by Šarić et al. (2012). It is a supervised system trained on manually labeled STS dataset, utilizing a rich set of text comparison features (incl. vector-space comparisons). Given two sentences, the system outputs a real-valued similarity score, which we use directly as the similarity between two argument statements.

[1] We use the pre-trained vectors available at `https://code.google.com/p/word2vec/`

Clustering. For clustering, we use the hierarchical agglomerative clustering (HAC) algorithm (see (Xu et al., 2005) for an overview of clustering algorithms). This is motivated by three considerations. First, HAC allows us to work directly with similarities coming from the STS systems, instead of requiring explicit vector-space representations as some other algorithms. Secondly, it produces hierarchical structures, allowing us to investigate the granularity of arguments. Finally, HAC is a deterministic algorithm, therefore its results are more stable.

HAC works with a distance matrix computed for all pairs of instances. We compute this matrix for all pairs of sentences s_1 and s_2 from the corresponding similarities: $1 - cos(v_1, v_2)$ for vector-space similarity and $1/(1 + sim(s_1, s_2))$ for STS similarity. Linkage criterion has been shown to greatly affect clustering performance. We experiment with complete linkage (farthest neighbor clustering) and Ward's method (Ward Jr, 1963), which minimizes the within-cluster variance (the latter is applicable only to vector-space similarity). Note that we do not cluster separately the statements from the pro and con stances. This allows us to investigate to what extent stance can be captured by semantic similarity of the arguments, while it also corresponds to a more realistic setup.

4 Cluster Analysis

4.1 Analysis 1: Clustering Models

Evaluation metrics. A number of clustering evaluation metrics have been proposed in the literature. We adopt the external evaluation approach, which compares the hypothesized clusters against target clusters. We use argument labels of Hasan and Ng (2014) as target clusters. As noted by Amigó et al. (2009), external cluster evaluation is a non-trivial task and there is no consensus on the best approach. We therefore chose to use two established, but rather different measures: the Adjusted Rand Index (ARI) (Hubert and Arabie, 1985) and the information-theoretic V-measure (Rosenberg and Hirschberg, 2007). ARI of 0 indicates clustering expected by chance and 1 indicates perfect clustering. The V-measure trade-offs measures of homogeneity (h) and completeness (c). It ranges from 0 to 1, with 1 being perfect clustering.

Results. We cluster the sentences from the four topics separately, using the gold number of clusters for each topic. Results are shown in Table 1. Overall, the best model is skip-gram with Ward's linkage, generally outperforming the other models considered in terms of both ARI and V-measure. This model also results in the most consistent clusters in terms of balanced homogeneity and completeness. Ward's linkage seems to work better than complete linkage for both BoW and skip-gram. STS-based clustering performs comparable to the baseline BoW model. We attribute this to the fact that the STS model was trained on different domains, and therefore probably does not extend well to the kind of argument-specific similarity we are trying to capture here.

We observe quite some variance in performance across topics. Arguments from the "Gay rights" topic seems to be most difficult to cluster, while "Marijuana" seems to be the easiest. In absolute terms, the clustering performance of the skip-gram model is satisfactory given the simplicity of the model. In subsequent analysis, we focus on the skip-gram model with Ward's linkage and the "Marijuana" topic.

4.2 Analysis 2: Clustering Quality

Cluster-class matching. To examine the cluster quality and clustering errors, we do a manual cluster-class matching for the "Marijuana" topic against the target clusters, using again the gold number of clusters (10). Cluster-matching is done on a class majority basis, resulting in six gold classes matched. Table 2 shows the results. We list the top three gold classes (and the percentage of sentences from these classes) in each of our clusters, and the top three clusters (and the percentage of sentences from these clusters) in each of the gold classes. Some gold classes (#4, #9) are frequently co-occurring, indicating their high similarity. We characterize each cluster by its medoid (the sentence closest to cluster centroid).

Error analysis. Grouping statements into coherent clusters proved a challenging task. Our preliminary analysis indicates that the main problems are related to (a) need for background knowledge, (b) use of idiomatic language, (c) grammatical errors, (d) opposing arguments, and (e) too fine/coarse gold argument granularity. We show some sample errors in Table 3, but leave a detailed error analysis for future work.

Ex. *#knowledge* demonstrates the need for background knowledge (exports are government regu-

Model (linkage)	"Obama"				"Marijuana"				"Gay rights"				"Abortion"			
	h	c	V	ARI	h	c	V	ARI	h	c	V	ARI	h	c	V	ARI
BoW (Complete)	.15	.15	.15	.03	.04	.04	.04	.00	.04	.04	.04	.01	.05	.04	.04	.01
BoW (Ward's)	.22	**.34**	.27	.04	.15	.20	.17	.02	.13	**.17**	**.15**	.04	.22	**.27**	**.24**	.07
Skip-gram (Complete)	.18	.26	.21	.04	.09	.22	.13	.02	.09	.10	.10	.04	.17	.24	.20	.03
Skip-gram (Ward's)	**.30**	.29	**.30**	**.10**	**.25**	**.24**	**.25**	**.19**	**.16**	.15	**.15**	**.07**	**.24**	.22	.23	**.08**
STS (Complete)	.11	.11	.11	.02	.05	.05	.05	.03	.05	.05	.05	.01	.06	.06	.06	.02

Table 1: External evaluation of clustering models on the four topics

lated). A colloquial expression (*pot*) is used in Ex. *#colloquial*. In *#oppose*, the statement is assigned to a cluster of opposing argument. In Ex. *#general* our model predicts a more coarse argument.

Another observation concerns the level of argument granularity. In the previous analysis, we used the gold number of clusters. We note, however, that the level of granularity is to a certain extent arbitrary. To exemplify this, we look at the dendrogram (Fig. 1) of the last 15 HAC steps on the "Marijuana" topic. Medoids of clusters divided at point *CD* are (1) *the economy would get billions of dollars (...) no longer would this revenue go directly into the black market.* and (2) *If the tax on cigarettes can be $5.00/pack imagine what we could tax pot for!*. These could well be treated as separate arguments about *economy* and *taxes*, respectively. On the other hand, clusters merged at *CM* consists mostly of gold arguments (1) *Damages our bodies* and (2) *Responsible for brain damage*, which could be represented by a single argument *Damaging our entire bodies*. The dendrogram also suggests that the 10-cluster cut is perhaps not optimal for the similarity measure used.

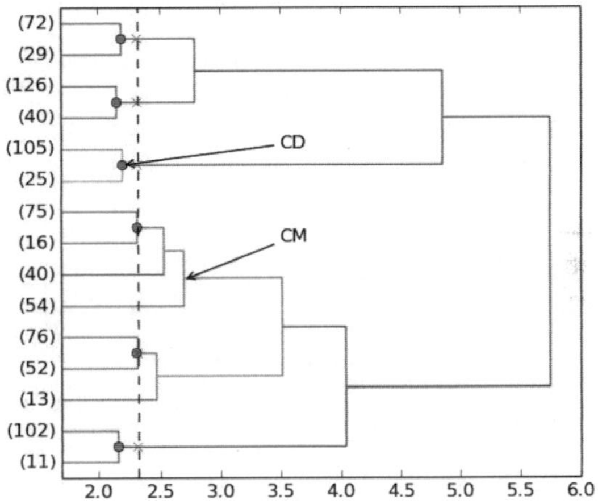

Figure 1: Dendrogram for the "Marijuana" topic (the dashed line shows the 10-clusters cut)

5 Conclusion

In this preliminary study, we addressed unsupervised identification of prominent arguments in online debates, using hierarchical clustering based on textual similarity. Our best performing model, a simple distributed representation of argument sentence, performs in a 0.15 to 0.30 V-measure range. Our analysis of clustering quality and errors on manually matched cluster-classes revealed that there are difficult cases that textual similarity cannot capture. A number of errors can be traced down to the fact that it is sometimes difficult to draw clear-cut boundaries between arguments.

In this study we relied on simple text similarity models. One way to extend our work would be to experiment with models better tuned for argument similarity, based on a more detailed error analysis. Also of interest are the internal evaluation criteria for determining the optimal argument granularity.

A more fundamental issue, raised by one reviewer, are the potential long-term limitations of the clustering approach to argument recognition. While we believe that there is a lot of room for improvement, we think that identifying arguments fully automatically is hardly feasible. However, we are convinced that argument clustering will prove valuable in human-led argumentative analysis. Argument clustering may also prove useful for semi-supervised argument recognition, where it may be used as unsupervised pre-training followed by supervised fine-tuning.

Acknowledgments. We thank the anonymous reviewers for their many comments and suggestions.

Hypothesized clustering			Gold classes		
Id	Classes	Cluster medoid	Id	Clusters	Gold argument
1	**10 (54%)** 2 (12%) 6 (10%)	*Tobacco and alcohol are both legal and widely used in the US, (...) If the abuse of marijuana is harmful, isn't the abuse of tobacco or alcohol equally life threatening? (...)*	1	5 (23%) 9 (19%) 10 (18%)	*Used as a medicine for its positive effects*
2	**4 (92%)** 9 (8%)	*The biggest effect would be an end to brutal mandatory sentencing of long jail times that has ruined so many young peoples lives.*	2	1 (33%) 9 (28%) 3 (15%)	*Responsible for brain damage*
3	**9 (44%)** 4 (25%) 7 (8%)	*Legalizing pot alone would not end the war on drugs. It would help (...) my personal opinion would be the only way to completely end the war on drugs would be to legalize everything.*	3	9 (41%) 3 (23%) 10 (23%)	*Causes crime*
4	**8 (37%)** 1 (22%) 10 (17%)	*What all these effects have in common is that they result from changes in the brain's control centers (...) So, when marijuana disturbs functions centered in the deep control centers, disorienting changes in the mind occur (...)*	4	9 (40%) 3 (26%) 10 (12%)	*Prohibition violates human rights*
5	**1 (45%)** 6 (18%) 8 (10%)	*People with pre-existing mental disorders also tend to abuse alcohol and tobacco. (...) the link between marijuana use and mental illness may be an instance when correlation does not equal causation.*	5	6 (25%) 7 (25%) 4 (18%)	*Does not cause any damage to our bodies*
6	**5 (63%)** 10 (31%) 1 (6%)	*There are thousands of deaths every year from tobacco and alcohol, yet there has never been a recorded death due to marijuana.*	6	9 (29%) 1 (19%) 7 (16%)	*Damages our bodies*
7	**10 (48%)** 5 (13%) 6 (12%)	*as far as it goes for medicinal purposes, marijuana does not cure anything (...) It is for the sole purpose of numbing the pain in cancer patients (...) and also making patients hungry so they eat more and gain weight on their sick bodies*	7	9 (39%) 3 (30%) 1 (9%)	*Highly addictive*
8	**9 (92%)**	*the economy would get billions of dollars in a new industry if it were legalized (...) no longer would this revenue go directly into the black market.*	8	4 (44%) 7 (16%) 9 (16%)	*If legalized, people will use marijuana and other drugs more*
9	**4 (30%)** 9 (13%) 10 (11%)	*(...) I think it ridiculous that people want to legalise something that has four - seven times the amount of tar (the cancer causing agent) in one cone than in one cigarette (...)*	9	8 (53%) 3 (25%) 9 (10%)	*Legalized marijuana can be controlled and regulated by the government*
10	**10 (30%)** 9 (19%) 4 (15%)	*But I'm not gonna tell anyone they can't smoke pot or do meth because I don't like it.*	10	1 (36%) 7 (21%) 10 (18%)	*Not addictive*

Table 2: Manual cluster-class matching for the "Marijuana" topic and the gold number of clusters

Id	Statement	Hypothesized clustering argument	Gold argument
#knowledge	*Pot is also one of the most high priced exports of Central American Countries and the Carribean*	*Not addictive*	*Legalized marijuana can be controlled and regulated by the government*
#colloquial	*If I want to use pot, that is my business!*	*Legalized marijuana can be controlled and regulated by the government*	*Prohibition violates human rights*
#opposing	*(...) immediately following the legalization of the drug would cause widespread pandemonium. (...)*	*Legalized marijuana can be controlled and regulated by the government*	*If legalized, people will use marijuana and other drugs more*
#general	*The user's psychomotor coordination becomes impaired (...), narrow attention span, "depersonalization, euphoria or depression (...)*	*Damages our bodies*	*Responsible for brain damage*

Table 3: Error analysis examples for the "Marijuana" topic

References

Eneko Agirre, Mona Diab, Daniel Cer, and Aitor Gonzalez-Agirre. 2012. SemEval-2012 task 6: A pilot on semantic textual similarity. In *Proceedings of the First Joint Conference on Lexical and Computational Semantics-Volume 1: Proceedings of the main conference and the shared task, and Volume 2: Proceedings of the Sixth International Workshop on Semantic Evaluation*, pages 385–393.

Enrique Amigó, Julio Gonzalo, Javier Artiles, and Felisa Verdejo. 2009. A comparison of extrinsic clustering evaluation metrics based on formal constraints. *Information retrieval*, 12(4):461–486.

Filip Boltužić and Jan Šnajder. 2014. Back up your stance: Recognizing arguments in online discussions. In *Proceedings of the First Workshop on Argumentation Mining*, pages 49–58.

Elena Cabrio and Serena Villata. 2012. Combining textual entailment and argumentation theory for supporting online debates interactions. In *Proceedings of the 50th Annual Meeting of the Association for Computational Linguistics: Short Papers-Volume 2*, pages 208–212.

Alexander Conrad, Janyce Wiebe, et al. 2012. Recognizing arguing subjectivity and argument tags. In *Proceedings of the Workshop on Extra-Propositional Aspects of Meaning in Computational Linguistics*, pages 80–88.

Debanjan Ghosh, Smaranda Muresan, Nina Wacholder, Mark Aakhus, and Matthew Mitsui. 2014. Analyzing argumentative discourse units in online interactions. In *Proceedings of the First Workshop on Argumentation Mining*, pages 39–48.

Kazi Saidul Hasan and Vincent Ng. 2014. Why are you taking this stance? Identifying and classifying reasons in ideological debates. In *Proceedings of the 2014 Conference on Empirical Methods in Natural Language Processing (EMNLP)*, pages 751–762.

Lawrence Hubert and Phipps Arabie. 1985. Comparing partitions. *Journal of classification*, 2(1):193–218.

Tomas Mikolov, Kai Chen, Greg Corrado, and Jeffrey Dean. 2013a. Efficient estimation of word representations in vector space. In *Proceedings of ICLR*, Scottsdale, AZ, USA.

Tomas Mikolov, Ilya Sutskever, Kai Chen, Greg S Corrado, and Jeff Dean. 2013b. Distributed representations of words and phrases and their compositionality. In *Advances in Neural Information Processing Systems*, pages 3111–3119.

Marie-Francine Moens, Erik Boiy, Raquel Mochales Palau, and Chris Reed. 2007. Automatic detection of arguments in legal texts. In *Proceedings of the 11th International Conference on Artificial Intelligence and Law*, pages 225–230.

Marie-Francine Moens. 2014. Argumentation mining: Where are we now, where do we want to be and how do we get there? In *Post-proceedings of the forum for information retrieval evaluation (FIRE 2013)*.

Joonsuk Park and Claire Cardie. 2014. Identifying appropriate support for propositions in online user comments. *ACL 2014*, pages 29–38.

Daniel Ramage, Anna N Rafferty, and Christopher D Manning. 2009. Random walks for text semantic similarity. In *Proceedings of the 2009 workshop on graph-based methods for natural language processing*, pages 23–31.

Andrew Rosenberg and Julia Hirschberg. 2007. V-measure: A conditional entropy-based external cluster evaluation measure. In *EMNLP-CoNLL*, volume 7, pages 410–420.

Frane Šarić, Goran Glavaš, Mladen Karan, Jan Šnajder, and Bojana Dalbelo Bašić. 2012. Takelab: Systems for measuring semantic text similarity. In *Proceedings of the Sixth International Workshop on Semantic Evaluation (SemEval 2012)*, pages 441–448, Montréal, Canada, 7-8 June.

Amine Trabelsi and Osmar R Zaïane. 2014. Finding arguing expressions of divergent viewpoints in online debates. In *Proceedings of the 5th Workshop on Language Analysis for Social Media (LASM)@ EACL*, pages 35–43.

Joe H Ward Jr. 1963. Hierarchical grouping to optimize an objective function. *Journal of the American statistical association*, 58(301):236–244.

Rui Xu, Donald Wunsch, et al. 2005. Survey of clustering algorithms. *Neural Networks, IEEE Transactions on*, 16(3):645–678.

And That's A Fact: Distinguishing Factual and Emotional Argumentation in Online Dialogue

Shereen Oraby*, **Lena Reed***, **Ryan Compton***,
Ellen Riloff †, **Marilyn Walker*** and **Steve Whittaker***
* University of California Santa Cruz
{soraby,lireed,rcompton,mawalker,swhittak}@ucsc.edu
† University of Utah
riloff@cs.utah.edu

Abstract

We investigate the characteristics of factual and emotional argumentation styles observed in online debates. Using an annotated set of FACTUAL and FEELING debate forum posts, we extract patterns that are highly correlated with factual and emotional arguments, and then apply a bootstrapping methodology to find new patterns in a larger pool of unannotated forum posts. This process automatically produces a large set of patterns representing linguistic expressions that are highly correlated with factual and emotional language. Finally, we analyze the most discriminating patterns to better understand the defining characteristics of factual and emotional arguments.

1 Introduction

Human lives are being lived online in transformative ways: people can now ask questions, solve problems, share opinions, or discuss current events with anyone they want, at any time, in any location, on any topic. The purposes of these exchanges are varied, but a significant fraction of them are argumentative, ranging from hot-button political controversies (e.g., national health care) to religious interpretation (e.g., Biblical exegesis). And while the study of the structure of arguments has a long lineage in psychology (Cialdini, 2000) and rhetoric (Hunter, 1987), large shared corpora of natural informal argumentative dialogues have only recently become available.

Natural informal dialogues exhibit a much broader range of argumentative styles than found in traditional work on argumentation (Marwell and Schmitt, 1967; Cialdini, 2000; McAlister et al., 2014; Reed and Rowe, 2004). Recent work has begun to model different aspects of these natural informal arguments, with tasks including stance classification (Somasundaran and Wiebe, 2010; Walker et al., 2012), argument summarization (Misra et al., 2015), sarcasm detection (Justo et al., 2014), and work on the detailed structure of arguments (Biran and Rambow, 2011; Purpura et al., 2008; Yang and Cardie, 2013). Successful models of these tasks have many possible applications in sentiment detection, automatic summarization, argumentative agents (Zuckerman et al., 2015), and in systems that support human argumentative behavior (Rosenfeld and Kraus, 2015).

Our research examines FACTUAL versus FEELING argument styles, drawing on annotations provided in the Internet Argument Corpus (IAC) (Walker et al., 2012). This corpus includes quote-response pairs that were manually annotated with respect to whether the response is primarily a FACTUAL or FEELING based argument, as Section 2.1 describes in more detail. Figure 1 provides examples of responses in the IAC (paired with preceding quotes to provide context), along with the response's FACTUAL vs. FEELING label.

FACTUAL responses may try to bolster their argument by providing statistics related to a position, giving historical or scientific background, or presenting specific examples or data. There is clearly a relationship between a proposition being FACTUAL versus OBJECTIVE or VERIDICAL, although each of these different labelling tasks may elicit differences from annotators (Wiebe and Riloff, 2005; Riloff and

Proceedings of the 2nd Workshop on Argumentation Mining, pages 116–126,
Denver, Colorado, June 4, 2015.

Wiebe, 2003; Saurí and Pustejovsky, 2009; Park and Cardie, 2014).

Class	Debate Forum Dialogue
FACT	**Quote:** Even though our planet is getting warmer, it is still a lot cooler than it was 4000 years ago. **Response:** *The average global temperature follows a sinusoidal pattern, the general consensus is we are supposed to be approaching a peak. Projections show that instead of peaking, there will be continue to be an increase in average global temperature.*
FACT	**Quote:** "When you go to war against your enemies...suppose you see a beautiful woman whom you desire...you shall take her..and she shall marry you." - Deut. 21:10 **Response:** *Read to the very end of the verse. "If you are not pleased with her, let her go wherever she wishes. You must not sell her or treat her as a slave, since you have dishonored her."*
FEEL	**Quote:** Talk about begging the question! I don't want your gun, and if such a law were passed it's not my job to enforce the law. **Response:** *I see you are willing to violate my constitutional rights yet you expect someone else to do your dirty work.... How typical.*
FEEL	**Quote:** "WASHINGTON – Supreme Court aspirant Sonia Sotomayor said Tuesday that she considers the question of abortion rights is settled precedent and says there is a constitutional right to privacy. The federal appeals court judge was asked at her confirmation...." **Response:** *While I'm still iffy on her with the whole New Haven case, and her off-the-bench comments on race, this is one thing I commend her for and agree completely with.*

Figure 1: Examples of FACTUAL and FEELING based debate forum Quotes and Responses. Only the responses were labeled for FACT vs. FEEL.

The FEELING responses may seem to lack argumentative merit, but previous work on argumentation describes situations in which such arguments can be effective, such as the use of emotive arguments to draw attention away from the facts, or to frame a discussion in a particular way (Walton, 2010; Macagno and Walton, 2014). Furthermore, work on persuasion suggest that FEELING based arguments can be more persuasive in particular circumstances, such as when the hearer shares a basis for social identity with the source (speaker) (Chaiken, 1980; Petty and Cacioppo, 1986; Benoit, 1987; Cacioppo et al., 1983; Petty et al., 1981). However none of this work has documented the linguistic patterns that characterize the differences in these argument types, which is a necessary first step to their automatic recognition or classification. Thus the goal of this paper is to use computational methods for pattern-learning on conversational arguments to catalog linguistic expressions and stylistic properties that distinguish Factual from Emotional arguments in these on-line debate forums.

Section 2.1 describes the manual annotations for FACTUAL and FEELING in the IAC corpus. Section 2.2 then describes how we generate lexico-syntactic patterns that occur in both types of argument styles. We use a weakly supervised pattern learner in a bootstrapping framework to automatically generate lexico-syntactic patterns from both annotated and unannotated debate posts. Section 3 evaluates the precision and recall of the FACTUAL and FEELING patterns learned from the annotated texts and after bootstrapping on the unannotated texts. We also present results for a supervised learner with bag-of-word features to assess the difficulty of this task. Finally, Section 4 presents analyses of the linguistic expressions found by the pattern learner and presents several observations about the different types of linguistic structures found in FACTUAL and FEELING based argument styles. Section 5 discusses related research, and Section 6 sums up and proposes possible avenues for future work.

2 Pattern Learning for Factual and Emotional Arguments

We first describe the corpus of online debate posts used for our research, and then present a bootstrapping method to identify linguistic expressions associated with FACTUAL and FEELING arguments.

2.1 Data

The IAC corpus is a freely available annotated collection of 109,553 forum posts (11,216 discussion threads). [1] In such forums, conversations are started by posting a topic or a question in a particular category, such as society, politics, or religion (Walker et al., 2012). Forum participants can then post their opinions, choosing whether to respond directly to a previous post or to the top level topic (start a new thread). These discussions are essentially dialogic; however the affordances of the forum such as asynchrony, and the ability to start a new thread rather than continue an existing one, leads to dialogic structures that are different than other multiparty informal conversations (Fox Tree, 2010). An additional source of dialogic structure in these discussions, above and beyond the thread structure, is the use of the quote mechanism, which is an interface feature that allows participants to optionally break down a previous post into the components of its argument and respond to each component in turn.

The IAC includes 10,003 Quote-Response (Q-R) pairs with annotations for FACTUAL vs. FEELING argument style, across a range of topics. Figure 2 shows the wording of the survey question used to collect the annotations. Fact vs. Feeling was measured as a scalar ranging from -5 to +5, because previous work suggested that taking the means of scalar annotations reduces noise in Mechanical Turk annotations (Snow et al., 2008). Each of the pairs was annotated by 5-7 annotators.

For our experiments, we use only the response texts and assign a binary FACT or FEEL label to each response: texts with score >1 are assigned to the FACT class and texts with score <-1 are assigned to the FEELING class. We did not use the responses with scores between -1 and 1 because they had a very weak Fact/Feeling assessment, which could be attributed to responses either containing aspects of *both* factual and feeling expression, or neither. The resulting set contains 3,466 FACT and 2,382 FEELING posts. We randomly partitioned the FACT/FEEL responses into three subsets: a training set with 70% of the data (2,426 FACT and 1,667 FEELING posts), a development (tuning) set with 20% of the data (693 FACT and 476 FEELING posts), and a test set with 10% of the data (347 FACT and 239 FEELING posts). For the bootstrapping method, we also used 11,560 responses from the unannotated data.

[1] https://nlds.soe.ucsc.edu/iac

Slider Scale -5,5: Survey Question
Fact/Emotion: Is the respondent attempting to make a fact based argument or appealing to feelings and emotions?

Figure 2: Mechanical Turk Survey Question used for Fact/Feeling annotation.

2.2 Bootstrapped Pattern Learning

The goal of our research is to gain insights into the types of linguistic expressions and properties that are distinctive and common in factual and feeling based argumentation. We also explore whether it is possible to develop a high-precision FACT vs. FEELING classifier that can be applied to unannotated data to find new linguistic expressions that did not occur in our original labeled corpus.

To accomplish this, we use the AutoSlog-TS system (Riloff, 1996) to extract linguistic expressions from the annotated texts. Since the IAC also contains a large collection of unannotated texts, we then embed AutoSlog-TS in a bootstrapping framework to learn additional linguistic expressions from the unannotated texts. First, we briefly describe the AutoSlog-TS pattern learner and the set of pattern templates that we used. Then, we present the bootstrapping process to learn more Fact/Feeling patterns from unannotated texts.

2.2.1 Pattern Learning with AutoSlog-TS

To learn patterns from texts labeled as FACT or FEELING arguments, we use the AutoSlog-TS (Riloff, 1996) extraction pattern learner, which is freely available for research. AutoSlog-TS is a weakly supervised pattern learner that requires training data consisting of documents that have been labeled with respect to different categories. For our purposes, we provide AutoSlog-TS with responses that have been labeled as either FACT or FEELING.

AutoSlog-TS uses a set of syntactic templates to define different types of linguistic expressions. The left-hand side of Figure 3 shows the set of syntactic templates defined in the AutoSlog-TS software package. PassVP refers to passive voice verb phrases (VPs), ActVP refers to active voice VPs, InfVP refers to infinitive VPs, and AuxVP refers to VPs where the main verb is a form of "to be" or "to have". Subjects (subj), direct objects (dobj), noun phrases (np), and possessives (genitives) can be extracted by the patterns. AutoSlog-TS applies the Sundance shallow parser (Riloff and Phillips, 2004) to each sentence and finds every possible match for each pattern template. For each match, the template is instantiated with the corresponding words in the sentence to produce a specific lexico-syntactic expression. The right-hand side of Figure 3 shows an example of a specific lexico-syntactic pattern that corresponds to each general pattern template.[2]

Pattern Template	Example Pattern
<subj> PassVP	<subj> was observed
<subj> ActVP	<subj> observed
<subj> ActVP Dobj	<subj> want explanation
<subj> ActInfVP	<subj> expected to find
<subj> PassInfVP	<subj> was used to measure
<subj> AuxVP Dobj	<subj> was success
<subj> AuxVP Adj	<subj> is religious
ActVP <dobj>	create <dobj>
InfVP <dobj>	to limit <dobj>
ActInfVP <dobj>	like to see <dobj>
PassInfVP <dobj>	was interested to see <dobj>
Subj AuxVP <dobj>	question is <dobj>
NP Prep <np>	origins of <np>
ActVP Prep <np>	evolved from <np>
PassVP Prep <np>	was replaced by <np>
InfVP Prep <np>	to use as <np>
<possessive> NP	<possessive> son

Figure 3: The Pattern Templates of AutoSlog-TS with Example Instantiations

In addition to the original 17 pattern templates in AutoSlog-TS (shown in Figure 3), we defined 7 new pattern templates for the following bigrams and trigrams: `Adj Noun`, `Adj Conj Adj`, `Adv Adv`, `Adv Adv Adv`, `Adj Adj`, `Adv Adj`, `Adv Adv Adj`. We added these n-gram patterns to provide coverage for adjective and adverb expressions because the original templates were primarily designed to capture noun phrase and verb phrase expressions.

The learning process in AutoSlog-TS has two phases. In the first phase, the pattern templates are applied to the texts exhaustively, so that lexico-syntactic patterns are generated for (literally) every instantiation of the templates that appear in the corpus. In the second phase, AutoSlog-TS uses the labels associated with the texts to compute statistics for how often each pattern occurs in each class of texts. For each pattern p, we collect P(FACTUAL $\mid p$) and P(FEELING $\mid p$), as well as the pattern's overall frequency in the corpus.

2.2.2 Bootstrapping Procedure

Since the IAC data set contains a large number of unannotated debate forum posts, we embedd AutoSlog-TS in a bootstrapping framework to learn additional patterns. The flow diagram for the bootstrapping system is shown in Figure 4.

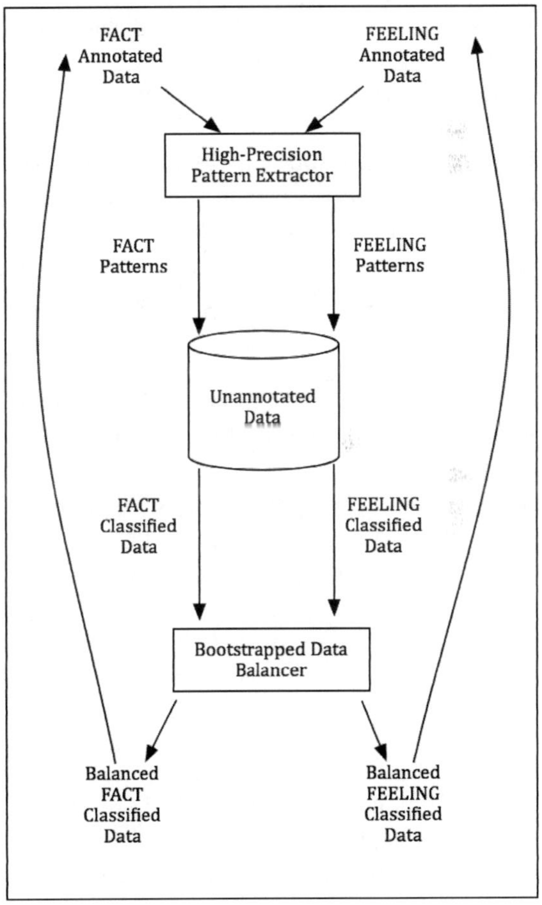

Figure 4: Flow Diagram for Bootstrapping Process

Initially, we give the labeled training data to AutoSlog-TS, which generates patterns and associated statistics. The next step identifies high-precision patterns that can be used to label some of the unannotated texts as FACTUAL or FEELING. We define two thresholds: θ_f to represent a mini-

[2]The examples are shown as general expressions for readability, but the actual patterns must match the syntactic constraints associated with the pattern template.

mum frequency value, and θ_p to represent a minimum probability value. We found that using only a small set of patterns (when θ_p is set to a high value) achieves extremely high precision, yet results in a very low recall. Instead, we adopt a strategy of setting a moderate probability threshold to identify reasonably reliable patterns, but labeling a text as FACTUAL or FEELING only if it contains at least a certain number different patterns for that category, θ_n. In order to calibrate the thresholds, we experimented with a range of threshold values on the development (tuning) data and identified θ_f=3, θ_p=.70, and θ_n=3 for the FACTUAL class, and θ_f=3, θ_p=.55, and θ_n=3 for the FEELING class as having the highest classification precision (with non-trivial recall).

The high-precision patterns are then used in the bootstrapping framework to identify more FACTUAL and FEELING texts from the 11,561 unannotated posts, also from 4forums.com. For each round of bootstrapping, the current set of FACTUAL and FEELING patterns are matched against the unannotated texts, and posts that match at least 3 patterns associated with a given class are assigned to that class. As shown in Figure 4, the Bootstrapped Data Balancer then randomly selects a balanced subset of the newly classified posts to maintain the same proportion of FACTUAL vs. FEELING documents throughout the bootstrapping process. These new documents are added to the set of labeled documents, and the bootstrapping process repeats. We use the same threshold values to select new high-precision patterns for all iterations.

3 Evaluation

We evaluate the effectiveness of the learned patterns by applying them to the test set of 586 posts (347 FACT and 239 FEELING posts, maintaining the original ratio of FACT to FEEL data in train). We classify each post as FACTUAL or FEELING using the same procedure as during bootstrapping: a post is labeled as FACTUAL or FEELING if it matches at least three high-precision patterns for that category. If a document contains three patterns for both categories, then we leave it unlabeled. We ran the bootstrapping algorithm for four iterations.

The upper section of Table 1 shows the Precision and Recall results for the patterns learned during bootstrapping. The Iter 0 row shows the performance of the patterns learned only from the original, annotated training data. The remaining rows show the results for the patterns learned from the unannotated texts during bootstrapping, added cumulatively. We show the results after each iteration of bootstrapping.

Table 1 shows that recall increases after each bootstrapping iteration, demonstrating that the patterns learned from the unannotated texts yield substantial gains in coverage over those learned only from the annotated texts. Recall increases from 22.8% to 40.9% for FACT, and from 8.0% to 18.8% for FEEL.[3] The precision for the FACTUAL class is reasonably good, but the precision for the FEELING class is only moderate. However, although precision typically decreases during boostrapping due to the addition of imperfectly labeled data, the precision drop during bootstrapping is relatively small.

We also evaluated the performance of a Naive Bayes (NB) classifier to assess the difficulty of this task with a traditional supervised learning algorithm. We trained a Naive Bayes classifier with unigram features and binary values on the training data, and identified the best Laplace smoothing parameter using the development data. The bottom row of Table 1 shows the results for the NB classifier on the test data. These results show that the NB classifier yields substantially higher recall for both categories, undoubtedly due to the fact that the classifier uses

[3]The decrease from 19.2% to 18.8% recall is probably due to more posts being labeled as relevant by *both* categories, in which case they are ultimately left unlabeled to avoid overlap.

Table 1: Evaluation Results

	Fact		Feel	
	Prec	Rec	Prec	Rec
Pattern-based Classification				
Iter 0	77.5	22.8	65.5	8.0
Iter 1	80.0	34.6	60.0	16.3
Iter 2	80.0	38.0	64.3	18.8
Iter 3	79.9	40.1	63.0	19.2
Iter 4	78.0	40.9	62.5	18.8
Naive Bayes Classifier				
NB	73.0	67.0	57.0	65.0

Table 2: Examples of Characteristic Argumentation Style Patterns for Each Class

Patt ID#	Probability	Frequency	Pattern	Text Match
FACT Selected Patterns				
FC1	1.00	18	NP Prep <np>	SPECIES OF
FC2	1.00	21	<subj> PassVP	EXPLANATION OF
FC3	1.00	20	<subj> AuxVP Dobj	BE EVIDENCE
FC4	1.00	14	<subj> PassVP	OBSERVED
FC5	0.97	39	NP Prep <np>	RESULT OF
FC6	0.90	10	<subj> ActVP Dobj	MAKE POINT
FC7	0.84	32	Adj Noun	SCIENTIFIC THEORY
FC8	0.75	4	NP Prep <np>	MISUNDERSTANDING OF
FC9	0.67	3	Adj Noun	FUNDAMENTAL RIGHTS
FC10	0.50	2	NP Prep <np>	MEASURABLE AMOUNT
FEEL Selected Patterns				
FE1	1.00	14	Adj Noun	MY ARGUMENT
FE2	1.00	7	<subj> AuxVP Adjp	BE ABSURD
FE3	1.00	9	Adv Adj	MORALLY WRONG
FE4	0.91	11	<subj> AuxVP Adjp	BE SAD
FE5	0.89	9	<subj> AuxVP Adjp	BE DUMB
FE6	0.89	9	Adj Noun	NO BRAIN
FE7	0.81	37	Adj Noun	COMMON SENSE
FE8	0.75	8	InfVP Prep <np>	BELIEVE IN
FE9	0.87	3	Adj Noun	ANY CREDIBILITY
FE10	0.53	17	Adj Noun	YOUR OPINION

all unigram information available in the text. Our pattern learner, however, was restricted to learning linguistic expressions in specific syntactic constructions, usually requiring more than one word, because our goal was to study *specific* expressions associated with FACTUAL and FEELING argument styles. Table 1 shows that the lexico-syntactic patterns did obtain higher precision than the NB classifier, but with lower recall.

Table 3: Number of New Patterns Added after Each Round of Bootstrapping

	FACT	FEEL	Total
Iter 0	1,212	662	1,874
Iter 1	2,170	1,609	3,779
Iter 2	2,522	1,728	4,520
Iter 3	3,147	2,037	5,184
Iter 4	3,696	2,134	5,830

Table 3 shows the number of patterns learned from the annotated data (Iter 0) and the number of new patterns added after each bootstrapping iteration. The first iteration dramatically increases the set of patterns, and more patterns are steadily added throughout the rest of bootstrapping process.

The key take-away from this set of experiments is that distinguishing FACTUAL and FEELING argumets is clearly a challenging task. There is substantial room for improvement for both precision and recall, and surprisingly, the FEELING class seems to be harder to accurately recognize than the FACTUAL class. In the next section, we examine the learned patterns and their syntactic forms to better understand the language used in the debate forums.

4 Analysis

Table 2 provides examples of patterns learned for each class that are characteristic of that class. We observe that patterns associated with factual arguments often include topic-specific terminology, explanatory language, and argument phrases. In contrast, the patterns associated with feeling based arguments are often based on the speaker's own beliefs or claims, perhaps assuming that they themselves are credible (Chaiken, 1980; Petty et al., 1981), or they involve assessment or evaluations of the arguments

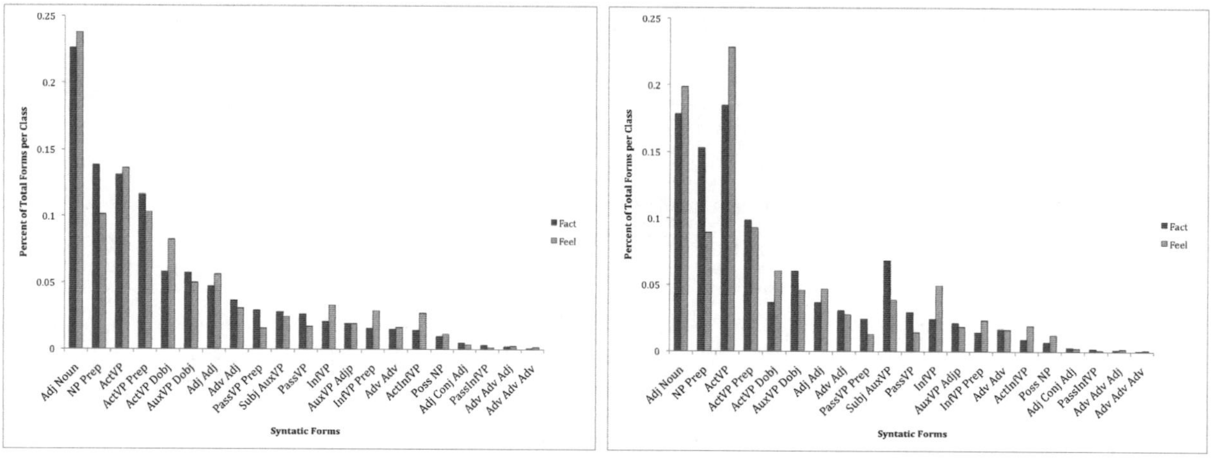

(a) Percentage of Each Unique Syntactic Form

(b) Percentage of Each Syntactic Form, by Instance Counts

Figure 5: Histograms of Syntactic Forms by Percentage of Total

of the other speaker (Hassan et al., 2010). They are typically also very creative and diverse, which may be why it is hard to get higher accuracies for FEELING classification, as shown by Table 1.

Figure 5 shows the distribution of syntactic forms (templates) among all of the high-precision patterns identified for each class during bootstrapping. The x-axes show the syntactic templates[4] and the y-axes show the percentage of all patterns that had a specific syntactic form. Figure 5a counts each lexico-syntactic pattern only once, regardless of how many times it occurred in the data set. Figure 5b counts the number of instances of each lexico-syntactic pattern. For example, Figure 5a shows that the *Adj Noun* syntactic form produced 1,400 different patterns, which comprise 22.6% of the distinct patterns learned. Figure 5b captures the fact that there are 7,170 instances of the *Adj Noun* patterns, which comprise 17.8% of all patterns instances in the data set.

For FACTUAL arguments, we see that patterns with prepositional phrases (especially *NP Prep*) and passive voice verb phrases are more common. Instantiations of *NP Prep* are illustrated by **FC1**, **FC5**, **FC8**, **FC10** in Table 2. Instantiations of *PassVP* are illustrated by **FC2** and **FC4** in Table 2. For FEELING arguments, expressions with adjectives and active voice verb phrases are more common. Almost every high probability pattern for FEELING includes an adjective, as illustrated by every pattern **except FE8** in Table 2. Figure 5b shows that three syntactic forms account for a large proportion of the instances of high-precision patterns in the data: *Adj Noun*, *NP Prep*, and *ActVP*.

Next, we further examine the *NP Prep* patterns since they are so prevalent. Figure 6 shows the percentages of the most frequently occurring prepositions found in the *NP Prep* patterns learned for each class. Patterns containing the preposition "of" make up the vast majority of prepositional phrases for both the FACT and FEEL classes, but is more common in the FACT class. In contrast, we observe that

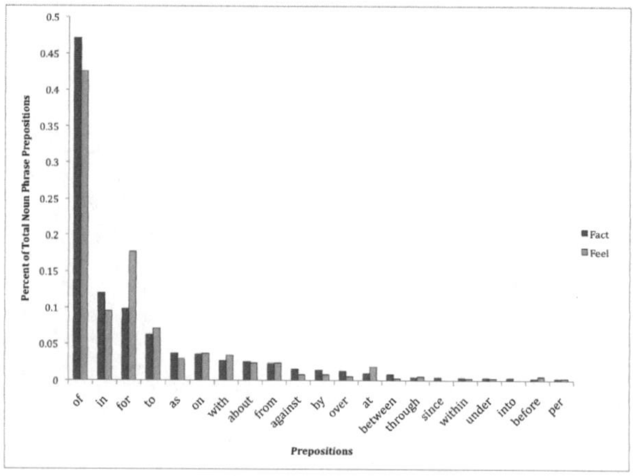

Figure 6: Percentage of Preposition Types in the *NP Prep* Patterns

[4] We grouped a few of the comparable syntactic forms together for the purposes of this graph.

patterns with the preposition "for" are substantially more common in the FEEL class than the FACT class.

Table 4 shows examples of learned *NP Prep* patterns with the preposition "of" in the FACT class and "for" in the FEEL class. The "of" preposition in the factual arguments often attaches to objective terminology. The "for" preposition in the feeling-based arguments is commonly used to express advocacy (e.g., *demand for*) or refer to affected population groups (e.g., *treatment for*). Interestingly, these phrases are subtle indicators of feeling-based arguments rather than explicit expressions of emotion or sentiment.

Table 4: High-Probability FACT Phrases with "OF" and FEEL Phrases with "FOR"

FACT "OF" Phrases	FEEL "FOR" Phrases
RESULT OF	MARRIAGE FOR
ORIGIN OF	STANDING FOR
THEORY OF	SAME FOR
EVIDENCE OF	TREATMENT FOR
PARTS OF	DEMAND FOR
EVOLUTION OF	ATTENTION FOR
PERCENT OF	ADVOCATE FOR
THOUSANDS OF	NO EVIDENCE FOR
EXAMPLE OF	JUSTIFICATION FOR
LAW OF	EXCUSE FOR

5 Related Work

Related research on argumentation has primarily worked with different genres of argument than found in IAC, such as news articles, weblogs, legal briefs, supreme court summaries, and congressional debates (Marwell and Schmitt, 1967; Thomas et al., 2006; Burfoot, 2008; Cialdini, 2000; McAlister et al., 2014; Reed and Rowe, 2004). The examples from IAC in Figure 1 illustrate that natural informal dialogues such as those found in online forums exhibit a much broader range of argumentative styles. Other work has on models of natural informal arguments have focused on stance classification (Somasundaran and Wiebe, 2009; Somasundaran and Wiebe, 2010; Walker et al., 2012), argument summarization (Misra et al., 2015), sarcasm detection (Justo et al., 2014), and identifying the structure of arguments such as main claims and their justifications (Biran and Rambow, 2011; Purpura et al., 2008; Yang and Cardie, 2013).

Other types of language data also typically contains a mixture of subjective and objective sentences, e.g. Wiebe et al. (2001; 2004) found that 44% of sentences in a news corpus were subjective. Our work is also related to research on distinguishing subjective and objective text (Yu and Hatzivassiloglou, 2003; Riloff et al., 2005; Wiebe and Riloff, 2005), including bootstrapped pattern learning for subjective/objective sentence classification (Riloff and Wiebe, 2003). However, prior work has primarily focused on news texts, not argumentation, and the notion of objective language is not exactly the same as factual. Our work also aims to recognize emotional language specifically, rather than all forms of subjective language. There has been substantial work on sentiment and opinion analysis (e.g., (Pang et al., 2002; Kim and Hovy, 2004; Wilson et al., 2005; Bethard et al., 2005; Wilson et al., 2006; Yang and Cardie, 2014)) and recognition of specific emotions in text (Mohammad, 2012a; Mohammad, 2012b; Roberts et al., 2012; Qadir and Riloff, 2013), which could be incorporated in future extensions of our work. We also hope to examine more closely the relationship of this work to previous work aimed at the identification of nasty vs. nice arguments in the IAC (Lukin and Walker, 2013; Justo et al., 2014).

6 Conclusion

In this paper, we use observed differences in argumentation styles in online debate forums to extract patterns that are highly correlated with factual and emotional argumentation. From an annotated set of forum post responses, we are able extract high-precision patterns that are associated with the argumentation style classes, and we are then able to use these patterns to get a larger set of indicative patterns using a bootstrapping methodology on a set of unannotated posts.

From the learned patterns, we derive some characteristic syntactic forms associated with the FACT and FEEL that we use to discriminate between the classes. We observe distinctions between the way that different arguments are expressed, with respect to the technical and more opinionated terminologies used, which we analyze on the basis of grammatical forms and more direct syntactic patterns, such as the use of different prepositional phrases. Overall, we demonstrate how the learned patterns can be used to more precisely gather similarly-styled argument responses from a pool of unannotated responses, carrying the characteristics of factual and emotional argumentation style.

In future work we aim to use these insights about argument structure to produce higher performing classifiers for identifying FACTUAL vs. FEELING argument styles. We also hope to understand in more detail the relationship between these argument styles and the heurstic routes to persuasion and associated strategies that have been identified in previous work on argumentation and persuasion (Marwell and Schmitt, 1967; Cialdini, 2000; Reed and Rowe, 2004).

Acknowledgments

This work was funded by NSF Grant IIS-1302668-002 under the Robust Intelligence Program. The collection and annotation of the IAC corpus was supported by an award from NPS-BAA-03 to UCSC and an IARPA Grant under the Social Constructs in Language Program to UCSC by subcontract from the University of Maryland.

References

W.L. Benoit. 1987. Argument and credibility appeals in persuasion. *Southern Speech Communication Journal*, 42(2):181–97.

S. Bethard, H. Yu, A. Thornton, V. Hatzivassiloglou, and D. Jurafsky. 2005. Automatic Extraction of Opinion Propositions and their Holders. In *Computing Attitude and Affect in Text: Theory and Applications*. Springer.

O. Biran and O. Rambow. 2011. Identifying justifications in written dialogs. In *2011 Fifth IEEE International Conference on Semantic Computing (ICSC)*, pages 162–168. IEEE.

C. Burfoot. 2008. Using multiple sources of agreement information for sentiment classification of political transcripts. In *Australasian Language Technology Association Workshop 2008*, volume 6, pages 11–18.

J.T. Cacioppo, R.E. Petty, and K.J. Morris. 1983. Effects of need for cognition on message evaluation, recall, and persuasion. *Journal of Personality and Social Psychology*, 45(4):805.

S. Chaiken. 1980. Heuristic versus systematic information processing and the use of source versus message cues in persuasion. *Journal of personality and social psychology*, 39(5):752.

Robert B. Cialdini. 2000. *Influence: Science and Practice (4th Edition)*. Allyn & Bacon.

J. E. Fox Tree. 2010. Discourse markers across speakers and settings. *Language and Linguistics Compass*, 3(1):1–13.

A. Hassan, V. Qazvinian, and D. Radev. 2010. What's with the attitude?: identifying sentences with attitude in online discussions. In *Proceedings of the 2010 Conference on Empirical Methods in Natural Language Processing*, pages 1245–1255. Association for Computational Linguistics.

John E. Hunter. 1987. A model of compliance-gaining message selection. *Communication Monographs*, 54(1):54–63.

Raquel Justo, Thomas Corcoran, Stephanie M Lukin, Marilyn Walker, and M Inés Torres. 2014. Extracting relevant knowledge for the detection of sarcasm and nastiness in the social web. *Knowledge-Based Systems*, 69:124–133.

Soo-Min Kim and Eduard Hovy. 2004. Determining the sentiment of opinions. In *Proceedings of the 20th International Conference on Computational Linguistics (COLING 2004)*, pages 1267–1373, Geneva, Switzerland.

Stephanie Lukin and Marilyn Walker. 2013. Really? well. apparently bootstrapping improves the performance of sarcasm and nastiness classifiers for online dialogue. *NAACL 2013*, page 30.

Fabrizio Macagno and Douglas Walton. 2014. *Emotive language in argumentation*. Cambridge University Press.

G. Marwell and D. Schmitt. 1967. Dimensions of compliance-gaining behavior: An empirical analysis. *sociomety*, 30:350–364.

Simon McAlister, Colin Allen, Andrew Ravenscroft, Chris Reed, David Bourget, John Lawrence, Katy Börner, and Robert Light. 2014. From big data to argument analysis. *Intelligence*, page 27.

Amita Misra, Pranav Anand, Jean E. Fox Tree, and Marilyn Walker. 2015. Using summarization to discover argument facets in dialog. In *Proceedings of the 2015 Conference of the North American Chapter of the Association for Computational Linguistics: Human Language Technologies*.

Saif Mohammad. 2012a. #emotional tweets. In **SEM 2012: The First Joint Conference on Lexical and Computational Semantics*.

Saif Mohammad. 2012b. Portable features for classifying emotional text. In *Proceedings of the 2012 Conference of the North American Chapter of the Association for Computational Linguistics: Human Language Technologies*.

Bo Pang, Lillian Lee, and Shivakumar Vaithyanathan. 2002. Thumbs up? Sentiment Classification using Machine Learning Techniques. In *Proceedings of the 2002 Conference on Empirical Methods in Natural Language Processing (EMNLP)*, pages 79–86.

Joonsuk Park and Claire Cardie. 2014. Identifying appropriate support for propositions in online user comments. *ACL 2014*, page 29.

R.E. Petty and J.T. Cacioppo. 1986. The elaboration likelihood model of persuasion. *Advances in experimental social psychology*, 19(1):123–205.

R.E. Petty, J.T. Cacioppo, and R. Goldman. 1981. Personal involvement as a determinant of argument-based persuasion. *Journal of Personality and Social Psychology*, 41(5):847.

S. Purpura, C. Cardie, and J. Simons. 2008. Active learning for e-rulemaking: Public comment categorization. In *Proceedings of the 2008 international conference on Digital government research*, pages 234–243. Digital Government Society of North America.

Ashequl Qadir and Ellen Riloff. 2013. Bootstrapped learning of emotion hashtags# hashtags4you. In *Proceedings of the 4th workshop on computational approaches to subjectivity, sentiment and social media analysis*, pages 2–11.

Chris Reed and Glenn Rowe. 2004. Araucaria: Software for argument analysis, diagramming and representation. *International Journal on Artificial Intelligence Tools*, 13(04):961–979.

Ellen Riloff and William Phillips. 2004. An introduction to the sundance and autoslog systems. Technical report, Technical Report UUCS-04-015, School of Computing, University of Utah.

E. Riloff and J. Wiebe. 2003. Learning Extraction Patterns for Subjective Expressions. In *Proceedings of the 2003 Conference on Empirical Methods in Natural Language Processing*.

E. Riloff, J. Wiebe, and W. Phillips. 2005. Exploiting Subjectivity Classification to Improve Information Extraction. In *Proceedings of the 20th National Conference on Artificial Intelligence*.

Ellen Riloff. 1996. Automatically generating extraction patterns from untagged text. In *AAAI/IAAI, Vol. 2*, pages 1044–1049.

Kirk Roberts, Michael A. Roach, Joseph Johnson, Josh Guthrie, and Sanda M. Harabagiu. 2012. Empatweet: Annotating and detecting emotions on twitter. In *Proceedings of the Eighth International Conference on Language Resources and Evaluation (LREC-2012)*. ACL Anthology Identifier: L12-1059.

Ariel Rosenfeld and Sarit Kraus. 2015. Providing arguments in discussions based on the prediction of human argumentative behavior. AAAI.

Roser Saurí and James Pustejovsky. 2009. Factbank: A corpus annotated with event factuality. *Language resources and evaluation*, 43(3):227–268.

R. Snow, B. O'Connor, D. Jurafsky, and A.Y. Ng. 2008. Cheap and fast—but is it good?: evaluating non-expert annotations for natural language tasks. In *Proceedings of the Conference on Empirical Methods in Natural Language Processing*, pages 254–263. Association for Computational Linguistics.

S. Somasundaran and J. Wiebe. 2009. Recognizing stances in online debates. In *Proceedings of the Joint Conference of the 47th Annual Meeting of the ACL and the 4th International Joint Conference on Natural Language Processing of the AFNLP: Volume 1-Volume 1*, pages 226–234. Association for Computational Linguistics.

S. Somasundaran and J. Wiebe. 2010. Recognizing stances in ideological on-line debates. In *Proceedings of the NAACL HLT 2010 Workshop on Computational Approaches to Analysis and Generation of Emotion in Text*, pages 116–124. Association for Computational Linguistics.

M. Thomas, B. Pang, and L. Lee. 2006. Get out the vote: Determining support or opposition from Congressional floor-debate transcripts. In *Proceedings of the 2006 conference on empirical methods in natural language processing*, pages 327–335. Association for Computational Linguistics.

Marilyn Walker, Pranav Anand, , Robert Abbott, and Jean E. Fox Tree. 2012. A corpus for research on deliberation and debate. In *Language Resources and Evaluation Conference, LREC2012*.

Douglas Walton. 2010. *The place of emotion in argument*. Penn State Press.

J. Wiebe and E. Riloff. 2005. Creating Subjective and Objective Sentence Classifiers from Unannotated Texts. In *Proceedings of the 6th International Conference on Computational Linguistics and Intelligent Text Processing*, pages 486–497, Mexico City, Mexico, February.

Janyce Wiebe, Theresa Wilson, and Matthew Bell. 2001. Identifying collocations for recognizing opinions. In *Proceedings of the ACL-01 Workshop on Collocation: Computational Extraction, Analysis, and Exploitation*, pages 24–31, Toulouse, France.

Janyce Wiebe, Theresa Wilson, Rebecca Bruce, Matthew Bell, and Melanie Martin. 2004. Learning subjective language. *Computational Linguistics*, 30(3):277–308.

Theresa Wilson, Janyce Wiebe, and Paul Hoffmann. 2005. Recognizing contextual polarity in phrase-level sentiment analysis. In *Proceedings of the 2005 Human Language Technology Conference / Conference on Empirical Methods in Natural Language Processing*.

T. Wilson, J. Wiebe, and R. Hwa. 2006. Recognizing strong and weak opinion clauses. *Computational Intelligence*, 22(2):73–99.

Bishan Yang and Claire Cardie. 2013. Joint inference for fine-grained opinion extraction. In *ACL (1)*, pages 1640–1649.

B. Yang and C. Cardie. 2014. Context-aware learning for sentence-level sentiment analysis with posterior regularization. In *Proceedings of the Association for Computational Linguistics (ACL)*.

Hong Yu and Vasileios Hatzivassiloglou. 2003. Towards answering opinion questions: Separating facts from opinions and identifying the polarity of opinion sentences. In *Proceedings of the 2003 Conference on Empirical Methods in Natural Language Processing*, pages 129–136, Sapporo, Japan.

Inon Zuckerman, Erel Segal-Halevi, Avi Rosenfeld, and Sarit Kraus. 2015. First steps in chat-based negotiating agents. In *Next Frontier in Agent-based Complex Automated Negotiation*, pages 89–109. Springer.

Combining Argument Mining Techniques

John Lawrence
School of Computing
University of Dundee
UK
j.lawrence@dundee.ac.uk

Chris Reed
School of Computing
University of Dundee
UK
c.a.reed@dundee.ac.uk

Abstract

In this paper, we look at three different methods of extracting the argumentative structure from a piece of natural language text. These methods cover linguistic features, changes in the topic being discussed and a supervised machine learning approach to identify the components of argumentation schemes, patterns of human reasoning which have been detailed extensively in philosophy and psychology. For each of these approaches we achieve results comparable to those previously reported, whilst at the same time achieving a more detailed argument structure. Finally, we use the results from these individual techniques to apply them in combination, further improving the argument structure identification.

1 Introduction

The continuing growth in the volume of data which we produce has driven efforts to unlock the wealth of information this data contains. Automatic techniques such as Opinion Mining and Sentiment Analysis (Liu, 2010) allow us to determine the views expressed in a piece of textual data, for example, whether a product review is positive or negative. Existing techniques struggle, however, to identify more complex structural relationships between concepts.

Argument Mining[1] is the automatic identification of the argumentative structure contained within a piece of natural language text. By automatically identifying this structure and its associated premises and conclusions, we are able to tell not just *what* views are being expressed, but also *why* those particular views are held.

The desire to achieve this deeper understanding of the views which people express has led to the recent rapid growth in the Argument Mining field (2014 saw the first ACL workshop on the topic in Baltimore[2] and meetings dedicated to the topic in both Warsaw[3] and Dundee[4]). A range of techniques have been applied to this problem, including supervised machine learning (starting with (Moens et al., 2007)) and topic modelling ((Lawrence et al., 2014)) as well as purely linguistic methods (such as (Villalba and Saint-Dizier, 2012)); however, little work has currently been carried out to bring these techniques together.

In this paper, we look at three individual argument mining approaches. Firstly, we look at using the presence of discourse indicators, linguistic expressions of the relationship between statements, to determine relationships between the propositions in a piece of text. We then move on to look at a topic based approach. Investigating how changes in the topic being discussed relate to the argumentative structure being expressed. Finally, we implement a supervised machine learning approach based on argumentation schemes (Walton et al., 2008), enabling us to not only identify premises and conclusions, but to determine how exactly these argument components are working together.

Based on the results from the individual imple-

[1] Sometimes also referred to as Argumentation Mining

[2] http://www.uncg.edu/cmp/ArgMining2014/

[3] http://argdiap.pl/argdiap2014

[4] http://www.arg-tech.org/swam2014/

Proceedings of the 2nd Workshop on Argumentation Mining, pages 127–136,
Denver, Colorado, June 4, 2015.

mentations, we combine these approaches, taking into account the strengths and weaknesses of each to improve the accuracy of the resulting argument structure.

2 Dataset

One of the challenges faced by current approaches to argument mining is the lack of large quantities of appropriately annotated arguments to serve as training and test data. Several recent efforts have been made to improve this situation by the creation of corpora across a range of different domains; however, to apply each of the techniques previously mentioned in combination means that we are limited to analysed data containing complete argumentation scheme specifications and provided along with the original text.

Although there are a number of argument analysis tools (such as Araucaria (Reed and Rowe, 2004), Carneades (Gordon et al., 2007), Rationale (van Gelder, 2007) and OVA (Bex et al., 2013)) which allow the analyst to identify the argumentation scheme related to a particular argumentative structure, the vast majority of analyses which are produced using these tools do not include this information. For example, less than 10% of the OVA analyses contained in AIFdb (Lawrence et al., 2012) include any scheme structure.

AIFdb still offers the largest annotated dataset available, containing the complete Araucaria corpus (Reed et al., 2008) used by previous argumentation scheme studies and supplemented by analyses from a range of other sources. Limiting the data to analyses containing complete scheme specifications and for which the original text corresponds directly to the analysis (with no re-construction or enthymematic content (Hitchcock, 1985) added) leaves us with 78 complete analyses (comprised of 404 propositions and 4,137 words), including 47 examples of the argument from expert opinion scheme and 31 examples of argument from positive consequences (these schemes are discussed in Section 5.)

3 Discourse Indicators

The first approach which we present is that of using discourse indicators to determine the argumentative connections between adjacent propositions in a piece of text. Discourse indicators are explicitly stated linguistic expressions of the relationship between statements (Webber et al., 2011), and, when present, can provide a clear indication of its argumentative structure. For example, if we take the sentence "Britain should disarm because it would set a good example for other countries", then this can be split into two separate propositions "Britain should disarm" and "it (disarming) would set a good example for other countries". The presence of the word "because" between these two propositions clearly tells us that the second is a reason for the first.

Relation Type	**Words**
Support	because, therefore, after, for, since, when, assuming, so, accordingly, thus, hence, then, consequently
Conflict	however, but, though, except, not, never, no, whereas, nonetheless, yet, despite

Table 1: Discourse indicators used to determine propositional connections

Discourse indicators have been previously used as a component of argument mining techniques for example in (Stab and Gurevych, 2014), indicators are used as a feature in multiclass classification of argument components, with each clause classified as a major claim, claim, premise or non-argumentative. Similar indicators are used in (Wyner et al., 2012), along with domain terminology (e.g. camera names and properties) to highlight potential argumentative sections of online product reviews. By looking at discourse indicators in isolation, however, we aim to determine their ability to be used on their own as an argument mining method.

There are many different ways in which indicators can appear, and a wide range of relations which they can suggest (Knott, 1996). We limit our search here to specific terms appearing between two sequential propositions in the original text. These terms are split into two groups, indicating support and attack relations between the propositions. A list of these terms can be seen in Table 1.

	p	r	f1
Discourse Indicators	0.89	0.04	0.07

Table 2: Comparison of the connections between propositions determined by discourse indicators and manual analysis

By performing a simple search for these terms across the text of each item in our corpus, we were able to determine suggested connections between propositions and compare these to the manual analyses. The results of this comparison can be seen in Table 2. In this case we look at the connections between the component propositions in the manually analysed argument structure (385 connections in total), and consider a connection to have been correctly identified if a discourse indicator tells us that two propositions are connected, and that the relation between them (support or attack) is the same as that in the manual analysis.

The results clearly show that, when discourse indicators are present in the text, they give a strong indication of the connection between propositions (precision of 0.89); however, the low frequency with which they can be found means that they fail to help identify the vast majority of connections (recall of 0.04). Additionally, the approach we use here considers only those discourse indicators found between pairs of consecutive propositions and, as such, is unable to identify connected propositions which are further apart in the text. Because of this, discourse indicators may provide a useful component in an argument mining approach, but, unless supplemented by other methods, are inadequate for identifying even a small percentage of the argumentative structure.

4 Topical Similarity

The next approach which we consider looks at how the changes of topic in a piece text relate to the argumentative structure contained within it. This method is similar to that presented in (Lawrence et al., 2014), where it is assumed firstly that the argument structure to be determined can be represented as a tree, and secondly, that this tree is generated depth first. That is, the conclusion is given first and then a line of reasoning is followed supporting this conclusion. Once that line of reasoning is exhausted, the argument moves back up the tree to support one of the previously made points. If the current point is not related to any of those made previously, then it is assumed to be unconnected.

Based on these assumptions we can determine the structure by looking at how similar the topic of each proposition is to its predecessor. If they are similar, then we assume that they are connected and the line of reasoning is being followed. If they are not sufficiently similar, then we first consider whether we are moving back up the tree, and compare the current proposition to all of those made previously and connect it to the most topically similar previous point. Finally, if the current point is not related to any of those made previously, then it is assumed to be unconnected to the existing structure.

Lawrence et al. perform these comparisons using a Latent Dirichlet Allocation (LDA) topic model. In our case, however, the argument structures we are working with are from much shorter pieces of text and as such generating LDA topic models from them is not feasible. Instead we look at the semantic similarity of propositions. We use WordNet[5] to determine the similarity between the synsets of each word in the first proposition and each word in the second. This relatedness score is inversely proportional to the number of nodes along the shortest path between the synsets. The shortest possible path occurs when the two synsets are the same, in which case the length is 1, and thus, the maximum relatedness value is 1. We then look at the maximum of these values in order to pair a word in the first proposition to one in the second, and finally average the values for each word to give a relatedness score for the proposition pair between 0 and 1. Similar to in (Lawrence et al., 2014), the threshold required for two propositions to be considered similar can be adjusted, altering the output structure, with a lower threshold giving more direct connections and a higher threshold greater branching and more unconnected components.

The results of performing this process using a threshold of 0.2 are shown in Table 3, and an example of the output structure can be seen in Figure 1.

[5] `http://wordnet.princeton.edu/`

	p	r	f1
Non-directed	0.82	0.56	0.67
Current to previous	0.63	0.43	0.51
Previous to current	0.19	0.13	0.15

Table 3: Topic Similarity Edge Predictions

For the results in Table 3, we consider a connection to have been correctly identified if there is any connection between the propositions in the manual analysis, regardless of direction or type. The standard output we obtain does not give any indication of the directionality of the connection between propositions, and these results are given in the first row of the table. The other two rows show the results obtained by assuming that these connections are always in one direction or another i.e. that the connection always goes from the current proposition to its predecessor or vice-versa.

Figure 1: Topic Structure

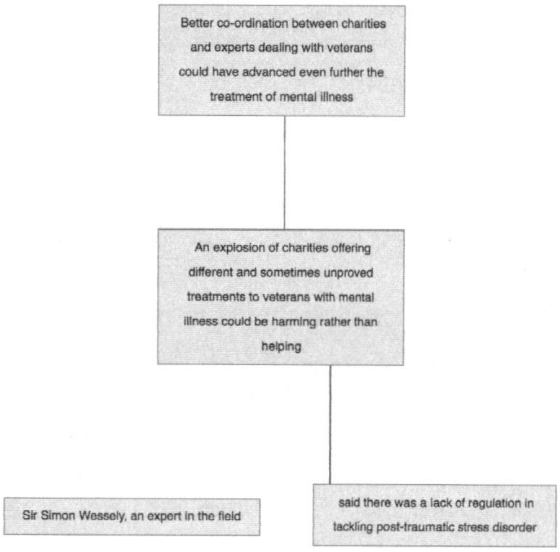

The results for non-directed connections are encouraging, as with the discourse indicators, precision (0.82) is higher than recall (0.56) suggesting that although this method may fail to find all connections, those that it does find can generally be viewed as highly likely. We can also see that the assumption of directionality from the current proposition to a previous proposition gives much better results than the other way around, suggesting that generally when a point is made it is made to support (or attack) something previously stated.

5 Argumentation Scheme Structure

Finally, we consider using a supervised machine learning approach to classify argument components and determine the connections between them. One of the first attempts to use this kind of classification is presented in (Moens et al., 2007), where a text is first split into sentences and then features of each sentence are used to classify them as "Argument" or "Non-Argument". This approach was built upon in (Palau and Moens, 2009), where each argument sentence is additionally classified as either a premise or conclusion. Our approach instead uses argumentation schemes (Walton et al., 2008), common patterns of human reasoning, enabling us to not only identify premise and conclusion relationships, but to gain a deeper understanding of how these argument components are working together.

The concept of automatically identifying argumentation schemes was first discussed in (Walton, 2011) and (Feng and Hirst, 2011). Walton proposes a six-stage approach to identifying arguments and their schemes. The approach suggests first identifying the arguments within the text and then fitting these to a list of specific known schemes. A similar methodology was implemented by Feng & Hirst, who produced classifiers to assign pre-determined argument structures as one in a list of the most common argumentation schemes.

The main challenge faced by this approach is the need to have already identified, not just that an argument is taking place, but its premises, conclusion and exact structure before a scheme can be assigned. By instead looking at the features of each component part of a scheme, we are able to overcome this requirement and identify parts of schemes in completely unanalysed text. Once these scheme components have been identified, we are able to group them together into specific scheme instances and thus obtain a complete understanding of the arguments being made.

Several attempts have been made to identify and classify the most commonly used schematic structures (Hastings, 1963; Perelman and Olbrechts-Tyteca, 1969; Kienpointner, 1992; Pollock, 1995;

Walton, 1996; Grennan, 1997; Katzav and Reed, 2004; Walton et al., 2008), though the most commonly used scheme set in analysis is that given by Walton. Here we look at two of Walton's schemes, Expert Opinion and Positive Consequences. Each scheme takes the form of a number of premises which work together to support a conclusion (the structure of the two schemes used can be seen in Table 4.)

Expert Opinion
Premise: Source E is an expert in subject domain S containing proposition A [FieldExpertise]
Premise: E asserts that proposition A is true (false) [KnowledgeAssertion]
Conclusion: A is true (false) [KnowledgePosition]

Positive Consequences
Premise: If A is brought about, then good consequences will (may plausibly) occur [PositiveConsequences]
Conclusion: Therefore, A should be brought about [EncouragedAction]

Table 4: Argumentation schemes

The features of these common patterns of argument provide us with a way in which to both identify that an argument is being made and determine its structure. By identifying the individual components of a scheme, we are able to identify the presence of a particular scheme from only a list of the propositions contained within the text. In order to accomplish this, one-against-others classification is used to identify propositions of each type from a set of completely unstructured propositions. Being able to successfully perform this task for even one of the proposition types from each scheme allows us to discover areas of the text where the corresponding scheme is being used.

This classification was performed with a Naïve Bayes classifier implemented using the *scikit-learn*[6] Python module for machine learning, with the features described in Table 5. Part Of Speech (POS) tagging was performed using the Python NLTK[7] POS-tagger and the frequencies of each tag added as individual features. The similarity feature was added to extend the information given by unigrams to include an indication of whether a proposition contains words similar to a pre-defined set of keywords. The keywords used for each type are shown in Table 6, and are based on the scheme definitions from Table 4 by manually identifying the key terms in each scheme component. Similarity scores were calculated using WordNet[8] to determine the maximum similarity between the synsets of the keywords and each word in the proposition. The maximum score for the words in the proposition was then added as a feature value, indicating the semantic relatedness of the proposition to the keyword.

Feature	**Description**
Unigrams	Each word in the proposition
Bigrams	Each pair of successive words
Length	The number of words in the proposition
AvgWLength	The average length of words in the proposition
POS	The parts of speech contained in the proposition
Punctuation	The presence of certain punctuation characters, for example " " indicating a quote
Similarity	The maximum similarity of a word in the proposition to pre-defined words corresponding to each proposition type

Table 5: Features used for scheme component classification

Table 7 shows the precision, recall and F-score obtained for each proposition type. The results show that even for a scheme where the classification of one proposition type is less successful, the results for the other types are better. If we consider being able to correctly identify at least one proposition type, then our results give F-scores of 0.93 and

[6] http://scikit-learn.org/stable/

[7] http://www.nltk.org/

[8] http://wordnet.princeton.edu/

Type	Keywords
Expert Opinion	
FieldExpertise	expert, experienced, skilled
KnowledgeAssertion	said
KnowledgePosition	be (to be)
Positive Consequences	
PositiveConsequences	occur, happen
EncouragedAction	should, must

Table 6: Keywords used for each proposition type

0.75 for locating an occurrence of each scheme type considered. This compares favourably with (Feng and Hirst, 2011), where the occurrence of a particular argumentation scheme was identified with accuracies of between 62.9% and 90.8%. Furthermore, Feng & Hirst's results only considered spans of text that were already known to contain a scheme of some type and required a prior understanding of the argumentative structure contained within the text, whereas the approach presented here does not have either of these requirements.

	p	r	f1
Expert Opinion			
FieldExpertise	0.95	0.90	0.93
KnowledgeAssertion	0.74	1.00	0.83
KnowledgePosition	0.93	0.55	0.62
Positive Consequences			
PositiveConsequences	0.75	0.67	0.71
EncouragedAction	0.86	0.67	0.75

Table 7: Classifying scheme components

By looking further at each set of three propositions contained within the text, we can locate areas where all of the component parts of a scheme occur. When these are found, we can assume that a particular scheme is being used in the text and assign each of its component parts to their respective role. This gives us an automatically identified structure as shown in Figure 2, where we can see that the component parts of the scheme are completely identified, but the remaining proposition is left unconnected.

Figure 2: Scheme Structure

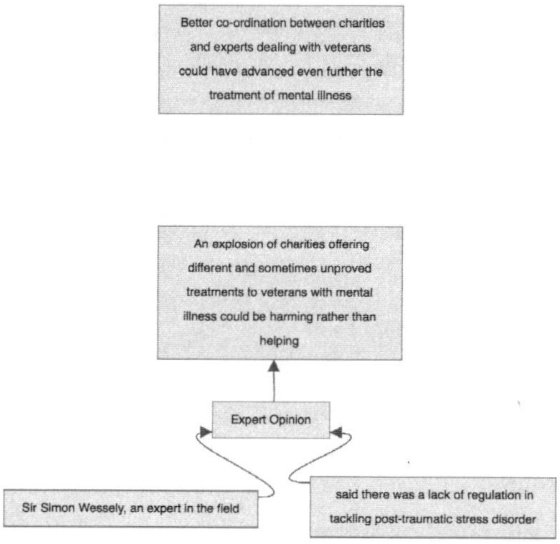

6 Combined Techniques

Having looked at three separate methods for automatically determining argument structure, we now consider how these approaches can be combined to give more accurate results than those previously achieved.

In order to investigate this, we tested a fixed subset of our corpus containing eight analyses, containing 36 pairs of connected propositions which we aim to identify. The remainder is used as training data for the supervised learning approach used to identify scheme instances. The use of such a fixed dataset allows us to compare and combine the computational methods used for discourse indicators and topical similarity with the supervised learning method used for scheme identification. The results of applying each approach separately are given in the first part of Table 8. In each case, the precision, recall and f1-score is given for how well each method manages to identify the connections between propositions in the set of analyses.

We can see from the results that, again, the precision for discourse indicators is high, but that the recall is low. This suggests that where indicators are found, they are the most reliable method of determining a connection.

The precision for using schematic structures is also high (0.82), though again the recall is lower. In this case, this is due to the fact that although this method can determine well the links between components in an argumentation scheme instance it gives no indication as to how the other propositions are connected.

Finally, topic similarity gives the poorest results, suggesting that this method be used to supplement the others, but that it is not capable of giving a good indication of the structure on its own.

Based on these results, we combine the methods as follows: firstly, if discourse indicators are present, then they are assumed to be a correct indication of a connection; next, we identify scheme instances and connect the component parts in accordance with the scheme structure; and finally, we look at the topic similarity and use this to connect any propositions that have previously been left out of the already identified structure. This combination of approaches is used to take advantage of the strengths of each. As previously discussed, discourse indicators are rare, but provide a very good indication of connectedness when they do occur, and as such, applying this method first gives us a base of propositions that are almost certainly correctly connected. Scheme identification offers the next best precision, and so is applied next. Finally, although topical similarity does not perform as well as scheme identification and does not give an indication of direction or type of connection, it allows us to connect those propositions which are not part of a scheme instance.

Carrying out this combined approach gives us the results shown in the last row of Table 8. Again, the results are based on correctly identified connections when compared to the manual analysis. We can see that by combining the methods, accuracy is substantially improved over any one individual method.

An example of the resulting structure obtained using this combined approach can be seen in Figure 3. If we compare this to a manual analysis of the same text (Figure 4), we can see that the structures are almost identical, differing only in the fact that the nature of the relationship between the premises "An explosion of charities offering different and sometimes unproved treatments to veterans with mental illness could be harming rather than helping" and "Better co-ordination between charities and experts dealing with veterans could have advanced even further the treatment of mental illness" is still unknown. We could make the further assumption, as detailed in section 3 that the second proposition supports or attacks the first as it appears later in the text, and in so doing obtain a picture almost identical to that produced by manual analysis.

	p	**r**	**f1**
Discourse Indicators	1.00	0.08	0.15
Topic Similarity	0.70	0.54	0.61
Schematic Structure	0.82	0.69	0.75
Combined Methods	**0.91**	**0.77**	**0.83**

Table 8: Identifying Argument Structure

Figure 3: Combined

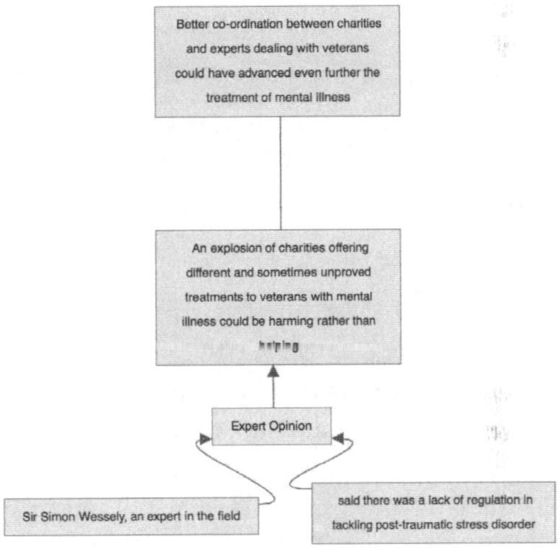

6.1 Proposition Boundary Learning

Until now, we have considered determining the argumentative structure from a piece of text which has already been split into its component propositions; however, in order to be able to extract structure from natural language, we must also be able to perform this segmentation automatically.

Text segmentation can be considered as the identification of a form of Elementary Discourse Units (EDUs), non-overlapping spans of text corresponding to the minimal units of discourse. (Peldszus and Stede, 2013) refers to these argument segments as 'Argumentative Discourse Units' (ADUs), and defines an ADU as a 'minimal unit of analysis', pointing out that an ADU may not always be as small as

Figure 4: Manual Analysis

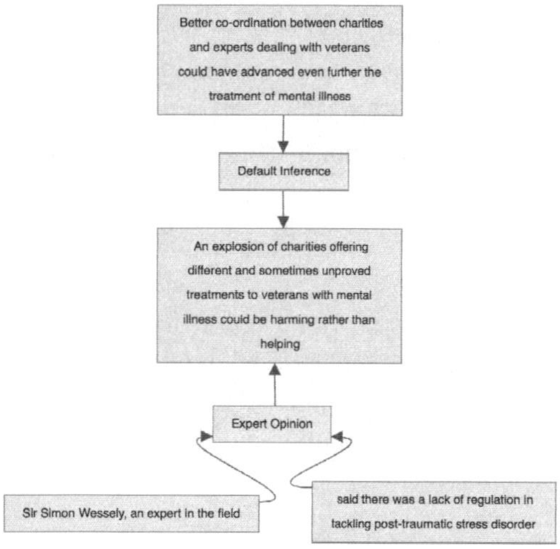

an EDU, for example, 'when two EDUs are joined by some coherence relation that is irrelevant for argumentation, the resulting complex might be the better ADU'.

We now look at how well our combined approach performs on text which is segmented using Propositional Boundary Learning. This technique, introduced in (Lawrence et al., 2014), uses two naïve Bayes classifiers, one to determine the first word of a proposition and one to determine the last. The classifiers are trained using a set of manually annotated training data. The text given is first split into words and a list of features calculated for each word. The features used are given below:

word The word itself.

length Length of the word.

before The word before.

after The word after. Punctuation is treated as a separate word so, for example, the last word in a sentence may have an after feature of '.'.

pos Part of speech as identified by the Python Natural Language Toolkit POS tagger[9].

Once the classifiers have been trained, these same features are then determined for each word in the test data and each word classified as either 'start' or 'end'. Once the classification has taken place, the individual starts and ends are matched to determine propositions, using their calculated probabilities to resolve situations where a start is not followed by an end (i.e. where the length of the proposition text to be segmented is ambiguous). Using this method, Lawrence et al. report a 32% increase in accuracy over simply segmenting the text into sentences, when compared to argumentative spans identified by a manual analysis process.

Performing this process on the text from the example in Figure 4, we obtain a list of five propositions:

1. An explosion of charities offering different and sometimes unproved treatments to veterans with mental illness could be harming

2. rather than helping, it was claimed last night.

3. Sir Simon Wessely, an expert in the field

4. there was a lack of regulation in tackling post-traumatic stress disorder

5. Better co-ordination between charities and experts dealing with veterans could have advanced even further the treatment of mental illness

Using these propositions as input to our scheme component classification identifies proposition 1 as an Expert Opinion KnowledgePosition, and proposition 3 as FieldExpertise, though fails to identify any of the propositions as a KnowledgeAssertion. Additionally, applying topical similarity to these propositions results in suggested connections from 1 to 4 and from 1 to 5.

The output from this process can be seen in Figure 5. Although this structure is not identical to that obtained using manually identified propositions, the similarity is strong and suggests that with improvement in the automatic segmentation of text into argument components, these techniques could be used to give a very good approximation of manual argument analysis.

[9] `http://www.nltk.org/`

Figure 5: Automatically Identified Propositions

7 Conclusion

We have implemented three separate argument mining techniques and for each achieved results comparable to those previously reported for similar methods.

In (Feng and Hirst, 2011), the occurrence of a particular argumentation scheme was identified with accuracies of between 62.9% and 90.8% for one-against-others classification. However, these results only considered spans of text that were already known to contain a scheme of some type and required a prior understanding of the argumentative structure contained within the text. By considering the features of the individual types of premise and conclusion that comprise a scheme, we achieved similar performance (F-scores between 0.75 and 0.93) for identifying at least one component part of a scheme.

We have shown that, although there are strengths and weaknesses to each of these techniques, by using them in combination we can achieve results that are remarkably close to a manual analysis of the same text. The accuracy we achieve for determining connections between propositions (f-score of 0.83) compares favourably with other results from the argument mining field. For example, in (Palau and Moens, 2009) sentences were classified as either premise (F-score, 0.68) or conclusion (F-score, 0.74), but in the case of our combined results, not only are we able to determine the premises and conclusion of an argument, but its schematic structure and the precise roles that each of the premises play in supporting the conclusion.

Finally, we have shown that by using Propositional Boundary Learning as an initial step in this process, we are able to take a piece of natural language text and automatically produce an argument analysis that still remains close to that determined by a manual analyst.

As the field of argument mining continues its dramatic growth, there are an increasing number of strategies being explored for contributing to the task. In building a simple algorithm for combining these techniques, we have demonstrated that it is quite possible to yield significant increases in performance over any single approach. This is in contrast to some other areas of text mining and machine learning in general, where combining different techniques is either not possible or else yields only marginal improvements. It seems likely that this strong complementarity in techniques for argument mining reflects a deep diversity not just in the techniques but in the underlying insights and strategies for identifying argument, which in turn reflects the breadth of philosophical, linguistic and psychological research in argumentation theory. We might hope as a consequence that as that research is increasingly tapped by algorithms for extracting various aspects of argument, so the combinations of algorithms become more sophisticated with ever better argument mining performance on unconstrained texts.

Acknowledgments

This research was supported in part by the RCUK Lifelong Health and Wellbeing Programme grant number EP/K037293/1 - BESiDE: The Built Environment for Social Inclusion in the Digital Economy.

References

Floris Bex, John Lawrence, Mark Snaith, and Chris Reed. 2013. Implementing the argument web. *Communications of the ACM*, 56(10):66–73, Oct.

Vanessa Wei Feng and Graeme Hirst. 2011. Classifying arguments by scheme. In *Proceedings of the 49th Annual Meeting of the Association for Computational Linguistics: Human Language Technologies-Volume 1*, pages 987–996. Association for Computational Linguistics (ACL).

Thomas F Gordon, Henry Prakken, and Douglas Walton. 2007. The Carneades model of argument and burden of proof. *Artificial Intelligence*, 171(10):875–896.

Wayne Grennan. 1997. *Informal Logic: Issues and Techniques*. McGill-Queen's Press-MQUP.

Arthur C Hastings. 1963. *A Reformulation of the Modes of Reasoning in Argumentation*. Ph.D. thesis, Northwestern University.

David Hitchcock. 1985. Enthymematic arguments. *Informal Logic*, 7(2):289–98.

Joel Katzav and Chris Reed. 2004. On argumentation schemes and the natural classification of arguments. *Argumentation*, 18(2):239–259.

Manfred Kienpointner. 1992. *Alltagslogik: struktur und funktion von argumentationsmustern*. Frommann-Holzboog.

Alistair Knott. 1996. *A data-driven methodology for motivating a set of coherence relations*. Ph.D. thesis, Department of Artificial Intelligence, University of Edinburgh.

John Lawrence, Floris Bex, Chris Reed, and Mark Snaith. 2012. AIFdb: Infrastructure for the argument web. In *Proceedings of the Fourth International Conference on Computational Models of Argument (COMMA 2012)*, pages 515–516.

John Lawrence, Chris Reed, Colin Allen, Simon McAlister, and Andrew Ravenscroft. 2014. Mining arguments from 19th century philosophical texts using topic based modelling. In *Proceedings of the First Workshop on Argumentation Mining*, pages 79–87, Baltimore, Maryland, June. Association for Computational Linguistics (ACL).

Bing Liu. 2010. Sentiment analysis and subjectivity. *Handbook of natural language processing*, 2:627–666.

Marie-Francine Moens, Eric Boiy, Raquel Mochales Palau, and Chris Reed. 2007. Automatic detection of arguments in legal texts. In *Proceedings of the 11th international conference on Artificial intelligence and law*, pages 225–230. ACM.

Raquel Mochales Palau and Marie-Francine Moens. 2009. Argumentation mining: the detection, classification and structure of arguments in text. In *Proceedings of the 12th international conference on artificial intelligence and law*, pages 98–107. ACM.

Andreas Peldszus and Manfred Stede. 2013. From argument diagrams to argumentation mining in texts: a survey. *International Journal of Cognitive Informatics and Natural Intelligence (IJCINI)*, 7(1):1–31.

Chaim Perelman and Lucie Olbrechts-Tyteca. 1969. *The New Rhetoric: A Treatise on Argumentation*. University of Notre Dame Press.

John L Pollock. 1995. *Cognitive carpentry: A blueprint for how to build a person*. MIT Press.

Chris Reed and Glenn Rowe. 2004. Araucaria: Software for argument analysis, diagramming and representation. *International Journal on Artificial Intelligence Tools*, 13(4):961–980.

Chris Reed, Raquel Mochales Palau, Glenn Rowe, and Marie-Francine Moens. 2008. Language resources for studying argument. In *Proceedings of the 6th Language Resources and Evaluation Conference (LREC-2008)*, pages 91–100, Marrakech.

Christian Stab and Iryna Gurevych. 2014. Identifying argumentative discourse structures in persuasive essays. In *Proceedings of the 2014 Conference on Empirical Methods in Natural Language Processing (EMNLP)*, pages 46–56, Doha, Qatar, October. Association for Computational Linguistics (ACL).

Tim van Gelder. 2007. The rationale for rationale. *Law, probability and risk*, 6(1-4):23–42.

M.G. Villalba and P. Saint-Dizier. 2012. Some facets of argument mining for opinion analysis. In *Proceedings of the Fourth International Conference on Computational Models of Argument (COMMA 2012)*, pages 23–34.

Douglas Walton, Chris Reed, and Fabrizio Macagno. 2008. *Argumentation Schemes*. Cambridge University Press.

Douglas Walton. 1996. *Argumentation schemes for presumptive reasoning*. Lawrence Erlbaum Associates, Mahwah, New Jersey.

Douglas Walton. 2011. Argument mining by applying argumentation schemes. *Studies in Logic*, 4(1):38–64.

Bonnie Webber, Markus Egg, and Valia Kordoni. 2011. Discourse structure and language technology. *Natural Language Engineering*, 18(4):437–490.

Adam Wyner, Jodi Schneider, Katie Atkinson, and Trevor Bench-Capon. 2012. Semi-automated argumentative analysis of online product reviews. In *Proceedings of the Fourth International Conference on Computational Models of Argument (COMMA 2012)*, pages 43–50.

Author Index